The End of Politics

New Labour and the Folly of Managerialism

by Chris Dillow

HARRIMAN HOUSE LTD

3A Penns Road
Petersfield
Hampshire
GU32 2EW
GREAT BRITAIN

Tel: +44 (0)1730 233870
Fax: +44 (0)1730 233880
Email: enquiries@harriman-house.com
Website: www.harriman-house.com

First published in Great Britain in 2007
Copyright © Harriman House Ltd

ISBN: 1-905641-17-6
ISBN 13: 978-1905641-17-8

British Library Cataloguing in Publication Data
A CIP catalogue record for this book can be obtained from the British Library.

Printed and bound by Biddles Ltd, Kings Lynn, Norfolk

Contents

Preface

This is not a book about politics, as politics is understood today. It contains no "revelations" about how Gordon hates Tony or about the size of John Prescott's membrum virile. You can get that sort of stuff in any schoolyard, and it'll probably be more eloquently expressed and about more interesting people.

Instead, this is a book about political ideas.

You might reply that there are no ideas in politics today.

But there are. And that is the point. Since its inception in the 1990s, New Labour has consistently held a big idea. It believes that, as Tony Blair put it, equality "is the partner of economic efficiency and not its enemy".[1]

This belief motivates most of the characteristic New Labour policies. The minimum wage is meant to raise the pay of worst-off workers whilst improving productivity and labour turnover. Tax credits are intended to top up the incomes of the low-paid whilst increasing incentives to work. Macroeconomic stability is supposed to increase the security of the worst-off workers whilst encouraging companies to invest. And better education should raise the pay of those on low incomes, by increasing their skills, as well as reducing skill shortages, thus allowing the economy to grow more quickly.

This notion that equality and efficiency are compatible contradicts two traditions into which many of us were educated. We were brought up to think the two conflicted – hence the title of Arthur Okun's influential book, *Equality and Efficiency: The Big Trade-Off*. And didn't Isaiah Berlin tell us that there were always trade-offs and tragic choices among values?

So who's right? New Labour or Okun and Berlin? This was the first question I asked myself; my answers are in chapters 4 to 9.

But as I investigated this question, others emerged. Why is voter turnout collapsing at the same time as our biggest political party is offering a new and interesting programme? Are there really single coherent and attractive concepts of equality or efficiency as New Labour seems to believe? Why are New Labour's critics, from both the "left" and "right," so ineffective?

As I thought about these questions, the book grew into something more ambitious, and I hope, more interesting, than I originally planned.

Hence the title of the book. By "end of politics", I mean three distinct things.

First, I mean that New Labour aspires to put an end to politics. In claiming that efficiency and equality are compatible, New Labour rules out a lot of traditional political debate, much of which is about which ideals we should choose in preference to others. Also, New Labour believes that an enlightened group of experts have sufficient understanding of the laws of history and the nature of the economy to intervene for the better. New Labour, therefore, tries to replace politics with management. This, I argue in chapter 1, is an ideological position. It's the ideology of managerialism – the belief that management and leadership can solve our problems.

However, New Labour is not alone in having this ideology. Many of its opponents, on "left" and "right", are also managerialists, in that they believe that public services and society can be managed from the top.

And herein lies my second meaning of the "end of politics." I intend to show that conventional party politics, in the sense of a competition between managerialist parties, should be killed off. Managerialist ideology should have no place in politics. It probably doesn't even have a legitimate place in companies any more.

This, I think, is one reason why voter turnout is falling. People are dissatisfied with this ideology.[2] This book is an attempt to articulate this dissatisfaction.

On this point, the political class is being (deliberately?) obtuse. It blames falling turnout on "apathy." This is nonsense. It's like asking Gordon Ramsey whether he prefers McDonalds to Burger King and, on hearing "neither", inferring that he is apathetic about food. Our alienation from conventional managerialist politics is not apathy. It's contempt.

But there are alternatives to managerialist politics. And this is where my third meaning of "end of politics" comes in. We can and should ask: what are the ends, or aims, to which politicians should strive? What exactly do we mean by equality and efficiency? Why are they so attractive? New Labour and managerialism do not answer these questions. They seem to think that passionate assertion is a good substitute for reasoned analysis. I disagree.

In a (probably vain) attempt to establish all this, I proceed in four stages.

First, I try to define New Labour and analyse its intellectual origins. In chapter one I reject two popular hostile depictions of New Labour – as "all spin and no substance" and as an accommodation to Thatcherism. Instead, I propose to take Mr Blair seriously. His description of New Labour as "modernized social democracy" is the most useful we have. Although I like the description, I don't like the thing. "Modernized social democracy" is a manifestation of managerialist ideology. In this chapter I describe aspects of New Labour's managerialism, and sketch a few of its weaknesses.

One of the most pernicious of these weaknesses is New Labour's pretence that its "modernizing" of social democracy is a necessary response to globalization. This is false. It's an attempt to present as necessary and inevitable some changes that are in fact debatable. It's an example of the managerialist habit of trying to suppress political discussion by claiming superior insights into the economic future. Chapter 2 argues this point. I show that globalization provides no justification for putting the "new" into New Labour.

Instead, the real justification for doing so is that post-war social democracy proved to be unsustainable, as I show in chapter 3. There are two purposes to this chapter. First, much of the misunderstanding of New Labour – by critics and supporters alike – is rooted in a woeful misrepresentation of Labour's past. There's a tendency to regard Old Labour as soft-headed and soft-hearted – generous to the welfare state and committed to equality, but reckless about public finances and inflation. This leads New Labour's critics to sometimes regard any sign of economic "prudence" or any reluctance to squeeze the rich until the pips squeak as a betrayal of a noble inheritance and a concession to Thatcherism.

This is gibberish. Old Labour did not choose equality over efficiency. Like New Labour, it thought it could have both. But it couldn't. And that raises the question: if Old Labour's attempt to reconcile equality and efficiency led to disaster, why should New Labour's efforts to do so fare any better?

Chapters 4-9 tackle this question. These address questions such as: What exactly is the link between education and economic growth? Do minimum wages really not destroy jobs? What is the response of labour supply to tax and the benefit system? What are the causes of income inequality? How, if at all, does macroeconomic stability lead to higher investment?

These are essays in empirical economics. Subsequent chapters take a philosophical turn, and investigate the philosophy behind New Labour's cherished ideals of equality and efficiency.

In chapters 10 and 11 I ask: what exactly do we mean by efficiency or the national interest? Chapter 10 shows that Gordon Brown's preferred conception of it – faster economic growth – is really not attractive. There's abundant evidence that, in rich countries, higher incomes don't make us very much happier.

Chapter 11 considers four other notions of efficiency – utilitarianism, Pareto efficiency, majority rule and the maximization of primary goods or capabilities. These four all conflict with each other in some ways. Efficiency, or the "national interest," is not therefore a clear self-evident ideal, as managerialists like to pretend. It's a multifaceted concept.

If efficiency isn't a hard-headed unarguable idea, what about equality? In chapter 12, I show that this too has many competing and conflicting conceptions. The problem with New Labour is that, far from abandoning equality, it has actually committed itself to too many conflicting notions of it.

Chapters 13 and 14 tackle managerialism head-on. I try to revive an unjustly neglected strand of conservatism – a scepticism about our powers of rationality.

In chapter 13, I show how governments often act irrationally, because they are prone to the cognitive biases and errors identified by Daniel Kahneman and his colleagues.

This chapter assumes that there is a single coherent conception of rationality, from which we fall short because of psychological and intellectual weakness. Chapter 14 shows that this assumption is wrong. There, I show that rationality is itself an ambiguous ideal that can sometimes often justify competing courses of action.

These two chapters, when read with chapters 10 and 11, amount to a simple argument - efficiency and rationality are not hard-headed incontestable ideals. In this sense, technocracy and managerialism are simply incoherent.

Although I like to think that this constitutes a coherent linear narrative, you needn't read it this way. You could start with chapters 13, 14 and 1, and read chapters 4-9 as empirical evidence for them. And perhaps chapter 1 contains too many bald claims that are only defended (if at all) in later chapters. So you could save it for last. And non-economists might want to skip chapters 2-8, which are heavy on economics.

Of course, books on politics are only of any merit if they support the prejudices of their readers. With this in mind, I recommend supporters of New Labour to read chapters 3 and the early parts only of chapters 4-8. They could also safely read chapter 11.

Conservatives might enjoy chapters 1, 3, the later parts of chapters 4-8 and – if they are traditional Burkeans or Oakeshottians – chapter 13. Supporters of David Cameron might not like chapter 13, but could enjoy chapter 10, which sort of endorses his view that "general well-being" matters, and not just GDP growth.

Leftist readers should avoid chapter 3. But there'll be large parts of chapter 6 they'll like, and chapter 14 might appeal to the relativists among them; I tried to discard Foucault and Feyerbend along with the equations, but failed.

In not falling neatly into a "left" or "right" tribe, I'm breaking with convention. And there's another convention I want to break

Many writers thank a vast number of eminent people "who read and commented upon the manuscript." This only invites readers to ask: if so many clever people read the wretched thing, why did none spot that it was utter rubbish? I'm not going to pretend I have lots of clever but careless friends. My acknowledgements are the footnotes.

Notes

1. *New Britain: My Vision of a Young Country*, px.

2. I should stress the distinction between justification and explanation here. I am not trying to explain why voter turnout is collapsing – merely to justify it.

1.

New Labour and Managerialism

What exactly is New Labour?

It's a simple enough question, but one that has aroused a lot of debate and confusion. In this chapter, I propose a radical answer – we should believe what Tony Blair says. New Labour is indeed best described as a "modernized social democracy".[1]

Before defending and analysing this claim, let's consider two popular alternative descriptions of New Labour – that it is "all spin and no substance", or a form of accommodation to Thatcherism.

The first of these notions has an obvious flaw – New Labour's spin-doctors have in fact been appallingly bad.

One measure alone proves this – that almost 1.9 million fewer people voted Labour in 2005 than in 1979. A party that presided over the lowest unemployment and inflation rates for a generation, and which had delivered economic and social stability, won fewer supporters than the party that presided over double-digit inflation and the winter of discontent.

Put this another way. Between 1997 and 2005 New Labour lost the support of 3.9 million voters. The 1974-79 government lost just 140,000 voters, the 1964-70 government lost just 30,000 voters and the 1945-51 government actually won an extra 2 million voters.

Judged by its ability to maintain voters' support, therefore, New Labour has been the worst Labour government in post-war history. Its spin doctors might have been good at persuading the halfwits who write for newspapers to give them good headlines. But if we judge them by the standard that really matters – the ability to persuade voters – they have been as useful as a chocolate fireguard.

And herein lies the paradox. There is much to be said for many of New Labour's most distinctive economic policies. As I show at the start of chapters 4 to 8, there's a lot of substance to them. And yet New Labour hasn't really made out the case for these in public. It seems to think the repetition of slogans – "no return to boom and bust", "making work pay", "education, education, education" – is a good substitute for coherent argument. The ballot box says otherwise.

It's not just in economic policy that this is true. Howard Glennerster has complained: "Selling its strategic social policy vision is something this government has been surprisingly bad at."[2]

Rather than regard New Labour as "all spin and no substance", perhaps we should see it as the exact opposite: all substance and no (useful) spin.

One of the gravest failings of New Labour's presentation of itself has been to misrepresent its reasons for calling itself "new." It has often attributed the need for new policies to the need to adapt to the new forces of globalization. As we'll see in chapter 2, this is wrong. And because many critics have recognised it to be wrong, they have leapt to the conclusion that these new policies represent simply a betrayal of Labour's traditions and the embracing of Thatcherite neoliberalism. "What Tony Blair does with a smile, Margaret Thatcher used to do with a snarl. Their policies are the same," Dave Nellist of the Socialist Alliance has complained[3].

One academic proponent of this view has been Colin Hay. He has argued that "the Labour government conceives neither of the need for, nor indeed the possibility of...an alternative to the ascendant neoliberalism of the times".[4]

Other proponents have been Stephen Driver and Luke Martell. New Labour, they write, is an "accommodation with Thatcherism." "Labour in government has pursued an anti-inflationary macroeconomic policy, drawn lines under the Thatcherite supply-side reforms, promoted work not welfare, continued the managerial revolution in the public services...and retained some of the internal market reforms to health and education" they say[5]. And, they add, "Brown's prudence echoes Thatcherite economic philosophy".[6]

There are three flaws in this "accommodation with neoliberalism" thesis.

First, any non-revolutionary government will have many points of similarity with its predecessor.

Consider Thatcherism as it looked after a few years in power.

In the mid-80s, the government spent more than two-fifths of GDP – much the same as the Labour government spent in the 1970s, and more than the 1964-70 Labour government spent. There was a top rate of income tax of 60 per cent. Welfare services such as health and education were free at the point of use, and the main utilities were still nationalized industries. The evidence that Thatcherism was an "accommodation to social democracy" was therefore about as strong as the evidence that New Labour is an accommodation to Thatcherism.

But nobody seriously defined Thatcherism as a continuation of social democracy. So why should they define New Labour as a continuation of Thatcherism? A few points of similarity are not sufficient for a definition; you don't call a panda a cat because it's cute, furry and has four legs.

The second failing is that the accommodation thesis hugely understates New Labour's egalitarian principles. Many New Labour policies – the pensioners' Minimum Income Guarantee, the Working Families Tax Credit and the National Minimum Wage – have the old-fashioned aim of raising the incomes of the worst-off. I'll show in chapter 9 that these measures have – so far – not greatly increased equality, but this is because equality is harder to achieve than generally thought, not because New Labour has not been trying.

What's more, New Labour leaders have a strong ideological commitment to some sort of equality: you won't find many speeches on New Labour's principles without reference to social justice or equality. Indeed, I show in chapter 12 that the problem with New Labour's commitment to equality is not that it's lacking, but rather that it is committed to too many different and competing ideals of equality.

Thirdly, the accommodation thesis grotesquely misunderstands Old Labour. A commitment to "prudent" macroeconomic policies – low inflation and balanced budgets – is not a departure from Old Labour and a concession to Thatcherism. Quite the opposite. Old Labour Chancellor Hugh Dalton argued for a "stable cost of living index" (my emphasis). That makes him tougher on inflation than any Thatcherite Chancellor. And Gordon Brown's "golden rule" – that governments should borrow only to invest rather than to finance current spending – can be seen as a rejection of the Tory "imprudence" of the early 1990s and a return to the sound public finance principles of Old Labour Chancellors Stafford Cripps and Roy Jenkins.

Nor is there anything neoliberal about promoting "work not welfare." As we'll see in chapter 3, a key purpose of the Beveridge report was to "make and keep men fit for service."

It's only if you regard Old Labour as an economically reckless party of scroungers that you can regard New Labour's "prudence" and belief in work as an accommodation with Thatcherism. This, though, would be a travesty of history.

All this raises the question. If New Labour is neither an accommodation with Thatcherism nor all spin and no substance, what is it?

Reconciling equality and efficiency

The key feature of New Labour – and what represents a complete break with Thatcherism – is a belief that equality and efficiency are mutually compatible. Gordon Brown says: "With a Labour government economic progress and social justice can advance together."[7] And in his preface to New Britain: my vision of a young country, Tony Blair said: "Social justice, the extension to all of a stake in a fair society, is the partner of economic efficiency and not its enemy[8]." These are no isolated soundbites. The belief has been a consistent one of Blair's. For example:

> The purpose of this Government has always been to bring together economic efficiency and a social justice agenda on which we can continue to deliver. (July 18 2000)
>
> I stand as New Labour, seeking for the first time in a century of British politics to marry together a well-run economy and a just and fair society. (May 13 2001)
>
> It is the combination of economic efficiency and social justice that marks this government out from its predecessors. (30 July 2003)
>
> The old choice that you had to choose between economic efficiency and social justice no longer applies. You can in fact have both. (February 25 2005)

This is a big, distinctive idea. It contradicts the view of several traditional economists who have been sympathetic to social democracy – a view embodied in the title of an influential book written by Arthur Okun in 1975 – *Equality and Efficiency: The Big Trade-Off*.

Attempts to increase equality, said Okun, could be inefficient for three reasons: because of the administrative costs of a welfare state; because increases in the incomes of the worst-off reduced their incentives to find work; and because taxes on the rich sent the message that economic success was ethically undesirable.[9] James Meade pointed out other ways in which equality and efficiency might conflict. An unhindered price mechanism, he said, was necessary for economic efficiency because this would ensure that resources were allocated to their most valuable use. But it would also lead to insecurity and an undesirable distribution of income. Or, he added, low wages might be necessary to price everyone into work, but would lead to large income inequalities.[10]

Of course, neither Okun nor Meade argued that one should always choose efficiency over equality. Their point was merely that you cannot often have both.

However, much of New Labour's thinking is an effort to show that, in many cases, you can. Major New Labour policies – such as tax and benefit reform, a minimum wage, the emphasis on education and macroeconomic stability – are all intended to promote both efficiency and equality, as we'll see in chapters 4-8.

So what changed? How was the conventional thinking of Meade and Okun – two of the greatest economists of their generation – so easily overturned?

One reason is that some inegalitarian policies of the 1980s did not have their desired effects on efficiency. The Thatcher and Reagan administrations slashed top rates of income tax and taxes on savings. And yet there is little evidence that the rich worked harder or that aggregate savings or productivity rose.[11]

Also, researchers found increasing evidence in the early 1990s that inequality was actually damaging the economy. Here, an unjustly neglected book is *Paying for Inequality: The Economic Costs of Social Injustice*, edited by Andrew Glyn and David Miliband. It documents ways in which inequality is economically inefficient. For example:

- The long-term unemployed and those out of the labour force – whose numbers soared in the 1980s and 1990s – are not competing in the labour market sufficiently strongly to bid down wages. This means that if they could be put back to work, output would rise without raising inflation. "Long-term unemployment appears to be a total waste since it fails even to offer a payoff in terms of controlling inflation" says John Philpott.[12]
- Some low-paid workers were being paid less than the marginal product of their work. In such cases, a National Minimum Wage would be both egalitarian and efficient, because it would attract more people into the labour market and increase employment.[13]
- The UK has traditionally had a shortage of skilled workers. This restrained output – because labour shortages led to rising wage inflation which in turn caused the Bank of England to raise interest rates. It also led to inequality, as the unskilled found it hard to get decent jobs. Improved education and training could therefore be both efficient and equitable.

For reasons such as these, concluded Glyn and Miliband, "greater equality and greater efficiency can go hand in hand".[14]

A good reason to put the "new" into New Labour back in the mid-90s was to draw attention to this new evidence which strengthened the case for social democracy.

So, what can be wrong with this?

The answer, I think, lies in the defining feature of New Labour – its managerialism.

By "managerialism" I mean an ideology which tries to eliminate political debate about the rival merits of competing ideals. In its stead, managerialism relies on a central elite which believes that it, and it alone, has the skill and know-how to devise policies to cope with the inexorable forces of economic change. And this skill allows apparently conflicting objectives, such as equality and efficiency, to be reconciled through the design of clever policies.

In short, New Labour believes it can run a country in the same way that executives run a business.

Now, you might object here that it's odd to call New Labour "managerialist" when in fact it has been quite awful at managing pretty much every major government department. To take just a few examples:

- The Rural Payments Agency paid only 15% of its subsidies to farmers on time in 2005-06. The National Audit Office found that, of 363 cases it investigated, there were overpayments in 34 and under-payments in 79, an error rate of almost one-in-three.[15]

- Home Secretary John Reid described the Immigration and Nationality Directorate as "not fit for purpose...It is inadequate in terms of its scope, it is inadequate in terms of its information technology, leadership, management, systems and processes".[16]

- The NHS's Connecting for Health programme – the largest IT project ever undertaken – is hugely behind schedule and over budget.[17]

- "The performance of the Defence Procurement Agency in 2002-03 can only be described as woeful. On the somewhat optimistic assumption that no further slippage is experienced, major equipment projects will on average be delivered to the end user a year and a half late. The substantial in-year cost increases of some £3.1 billion will have a major impact on the current equipment plan and must inevitably lead to cancellations or cuts in equipment projects".[18]

- There is "substantial" fraud and error – of £2.7bn – in benefit payments by the Department for Work and Pensions. The NAO has qualified its accounts (that is, doubted their accuracy) for 17 consecutive years.[19]

- Fraud and error led to over £1bn of overpayments of tax credits in 2003-04. The NAO has qualified the accounts of HMRC for four successive years.[20]

We could of course, multiply these examples many-fold; see, for example, Matthew Elliott and Lee Rotherham's *The Bumper Book of Government Waste* or David Craig and Richard Brooks' *Plundering the Public Sector*.

What these examples show is that there's a big difference between management and managerialism. Management is a technique, the skill of organizing resources effectively, which may be done well or badly. Managerialism is an ideology, the belief that government should behave like company managers and has the skill to do so. The purpose of this book is to show that this belief is false. Even if all managers were perfectly honest, and as clever as any reasonable human being could possibly be, there would still be huge flaws in managerialism. It's not enough to give a list of instances of poor management. It's the ideology that's the problem, not just the practice.

In the rest of this chapter, I'll show some aspects of New Labour's managerialist ideology.

"New, new, new": the rhetoric of modernity

One of the key buzzwords of New Labour is 'modern'. New Labour, Blair has said, is a "modernized social democracy." He says he's attempting "to take traditional Labour values – equality, liberty, solidarity, democracy, justice – but find modern means to give them expression".[21] Here are some other of Blair's uses of the M word:

This is what a modern welfare state should do. Be on the side of people, when they need it – allowing them greater freedom, greater choice and greater power over the things that they want to do. (October 5 2006)

The purpose of the reforms is to create a modern education system and a modern NHS. (October 24 2005)

The UK will develop a strong, modern knowledge-based economy. (November 17 2004)

We want a modern police service more responsive to local communities. (March 30 2004)

As Alan Finlayson says: "If there is a single word that might capture the essence of New Labour's social and political project, then it is 'modernization'".[22]

This is because Blair believes there are deep historical forces – globalization and technical change – that dictate what policy should be. As he said, much of the change in New Labour's economic thinking in the 1990s "was to do not with ideology but with the altered circumstances of the world economy".[23]

But it's not just economic policy that's determined by globalization. So is foreign policy:

The rule book of international politics has been torn up. Interdependence – the fact of a crisis somewhere becoming a crisis everywhere – makes a mockery of traditional views of national interest.[24]

And so is criminal justice policy:

What is happening is simply another facet of globalization and a changing world...As a result of the scale and nature of this seismic change, the challenges faced by the criminal justice and immigration systems have grown exponentially, not in a small way but in a way that, frankly, mocks a system built not for another decade but another age. So we end up fighting 21st century problems with 19th century solutions.[25]

Blair's love of this theme of constant change is so strong that he seems to be keeping up with the parodies of his rhetoric. In 2002 Alan Finlayson wrote that New Labour has "an absolute conviction in the newness of the new world of new things".[26] A year later Mr Blair said: "Look around the world today, at every institution or community, and the chief characteristic is rapid change. The forces of change outside our country drive the need for change within it. We are the party of change. But our historic mission is to turn change into progress."[27]

All this is pure managerialism. Managerialists like to pretend that we face big challenges in a fast-moving environment. They invite us to believe that they alone are equipped to address such challenges (in managerialism, problems are never solved, only addressed). And they like to present policies as necessary responses to external events – just as company bosses present mass redundancies as inevitable measures over which they have little choice.

New Labour tries to replace reasoned debate with an appeal to economic necessity, and with a claim to possess superior managerialist skills. As Finlayson put it, the rhetoric of newness, rapid change and modernity "helps to make 'natural' and uncontestable that which is not necessarily so".[28] David Marquand put it well:

> 'New, new, new' Tony Blair told a meeting of European socialist leaders in a characteristic outburst shortly after entering office, 'everything is new.' This is the myth in a nutshell. The world is new, the past has no echoes, modernity is unproblematic, the path to the future is linear. There is one modern condition, which all rational people would embrace if they knew what it was. The Blairites do know. It is on that knowledge that their project is based, and by it that their claim to power is validated.[29]

There's a strain of vulgar Marxist-Leninism here: New Labour seems to believe in a crude economic determinism, in which the laws of economic development determine social change, and that only a self-appointed vanguard understands these laws.

The comparison shouldn't be surprising. Managerialists come from the left and the right – whatever those terms mean. Lenin was as much a managerialist as Henry Ford. Both believed in hierarchy and technological determinism rather than democracy and debate.[30]

There's another managerialist function served by this rhetoric of globalization. Managerialists love certainty. They are like doctors, often wrong but never in doubt. The rhetoric of globalization preserves this sense of certainty.

To see how, think back to 1983. Then, several senior New Labour figures

– Tony Blair and Gordon Brown among them – were elected to parliament on a manifesto which called for, among other things, more nationalization and the UK's withdrawal from the European Union. Within 10 years, they believed the opposite of this.

For many of us, being compelled to reverse publicly held positions such as these would be a disturbingly dissonant experience. It would compel us to question which other of our beliefs might be false.

Many New Labour figures, however, seem not to have suffered any such crisis of confidence. Could this be because they have persuaded themselves that their change of mind was due to a change in the facts about the outside world, rather than the fact that they were wrong all along? If so, then globalization is significant not (just) because it is an important economic fact, but because it is a mechanism for preserving the self-image of New Labour's leaders. New Labour's rhetoric of modernity, says Marquand, "airbrushes an embarrassing past".[31]

Now, you might object here that New Labour's claim that globalization has forced it to change is not managerialist rhetoric, but merely the truth.

It's not. I'll show in chapter 2 that globalization has not rendered old-style social democracy infeasible – if anything quite the opposite.

But let's say I'm wrong. Let's assume New Labour's diagnosis of the inevitability of economic change is correct. Does this diagnosis justify its economic policies?

Not at all. The diagnosis is consistent with some anti-managerialist alternatives. Consider some of the most common claims about the "modern" economy made by New Labour:

- *"We live in an age of rapid economic change and insecurity."* New Labour believes this strengthens the case for macroeconomic stability, and for greater education, so that workers can be better prepared for changes in their careers. However, it is also a case for encouraging the creation of what Robert Shiller calls "macro markets" – ways of insuring ourselves against economic changes.

- *"Human capital is increasingly important."* To New Labour, this is why we should pay more attention to education. However, it's also a case for breaking down corporate hierarchies. It's no coincidence that businesses that are traditionally dependent upon human capital – such as law firms, accountancy firms or medical practices – are partnerships rather than autocratic companies with external shareholders.

- *"Traditional family structures and employment practices are breaking down."* To New Labour, this is a reason to reform the traditional welfare state. However, it's also a good argument for introducing a citizen's basic income – something paid to every adult regardless of their circumstances. Such an income is a better way than traditional welfare benefits of helping people in part-time or temporary work, or in non-traditional family structures.

- *"Information technologies are transforming our lives."* Fair enough. But a key idea among theorists of the new economy – such as Manuel Castells or Kevin Kelly – is that the new economy creates a "network society" – a society in which loose temporary alliances can replace rigid hierarchies. You hear none of this from New Labour, which sticks to a faith in hierarchic government and hierarchic companies.

This list shows two things. First, it's just not true that modernity, "new times" or globalization suffice to determine a single set of policies.

The leadership myth

Secondly, in each of these cases, the "new economy" suggests a case for a market or egalitarian policy on the one hand, and a managerialist, hierarchical policy on the other. And in every case, New Labour has chosen the managerialist alternative over the non-managerialist one.

And herein lies another aspect of New Labour's managerialism – its faith in leadership as a force for transforming society. As Blair told Rupert Murdoch's News Corp executives: "For heaven's sake, above all else, lead."[32]

But why is leadership so important? New Labour seems to take it for granted, perhaps because it thinks that only a special elite can understand the deterministic power of economic and technical change.

But this assumption is doubtful. People at the top of hierarchies just don't have sufficient knowledge and judgment to control complex organizations and society. The widespread management failures across almost all government departments testify to this; I'll return to this in chapters 13 and 14. And as Jeffrey Nielson argued in *The Myth of Leadership*, hierarchies are a terrible way of structuring organizations. They pervert internal communication, demotivate employees and encourage selfishness at all levels, under-utilize skills and discourage innovation.

Empirical evidence on this point is weak, simply because we rarely see leadership-dominated organizations compete directly with egalitarian ones. However, in two cases where they do, egalitarianism seems to do well. In retailing, John Lewis has been voted the UK's favourite retailer. And in the City hedge funds – which tend to be small partnerships have been growing rapidly relative to more traditional hierarchical fund managers.

It's therefore at least questionable whether organizations need leadership rather than more democratic control. But it's a question New Labour never asks.

This has led to a sheer absurdity. The Department of Health has said: "Delivering effective policy to support good health requires strong leadership across government[33]." This contrives to overlook the message of government-sponsored research which suggests that leadership can cause poor health. The Whitehall Studies concluded that: "The more senior you are in the employment hierarchy, the longer you might expect to live compared to people in lower employment grades."[34]

New Labour has a blind spot – it just cannot see alternatives to leadership, even when its own research shows that hierarchies can be fatal. Consider a remark made by Gordon Brown in 1999. Increasing opportunity, he said, must include "a redistribution of power that offers people real control over the decisions that affect their lives".[35] Now, many of the decisions that affect our lives are taken in company boardrooms. But has New Labour offered people "real control" over these? New Labour's commitment to equality and empowerment seems to stop when these ideals challenge corporate hierarchy. "Leadership", New Labour believes, is always necessary.

New Labour as human resources department

This faith in leadership suggests that New Labour regards people as objects to be managed, rather than as subjects who have a right to control their own lives. As Stuart Hall has complained, New Labour tries to change people to fit into the interests of the economy, rather than to change the economy to fit the interests of people.[36]

One example of this is that New Labour thinks that government should serve as a human resources department. The New Deal, tax credits and its attempts to improve education are all aimed at increasing and improving the labour supply. As Tony Blair and Gerhard Schroder said: "The most important task of modernization is to invest in human capital."[37]

A further example of this mindset was clear in the creation of two influential bodies in the early 1990s, under the auspices of the Institute for Public Policy Research, a think-tank closely linked to New Labour: the Commission on Social Justice, which studied ways of reforming the welfare state; and the Commission on Public Policy and British Business, which considered how to improve UK competitiveness. Now, the curious thing here is that the latter contained many leading businessmen, but the Commission on Social Justice did not contain any welfare recipients. Businessmen, it was assumed, are good judges of what's good for business, but welfare claimants are not good judges of what's good for the welfare state.

In this regard, there is a continuity not only within New Labour, but from New Labour's antecedents to today's party.

Consider this from Mr Blair's speech to 1997's Labour party conference: "My heroes aren't just Ernie Bevin, Nye Bevan and Attlee. They are also Keynes, Beveridge and Lloyd George."[38]

Most people interpret this remark as evidence that Mr Blair is not truly rooted within the Labour tradition – he's more ecumenical than that.

However, it shows that he is truly rooted in managerialism – because Keynes and Beveridge believed the man in Whitehall should dictate not just our fates but our characters. It was Beveridge who wrote, in the blueprint for the post-war welfare state, that the purpose of his plan was "to make and keep men fit for service."[39] And Keynes' interest in eugenics led him to write that "the time may arrive a little later when the community as a whole must pay attention to the innate quality as well as to the mere numbers of its future members."[40]

Indeed, there's a continuity here right back to the 17th century. Then, the poor were regarded as objects, not subjects. C.B. Macpherson has explained:

> Puritan individualism, to the extent that it superseded the paternalism of the Tudor and early Stuart state, did nothing to raise the estimation of the political capacity of the dependent working class. On the contrary, the Puritan doctrine of the poor, treating poverty as a mark of moral shortcoming, added moral obloquy to the political disregard in which the poor had always been held. The poor might deserve to be helped, but it must be done from a superior moral footing. Objects of solicitude or pity or scorn or sometimes of fear, the poor were not full members of a moral community... But while the poor were, in this view, less than full members, they were certainly subject to the jurisdiction of the political community.[41]

New Labour's rhetoric of responsibilities as well as rights can be regarded as a continuation of this theme.

The crooked timber of humanity

Another failing in this aspect of managerialism is that it ignores what Isaiah Berlin called the crooked timber of humanity.

To the managerialist, there is just one ideal of human nature – the notion of a "career" – a life planned in advance, in pursuit of chosen goals. Just as managerialists think a single central organization can control the world, so they think a single central self can control the individual's life.

But as thinkers as varied as George Ainslie, Daniel Dennett and Michael Walzer have shown in several ways, this is a fiction. The self is always divided: between roles (worker, parent, citizen or creative spirit); between identities (man, Englishman, agnostic, European); and between ideals (peace, justice, freedom.) Doubt, anguish, anxiety, and ambiguity arise from these divisions.[42]

Managerialists ignore this. They believe we have clear careers, and no ambiguity, no doubt. To them, everything is planned. Goals and targets are all. They are oblivious to the fact that this conception of human nature is a very modern one. The word "career" – in its modern sense – first appears in the English language in only 1803. Before then, people thought about their lives – insofar as they did so at all – as following inherited traditions, divine pre-ordination, or social regulations. Those who rebelled against this were spontaneous libertines, not monomanical climbers of ladders.

Pro-business, not pro-market

New Labour likes to claim that it is "pro-business." The significance of this is that one rarely hears that it is "pro-market".

The distinction is important. Markets are tumultuous, unpredictable and uncontrollable processes, which often make fools of the most esteemed expert – as anyone who has spent more than a few days working in the foreign exchange or stock markets will testify. Businesses, however, are hierarchical bureaucracies and their leaders are often more like senior civil servants than buccaneering entrepreneurs.

New Labour's preference for business over markets shows its managerialist bias – because to any managerialist, businesses, with their mission statements and their illusions of control, are much more congenial than the disruptive anarchic forces of the market.

However, it is markets, not hierarchies, that deliver economic efficiency, because it is these that weed out poor performers and give the others incentives to perform. Tesco is not a more efficient organization than London Underground because its executives are cleverer than London Underground's (though being sentient creatures they probably are). It's because market pressures force it to be so. Businesses are the price we must pay for what is truly valuable – markets. Managerialists ignore this.

The state as enterprise association

There's a big problem with adopting managerialism as a governing ideology. It's that, as Anthony Barnett has said: "A country is not like a company and cannot be run as if it were."[43]

The difference is that companies have only one goal – to maximise profits – whereas governments do not. In a company conflicts of interest and ideals are obstacles to be removed, whereas in a country they are inevitable. And what's more – as I'll show in chapter 11 – it's far from easy to aggregate these competing interests, so we cannot easily speak of a "national interest" in the same way we can speak of a company's interest.

So, whilst it might make sense for a chief executive to speak of "moving Tesco forward", it makes no sense to speak of "moving Britain forward." This, though, is precisely the title of a recent book by Gordon Brown.

The presumption which that title – and its contents – embodies is that government should lead us towards a collective goal. But even if there is such a thing as effective leadership, is there such a goal? Should there be? Some have thought not. They've considered the job of government to be a more limited one. Here's Michael Oakeshott:

> The office of government is not to impose other beliefs and activities upon its subjects, not to tutor or to educate them, not to make them better or happier in another way, not to direct them, to galvanize them into action, to lead them or to coordinate their activities so that no occasion of conflict shall occur; the office of government is merely to rule. This is a specific and limited activity, easily corrupted when it is combined with any other, and, in the circumstances, indispensable. The image of the ruler is the umpire whose business is to administer the rules of the game, or the chairman who governs the debate according to known rules but does not himself participate in it.[44]

Now, my point here is not that Oakeshott was right, though I think he was. It's that New Labour doesn't even consider the possibility that he might be. Just as New Labour never considers the egalitarian alternatives to managerialism, so it never even considers the possibility that government should be an umpire not a player. In this sense, its managerialist ideology is totalitarian, in that it doesn't seem to permit the possibility of alternatives.

There are no trade-offs: having it all

Perhaps one reason for this tendency to regard the state as a player rather than umpire is that New Labour's managerialism leads it to think that it can manage away conflicts of interest.

It's not just equality and efficiency that New Labour believes to be compatible. Blair has also, for example, claimed that there are no trade-offs between prosperity, peace and democracy:

> Ever since I saw 9/11 change the world, I have believed that the greatest danger is that global politics divides into "hard" and "soft". The "hard" get after the terrorists. The "soft" campaign against poverty. The divide is dangerous because interdependence makes all these issues just that: interdependent....Without progress – in democracy and in prosperity – security is at risk. Without security, progress falters.[45]

This belief that our ideals are all mutually compatible flatly contradicts a long intellectual tradition, associated with Sir Isaiah Berlin, which says our cherished ideals do indeed conflict. As he wrote:

> The notion of the perfect whole, the ultimate solution, in which all the good things co-exist, seems to me not merely unattainable – that is a truism – but conceptually incoherent. I do not know what is meant by a harmony of this kind. Some among the great goods cannot live together. That is a conceptual truth. We are doomed to choose, and every choice may entail an irreparable loss...we must engage in trade-offs – rules, values, principles must yield to each other in varying degrees in specific situations.[46]

In this tradition, John Gray has recently written that "coping with tragic contingencies" is an essential fact of political life, and that the aim of politics must be to achieve a rough and messy compromise between competing ideals and interests rather than any greater utopia.[47] In similar vein – though he and Gray disagree on much else – John Rawls recommended that political philosophy cannot be over-ambitious. A theory of justice, he said, must aim at being reasonable, rather than true, and must be a partial rather than a comprehensive world view.[48]

New Labour rejects this politics of tragic choices and limited ambition. It does so because it believes governments are clever enough to design policies that achieve both justice and efficiency. For example, governments know how labour supply decisions respond to tax and benefit rates, so they can design a tax and benefit system that encourages people to work. They know how to set the minimum wage at a high enough level to raise incomes, but not so high as to destroy employers' willingness to employ people. They know enough about what determines companies' capital spending decisions, so they can promote investment by striving for macroeconomic stability. And they know how to improve education, and how education affects earnings, so they can use better schooling to reduce wage inequality and promote economic growth by providing a bigger supply of skilled workers.

Sadly, though, this knowledge is illusory. As we'll see in chapters 4 to 8, the evidence in favour of New Labour's main economic policies is missing or ambiguous.

New Labour's response to these ambiguities or lacunae is classic managerialism – they simply ignore the problem by a selective reading of the research and a selective presentation of the evidence.

For example, New Labour's enthusiasms for more education and for greater macroeconomic stability are based on studies comparing economic growth across a large number of countries. Some of these have found that education and economic stability are indeed associated with faster growth. However, other cross-country studies have found that big government, and lots of lawyers, are associated with slower growth. New Labour ignores these.

A more deadly example of the sloppiness of managerialist thought came when New Labour made the case for the war against Iraq in 2003. A rigorous argument for going to war would have consisted of a cost-benefit analysis, weighing the benefits of war – removing a vicious dictator and the threat of weapons of mass destruction – against the costs, both financial and human. However, this was never done, at least in public. No-one calculated how many lives it was worth destroying in order to achieve the benefits of victory.[49] All we got from New Labour managerialists were fragments of an argument for war.

This reveals one of the paradoxes of managerialism. It pretends to be clear-thinking and hard-headed. But it isn't. Awkward or contradictory evidence and dissonant facts are ignored. As Robert Protherough and John Pick wrote in their splendid *Managing Britannia*, managerialism, despite its claim to be rational, rests upon a myth – "an obsessive and irrational belief in the 'reality' of a fictive, wholly-manageable universe".[50] This in turn raises the suspicion that managerialists use evidence as drunks use lamp-posts – for support, not illumination. As George Ainslie has written: "Executives don't function effectively so much by rationally analyzing facts as by finding facts that make good rallying points."[51]

Maybe, then, managerialism is just a fig-leaf for the pursuit of power.

A moral vacuum

In pretending that trade-offs can be avoided, managerialism prevents its adherents from thinking deeply about fundamental values. After all, if we don't have to choose between liberty, equality or efficiency, we don't have to think about why these are valuable, or even about what they mean.

What's more, if you believe that "new times", globalization and modernity are sufficient to determine a single political response, there's no point in moral argument anyway. Again, Marquand puts it well. New Labour's myth of modernity, he says:

...rescues the mythologists from the need to base their politics on moral choices and to offer moral arguments. The new is by definition good, or at any rate inescapable. Change is an irresistible force, operating independently of human agency. Moral and ideological arguments for the Third Way are unnecessary; it does not have to be defended against alternative visions of the future, based on different moral and ideological premises. There is only one future, and resistance to it is spitting into the wind. The choices it poses are technical, not moral or political.[52]

This moral and ideological vacuum is preserved by a further characteristic of managerialism – a love of action rather than contemplation. Read the adverts for managerial jobs and the same buzzwords appear: dynamism, energy, desire. Rarely do you see a request for intelligence, wisdom or thoughtfulness.

The upshot is often a futile hyperactivity. In rushing from initiative to initiative, meeting to meeting and think-tank to think-tank, policy-makers distract themselves from the big questions: what exactly am I trying to achieve? What core values underlie what I am doing? Action is often a substitute for thought.

Perhaps the failure of old-style social democracy has also contributed to this reluctance to think about ultimate ends. Some New Labour politicians have the same attitude to moral principles as an embittered man has towards women – "they've let me down once, they'll always let me down." With this attitude, technocracy, or the pretence thereof, can be a cosy hiding place.

No limits: hubris

Another aspect of New Labour's managerialism is an apparently limitless confidence – at least in public – that government can do whatever it sets out to. For example, Blair and Schroder have told us that "for the new politics to succeed, it must promote a go-ahead mentality and a new entrepreneurial spirit at all levels of society" – as if it were possible to change the attitudes of over 100 million people.[53] And Gordon Brown has said:

Past generations could say:
If only we had the knowledge
If only we possessed the technology
If only we had discovered the medicine
If only we had pioneered the science
Yet today we have the knowledge, the technology, the medicine, the science, the financial system – all gifts, a capacity for change that no other generation has enjoyed.[54]

Not only does government have unbounded know-how, it also has the ability to do anything, such as changing a national culture that has taken decades to emerge. David Miliband and Douglas Alexander write: "We have to work harder at creating a culture...Britain needs to develop a learning culture."[55] What this omits is any discussion of the question: what policy tools does the government have with which to create any sort of culture?

The most famous example of New Labour's hubristic faith in the powers of government was, of course, Blair's claim before the 1997 election that we had "24 hours to save the NHS."

This claim, he has since recognised, was stupid. No-one can transform western Europe's largest employer in a few hours. But the claim is by no means the only example of New Labour's ambition. There is the asinine claim of Peter Mandelson and Roger Liddle that "our understanding of economics has greatly advanced this century, and in theory enables economic fluctuations to be damped and corrected". There is Tony Wright's idea that "the real issue is not whether there is too much regulation or too little, but whether particular regulation is sensible or necessary" – as if it were easy to tell.[56] And of course there are the countless day-to-day cases of "control freakery."

All this reveals another facet of managerialist ideology – a hubristic lack of awareness of the limits of one's abilities. As Protherough and Pick have written: "In the modern world there are no bounds to what governments think they can shape and manage. Modern governments now affect to be able to manage everything, from how ambitious we are to how fat women should be."[57]

This is clearly silly. But it has some unpleasant effects. To see them, contrast management – as it exists in its ideologized form – to proper crafts and professions.

I don't much care about the character of my doctor or plumber. All that matters is whether they have the necessary skills. Either they can do the job or they can't.

Managers, though, have no such benchmark for competence. So they haven't the self-awareness and self-confidence that comes from knowing their abilities and the limits thereof.

One consequence of this is an intrusion of personality into politics. Because managerialism isn't a demonstrable skill, its practitioners rely upon revealing their characters, as these, they hope, show competence and credibility. As Richard Sennett put it: "A political leader running for office is spoken of as 'credible' or 'legitimate' in terms of what kind of man he is, rather than in terms of the actions or programs he espouses."[58]

The result of this isn't just a "dumbing down" of politics, as idle gossip replaces rigorous policy analysis. It's also that politics becomes a series of crises: the NHS "crisis", the foot and mouth "crisis", the school exams "crisis" and so on. This happens because what's at stake in each issue isn't just a question of how to manage our affairs, but what this reveals about our rulers' personalities. In every issue, fitness to govern is called into question.

Worse still, politics becomes dominated by "spin." It's easier to give the impression of being a good manager than it is to genuinely be a good manager. And it is easier to manage the perceptions of a handful of journalists than it is to manage a vast government department or company. So it's no wonder that managers should invest so much effort in public relations.

In this sense the complaint that New Labour is "all spin and no substance" misses the point. What is "all spin and no substance" is not New Labour, but managerialism itself.

"History is bunk": You can't learn from the past

But how can anyone possibly have so much faith in the power of government to achieve its aims? Doesn't history show that most political projects end in failure?

It does. But herein lies another feature of managerialism –an ignorance of history. Blair has said: "I have no time for living in the past."[59]

This isn't just a pose. Blair has displayed his ignorance of history. In 2001 he said that New Labour is "seeking for the first time in a century of British politics to marry together a well-run economy and a just and fair society." Until New Labour came along, he has said, "the country faced a stark, inescapable choice between the cold but efficient and the caring but incompetent".[60]

Think about this. By "first time in a century" does he really mean the feat of marrying efficiency and fairness was achieved by Lord Salisbury? Probably not. And this is not the only way in which this claim is nonsense. It perpetuates the illiterate idea that Old Labour was "caring but incompetent." The truth is, though, that, as Jim Tomlinson reminds us, the search for ways of reconciling efficiency and equality is about as old as the Labour party itself[61]. In chapter 3, I'll show why these ways failed in the past.

This ignorance of history is no mere idiosyncrasy of Blair's. It's hard-wired into managerialism. After all, Henry Ford's most famous saying is: "history is bunk."

This is because, to the managerialist, the past is irrelevant. All that matters is the future, Management is always "moving forward", "striving", "progressing." To managerialists, say Protherough and Pick, "the best is always yet to come".[62] Managers are all gong and no dinner. As one wag put it, to New Labour, the future is certain; it's only the past that changes.

One effect of this is to make managerialism vulnerable to intellectual fads. This is a longstanding complaint about that oxymoron, management education. But it's also true of New Labour. In its own brief history it has enthusiastically taken up and then abandoned or downgraded ideas such as stakeholding, communitarianism, a payroll levy for training and "post-neo-classical endogenous growth theory." This alone should show that policies that once seem so promising can quickly seem unattractive.

A more striking example of this lies in an early predecessor of New Labour thinking, namely Alan Blinder's book, *Soft Hearts, Hard Heads: Tough-Minded Economics for a Just Society*. Writing in 1987, Blinder lamented the fact that the soft hearts of the traditional left were often accompanied by soft-headed thinking, whilst the hard heads of the right were often accompanied by hard hearts. Hence, he said, the need for "soft hearts and hard heads" – for policies which promoted both greater equality and greater efficiency. There was, he believed, no need to worry about Okun's dilemma, because: "Our present policies are so far from right that the need to trade equity for efficiency disappears...The trade-off need not be confronted because of the low quality base from which we start."[63]

The key to achieving greater equity and greater efficiency, Blinder believed, was to introduce more rigorous economic thinking into politics: "The critical problem is not that the limits of economic science are too confining, true as that is. Rather, it is that society makes such poor use of what economists really know."[64]

All this – the denial of a trade-off between equity and efficiency, the attempt to combine compassion and hard-headedness, and the technocratic faith in expertise – is quintessential New Labour. What are even more revealing, however, are the differences between Blinder and New Labour.

Blinder enthusiastically supported greater profit-sharing – an idea which had been advocated at the time by Martin Weitzman's briefly influential book, *The Share Economy* – and the exploitation of the short-run trade-off between inflation and unemployment to create more jobs. A little bit of inflation, he believed, "gives us elbow room to grow".[65] However, he dismissed minimum wages as "hare-brained",[66] and totally ignored policies such as improved education and central bank independence – even though he was himself to later become a vice-chairman of the US Federal Reserve.

In all this, Blinder and New Labour could not be further apart. This raises a disturbing possibility. Could it be that attempts to make better use of what economists know lead not to more equity and efficiency, but merely to support for the intellectual fashions of the day? Managerialism in companies is notoriously prone to fads and fashions – partly because managerialists lack the healthy scepticism engendered by historical perspective. Might the same be true of managerialism in government?

Emotivism

There's one final curious aspect of New Labour's managerialism we should consider – Blair's frequent stress upon feeling and emotion, rather than reason. He's said that "changing things requires *faith* in long term gain[66]", and that "political leaders have to back their *instinct*[67]." He has on various occasions said that he is "passionate" about: being pro-European; disarming Iraq's weapons of mass destruction; reconciling economic equality and efficiency; and religious equality. And, he said: "In the 1980s I stopped thinking about politics on the basis of what I had read or learnt, and started to think on the basis of what I felt."[68]

Again, these are not just examples of Blair's anti-intellectualism. They represent an ideological position. It's what philosophers call "emotivism" – the idea that moral judgments are no more than expressions of preference or feeling. Alasdair MacIntyre describes this position thus:

> Emotivism is the doctrine that all evaluative judgments and more specifically all moral judgments are *nothing but* expressions of preference, expressions of attitude or felling, insofar as they are moral or evaluative in character...Factual judgments are true or false; and in the realm of fact there are rational criteria by means of which we may secure agreement as to what is true and false. But moral judgments, being expressions of attitude or feeling, are neither true nor false; and agreement in moral judgment is not to be secured by any rational method, for there are none. It is to be secured, if at all, by producing certain non-rational effects on the emotions or attitudes of those who disagree with one...If this *is* true, *all* moral disagreement *is* rationally interminable.[69]

Naturally, if you believe talk about values is irrational and useless, it is tempting to resort to managerialism, which offers the comforting illusion that we can have all the values at once. If this is right, we can avoid dirty irrationality.

But feelings aren't enough. They're sufficient to make us believe in what Michael Walzer calls "thin" conceptions of political ideals, such as justice, equality and freedom. But these ideals are ambiguous, and little guide to policy. The upshot is that New Labour's attitudes towards equality seem confused.

So, for example, in 2001 Blair said that New Labour's philosophy "is based on a notion of equality that is not about outcomes or incomes; but about equal worth." However, he has also said: "I believe in greater equality. If the next Labour government has not raised the living standards of poorest by the end of its time in office it will have failed."[70]

This is just incoherent. And that's what you get when managerialism encourages emotivism.

"Being asked to die for the telephone company"

I hope by now to have established that New Labour believes in a managerialist ideology.

But New Labour is not alone. Almost all conventional politicians have been managerialists for a long time. We've seen managerialism in the Conservatives' re-organization of local government in 1973. We've seen it in Lady Thatcher's introduction of private management techniques into the civil service in the 1980s. We are seeing it in George W. Bush's belief that a liberal democracy can be built from scratch in Iraq. And we see it regularly in David Cameron's speeches.

Indeed, even people who think they are radical are just managerialists. When "anti-capitalist" protestors march on a G7 meeting, the bigwigs and the protestors may be divided by riot police and barriers, but they are united by a common ideology – the notion that the world can be controlled and managed for the better.

This raises the question: if so many are managerialists, why am I picking on New Labour? And why now?

I'm picking on New Labour simply because it's in power and we must always scrutinize government closely. Power is something to be checked, not worshiped.

As for why now? It's because the case against managerialism is stronger than ever now. It's clearer than ever before that human beings lack the cognitive skills to control the world. We have what Thomas Homer-Dixon has called "an ingenuity gap" – an almighty chasm between the complexity of our problems and the intellectual resources we have to solve them[71].

It is a cliché that people today suffer from an information overload. The cliché's wrong. We don't have too much information. We have too little understanding.

A few years ago, scepticism about the limits of rationality was largely confined to what are carelessly called right wingers – men like Edmund

Burke, Friedrich Hayek and Michael Oakeshott. Today, this is no longer the case. Since the 1970s thinkers such as Jon Elster, Daniel Kahneman, Paul Feyerabend, Richard Rorty, Robert Nozick, Alasdair MacIntyre and G.L.S Shackle, to name but a few, have all cast doubt in different ways upon our capacity to think rationally. These are not right wingers in any normal sense. All they have in common is an awareness that there is a big distinction between rationalism and rationality[72]. Rationalism says we can solve all problems by the application of reason and knowledge. Rationality tells us this is not so.

New Labour has not learnt this lesson. Indeed, as academics' doubts about the possibility and coherence of rationality have risen, Labour politicians' doubts have diminished. Many of its supporters like to think they have abandoned the woolly radicalism of their youth in favour of a hard-headed technocratic concern with efficiency. But just because you have lost your faith does not mean you have found your reason. Many 1960s radicals have replaced an irrational belief in the possibility of achieving a socialist utopia with an equally irrational belief in the powers of managerial rationalism.

There's one final, and very nasty, reason why I'm criticizing managerialism right now. It's that this is an increasingly important part of the attempt to legitimize state power.

Our rulers today cannot claim legitimacy by appealing to God's will or to the wisdom of past customs, as pre-democratic governments did. Nor even can they appeal to the will of the people, as democracies have traditionally done. In several western democracies, such as the UK, US and France, only around one-in-four adults voted for the ruling government.

Instead, governments' claims to legitimacy increasingly rest on the belief that they can manage society to make us happier and wealthier. As Alasdair MacIntyre has pointed out, the moral and political legitimacy of western governments now depends upon an issue in the philosophy of the social sciences: do governments have the knowledge to intervene in society for the better[73]?

They don't. Increasingly, voters are learning this.

And herein lies the fundamental political problem. Governments invite voters to ask the question: what can politicians do for me?

The reply is: "not enough to justify my tax bill."

Voters are turning away from party politicians for the same reason that customers desert incompetent shops – they just don't offer value for money.

We are, therefore, learning the wisdom of Edmund Burke's remarks 220 years ago – that no government can ever claim legitimacy by appealing only to our narrow self-interest; this would mean that we would only ever obey it when it was in our interests to do so, which would not be very often. A state based upon the "mechanic philosophy" of utilitarian efficiency, said Burke, was doomed to have only a partial and contingent legitimacy. In such a state, he wrote, "laws are to be supported only by their own terrors, and by the concern, which each individual may find in them, from his own private speculations, or can spare to them from his own private interests".[74]

Herein lies the justification for declining voter turnout and rising alienation from conventional politics, not just in the UK but around the developed world. Voters realize that the managerialist state is not delivering. It's not giving us "world class public services", not giving us "certainty not risk", and not "reconciling equality and efficiency." The nation-state, MacIntyre has said, presents itself as "a bureaucratic supplier of goods and services, which is always about to, but never actually does, give its clients value for money...it is like being asked to die for the telephone company".[75]

When people really are dying for the managerialist state, it's more important than ever that we point out its fundamental illegitimacy.

Notes

1. "The Third Way: New Politics for the New Century", reprinted in Andrew Chadwick and Richard Heffernan (eds), *The New Labour Reader*, p28.

2. "Social Policy" p394 in Anthony Seldon (ed), *The Blair Effect: The Blair Government 1997-2001*.

3. quoted in *The Independent*, May 17 2001.

4. *The Political Economy of New Labour*, p135.

5. *Blair's Britain*, p60.

6. *Blair's Britain*, p32.

7. Speech to Labour party conference, September 29, 2003. See also "Equality – Then and Now" written in 1999: "Today, we argue for equality not just because of our belief in social justice, but also because of our view of what is required for economic success." (Reprinted in Andrew Chadwick and Richard Heffernan (eds), *The New Labour Reader*, p134.)

8. *New Britain: My Vision of a Young Country* ps x, 97

9. *Equality and Efficiency: The Big Trade-Off* p96

10. *Efficiency, Equality and the Ownership of Property*, p13, 25.

11. Joel Slemrod and Jon Bakija, *Taxing Ourselves*, p108-9 and 112. One

reason why high top rates of tax are not inefficient is that they do not merely deter productive activity – if, indeed, they do even that. They may also deter rent-seeking activity such as engagement in office politics in an attempt to gain promotion. From the point of view of society, such behaviour is inefficient, because effort is spent in order to get resources transferred rather than produced. Anything that deters this is a good thing. Strangely, this point has been largely ignored.

12. "The incidence and cost of unemployment", p144, in Glyn and Miliband (eds), *Paying for Inequality*

13. Paul Gregg, Stephen Machin and Alan Manning, "High pay, low pay and labour market efficiency" in Glyn and Miliband (eds), *Paying for Inequality*.

14. *Paying for Inequality*, p8.

15. NAO press release October 18 2006.

16. *Daily Telegraph*, May 24 2006.

17. David Craig and Richard Brooks, *Plundering the Public Sector*, chs 10 and 11.

18. Defence Select Committee report, July 14 2004.

19. NAO press release November 7 2006.

20. NAO press release, July 11 2006.

21. Speech to Fabian society, June 17 2003.

22. *Making Sense of New Labour*, p66.

23. *New Britain: My Vision of a Young Country*, p124.

24. Speech on foreign policy, Georgetown, May 26 2006.

25. Speech on "Our Nation's Future", June 23 2006.

26. *Making Sense of New Labour*, p184.

27. Speech to Fabian society, June 17 2003.

28. *Making Sense of New Labour*, p67.

29. *The Progressive Dilemma: From Lloyd George to Blair*, p226.

30. This comparison is made by Harry Braverman in *Labour and Monopoly Capital*, p12.

31. *The Progressive Dilemma*, p226.

32. Speech on July 30 2006.

33. *Health Challenge England*, October 2006, p7.

34. *Work, Stress and Health: The Whitehall II Study*, p4.

35. "Equality – Then and Now" p136.

36. "The great moving nowhere show" p85, reprinted in Chadwick and Heffernan (eds), *The New Labour Reader*.

37. "Europe: the third way/die neue mitte", p111, reprinted in Chadwick and Heffernan (eds).

38. Quoted in Andrew Rawnsley, *Servants of the People*, p195.

39. *Social Insurance and Allied Services*, Cmnd 6404, November 1942, p170.

40. "The End of Laisser-Faire", p292 in *Essays in Persuasion*.

41. *The Political Theory of Possessive Individualism*, p226-27.

42. Michael Walzer, *Thick and Thin*, p85.

43 "Corporate populism and partyless democracy" p89, reprinted in Chadwick and Heffernan (eds).

44. "On being Conservative", p427 in *Rationalism in Politics and Other Essays*.

45. Speech on foreign policy, Georgetown, May 26 2006. Remember that the claim that the spread of democracy was compatible with the decline of terrorism came a few months after Hamas was democratically elected in Palestine and Mahmoud Ahmadinejad was elected president in Iran.

46. "The pursuit of the ideal", p11 in *The Proper Study of Mankind*, edited by Henry Hardy and Roger Hausheer.

47. *Straw Dogs*, p194 and passim.

48. *Political Liberalism*, p9, 196-7.

49. To have done this would, of course, have required the government to attach a price to human life. Although this is a necessary aspect of cost-benefit analysis – for example in deciding spending on road safety, it's something that governments are reluctant to admit doing. Such squeamishness shows that managerialism's hard-headedness is only superficial.

50. *Managing Britannia*, p29.

51. *Breakdown of Will*, p100.

52. *The Progressive Dilemma*, p226-7.

53. "Europe: the third way/die neue mitte", p112.

54. Speech at New York University, December 14, 2005.

55. *The Guardian*, September 25, 2006.

56. *Why Vote Labour?* p48.

57. *Managing Britannia*, p19.

58. *The Fall of Public Man*, p4.

59. *New Britain: my vision of a young country*, p129.

60. Sedgefield adoption speech, May 13 2001.

61. *Democratic Socialism and Economic Policy: The Attlee Years 1945-51*, passim

62. *Managing Britannia*, p64.

63. *Soft Hearts, Hard Heads*, p31.

64. *Soft Hearts, Hard Heads*, p199.

65. *Soft Hearts, Hard Heads*, p108.

66. Speech at CBI annual dinner, May 16, 2006.

67. Speech to News Corps, July 30, 2006

68. Sedgefield adoption speech, May 13 2001.

69. *After Virtue*, p11-12.

70. quoted in Andrew Glyn and Stewart Wood, "New Labour's economic policy", *University of Oxford Department of Economics discussion paper 49*, December 2000, p11.

71. *The Ingenuity Gap*, p1-2.

72. Deirdre McCloskey, *Knowledge and Persuasion in Economics*, p323.

73. *After Virtue*, p87.

74. *Reflections on the Revolution in France*, p171.

75. "A partial response to my critics", p303 in John Horton and Susan Mendus (eds), *After MacIntyre*.

2.

A Trojan Horse

We took far too long in the 1980s as a political party to face up to the need for change. Much of this change was to do not with ideology but with the altered circumstances of the world economy (Tony Blair)[1].

One of the reasons globalization gets a bad rap is that policymakers often fall into the trap of using 'competitiveness' as an excuse for needed domestic reforms. Large fiscal deficits or lagging domestic productivity are problems that drag living standards down in many industrial countries and would do so even in closed economies...Too often however the need to resolve fiscal or productivity problems is presented to the electorate as the consequence of global competitive pressures (Dani Rodrik).[2]

Why did Blair and Brown put the "New" into New Labour? Was this just a marketing gimmick? New Labour's supporters say not. Instead, they say, globalization – the fact that goods, services and financial capital now flow across borders much more freely than in recent years – has forced Labour to abandon old Labour economic policies. As John Gray said, "global capital markets...make social democracy unviable".[3]

There are, it's said, at least five ways in which this is the case.

First, governments can no longer use macroeconomic policy to maintain full employment. "The new international economy has greatly reduced the ability of any single government to use the traditional levers of economic policy in order to maintain high employment" say Peter Mandelson and Roger Liddle. "The days of simple home-based Keynesianism will not return"[4]. This is because any attempt by governments to borrow heavily to create jobs will cause international investors to sell their assets, causing a collapse of the currency and soaring interest rates, as French socialists discovered in 1981-82. "Full employment cannot be promoted by aggressive deficit financing because that is now being interdicted by global bond markets" says John Gray. "The global freedom of capital effectively demolishes the economic foundations of social democracy."[5]

Secondly, and relatedly, governments must retain the confidence of financial markets. "The rapid globalization of the world economy has made achieving credibility more rather than less important", Ed Balls has said.[6] This is not merely because they need to avoid repeating the French disaster.

It's also because "credible" governments can attract investment and hence get higher economic growth.

Thirdly, globalization limits the scope for redistributive taxation. Because highly skilled workers and companies can emigrate easily, high taxes will cause them to leave the country. That would deprive the economy of much-needed talent and expertise. "In a global economy our tax rates need to be conducive not only to keeping highly skilled labour, but to attracting it" says Tony Blair.[7] This means the tax system can no longer be used to equalize incomes.

Fourthly, globalization has cut demand for unskilled labour in the UK. Indian, Chinese and Romanian workers are cheaper than UK ones. So they are pricing unskilled British workers out of jobs; this can happen either through immigration, or the import of low-skill-intensive goods, or "offshoring" by indigenous firms. This has led to increased unemployment among unskilled workers, and lower wages for those who have clung onto their jobs.[8] The only solution to this, it's said, is to train and educate British workers so they are less vulnerable to competition. Hence Blair's famous statement that "education is the best education policy there is".[9]

Fifthly, says Blair, "with globalization comes its offspring – insecurity"[10]. One reason for this lies with the footloose nature of financial capital: "It is not new for financial markets to punish policies they believe unsustainable, but today when sentiment turns, it turns with a vicious alacrity" says Blair.[11] John Gray adds the unpredictable response of financial markets to government policy means that national economies have become "ungovernable".[12] Examples of this come readily to mind. The UK's traumatic exit from the European exchange rate mechanism in 1992, the collapse of currencies and stock markets in south east Asia in 1997 and the Argentine economic crisis of 2002 all testify to the fickle nature of financial markets.

But there's another form of insecurity which globalization brings – job insecurity. Around the advanced world, workers feel more insecure in their jobs.[13] "Old certainties like jobs for life or a skill for life can no longer be taken for granted" says Gordon Brown.[14]

The reason for this is not sufficiently appreciated. The greater potential for employers to switch production from country to country, or for consumers to switch from domestic goods to imports, means employment has become more sensitive to the level of wages. In other words, the demand for labour has become more price-elastic. This means wages and jobs are more sensitive to demand shocks. A simple diagram illustrates this. Imagine an initial equilibrium is at point A, with employment at E* and wages at W*. There is then a fall in demand for labour, so that employers will only maintain employment at E* if wages drop to W**. In a relatively closed economy, with an inelastic demand for labour, this shift results in a new equilibrium at B. With the more elastic demand curve caused by an open economy, however, the new equilibrium is at C. Both wages and employment, are lower. The message, says Dani Rodrik, is clear. "Openness magnifies the effects of shocks on the labour market."[15]

Fig. 1

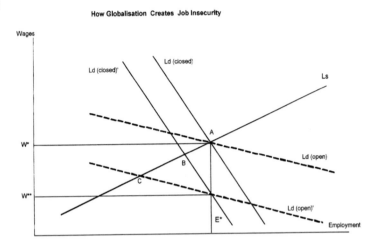

This can be especially bad news for those workers whose skills are specific to a particular job. If these lose their jobs, they will find it particularly hard to get a job which paid as much as their previous one. If such workers are less educated than others, globalization will increase the wage differential between educated and less educated workers.

All this means social democrats have felt compelled to re-assess the functions of government. "Old Labour" policies, such as high taxes and the use of macroeconomic policy levers to ensure full employment, are believed to be unworkable. Instead, governments must focus more upon retaining investors' confidence, training its workforce, and ensuring stability. In short, governments must become more like managers of companies.

The big government mystery

This sounds like devastating stuff. But is it true? There's one big fact that suggests it might not be. In the developed world, the most globalized economies are just as likely to have that hallmark of old-style social democracy – big government – as more closed economies.

Our chart shows this. Across the main 27 OECD economies in 2005, there's no correlation at all between the degree of globalization – measured by import penetration – and the size of government. Some open economies, such as Belgium and Sweden, have big governments. Some relatively closed ones – the US, Japan and Australia – have small governments.

Fig. 2

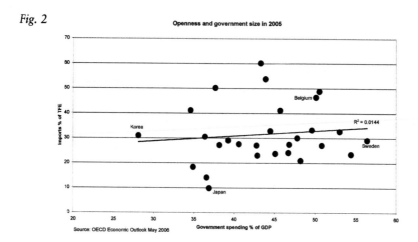

Of course, you can argue with this data in all sorts of ways. All I'm saying is that the claim that increasing globalization forces governments to change

What's more, there's no correlation between changes in globalization – again measured by import penetration and changes in the size of the state. Our third chart shows that some countries that have seen big increases in the degree of openness since 1990, such as Korea, have expanded the size of their government.

Fig. 3

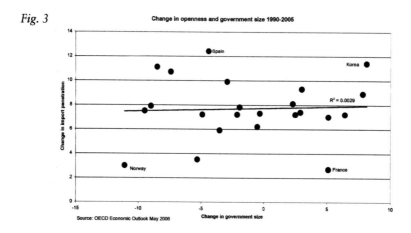

Of course, you can argue with this data in all sorts of ways. All I'm saying is that the claim that increasing globalization forces governments to change

doesn't leap out of the data. The idea that globalization must prevent big government – because taxpayers emigrate or because foreign investors lose confidence – seems inconsistent with the facts.

This is no coincidence. Open economies are more vulnerable to booms and busts as a result of fluctuations in world trade. Such fluctuations are even harder to predict than domestically generated fluctuations. Fiscal or monetary policy – the efficacy of which requires forecasts of future activity – will therefore often be unable to stabilise output. With discretionary stabilisation so tricky, governments must use "built-in stabilisers" more. But these require larger government spending and larger tax revenues. So open economies mean big government. "Societies that expose themselves to greater amounts of external risk demand (and receive) a larger government role as shelter from the vicissitudes of global markets" says Rodrik.[16] This mechanism seems to offset the mechanisms whereby globalization can shrink the state.

This raises the question. If globalization can be associated with big government, how can it undermine social democracy? The answer, says Rodrik, is simple:

> A strategy of compensating internationally immobile groups for accepting greater amounts of external risk can work as long as international economic integration is not too advanced. But once globalization moves beyond a certain point, the government can no longer finance the requisite income transfers because the tax base becomes too footloose.[17]

An imperfectly integrated world

But are we near this "certain point" at which globalization undermines conventional social democracy?

Maybe not. Despite the potent imagery conjured up by the fact that turnover on the world's foreign exchange markets now exceeds one trillion dollars a day many economists think globalization is exaggerated. "We do not live in a world in which all goods, services and factors of production move freely across national boundaries; nor are we rapidly becoming such a world" says Paul Krugman.[18] Instead, he believes we live in an "imperfectly integrated" economy.

One piece of evidence for this comes from the facts about trade in goods and services. The UK's exports of goods and services now account for just over a quarter of national income. Although that's much more than in the 1950s and 1960s, it is less than before World War One. In this sense, the UK economy is less globalized now than it was a century ago.

Fig. 4

UK exports as % of GDP

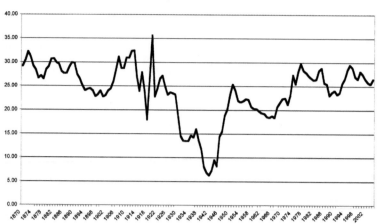

There are, though, objections to the relevance of this. One set of problems concerns measurement. Because export prices tend to rise less than prices of other goods and services, the same amount of money spent on exports is now worth a bigger volume of goods, relative to national income, than before. If we measure exports and GDP in constant prices, the UK economy is indeed more open than it has been for over a century[19]. Also, the increasing importance of services in advanced economies means one would expect international trade to decline in importance to the whole economy, even if manufacturing becomes more open because many services are hard to trade across borders. Measured as a share of manufacturing output rather than GDP, trade has indeed increased.

A further objection is that a given level of trade today might expose economies to more international influence than in the past. David Held and his colleagues point out that the textbook case where countries trade different products is becoming less true.[20] Around 30 per cent of trade now consists of exports and imports within the same industries. This means domestic companies are increasingly competing directly with foreign rivals – which means it is more important than ever before to maintain competitiveness.

A third objection is that trade now takes the form of companies out-sourcing low-skill production processes to low-wage countries. In this way, globalization can be a more powerful force for reducing the job prospects of the unskilled than it was a few decades ago.

It is, however, unclear how strong these objections are. Some believe they are not, and that trade does less to integrate national economies today than it did in the past. Years ago, international trade was mainly in commodity products. A drop in prices therefore led to a drop in national inflation. Today, however, trade is in differentiated goods. And producers of these often set their prices by reference to those in the national markets into which they are selling; this is called "pricing to market." The upshot is that domestic inflation is influenced less by import prices than used to be the case. "International considerations may today play less of a role in determining prices in Britain and (especially) the US that they did in the early years of the century" says Krugman.[21] Bank of England Governor Mervyn King seems to agree:

> Some of you may be tempted to think that because the growth of the Chinese economy has affected key prices in our own economy, inflation in Britain is now largely determined overseas. Low inflation in industrialized countries, it is argued, is made in China....That...is a myth....Inflation is made at home.[22]

There is, though, another thing about trade in goods that suggests we don't live in a well globalized world.

From the perspective of economic theory, the interesting fact about international trade is just how little of it goes on.

Consider the standard neoclassical theory of international trade – the Heckscher-Ohlin-Samuelson theory. This predicts countries will export those goods which use intensively the factors of production with which the nation is well endowed. So a country with abundant grazing land will export meat, whilst a country with many chemists will export pharmaceuticals.

This theory doesn't fit the facts. It fails in a very particular way – because much of the trade that should happen does not.[23] Billions of pounds of trade is missing, because countries with large factor endowments often do not export those goods which use these factors intensively.

One reason for this is that there seems to be a "home bias." Customers prefer domestic goods and services. Maurice Obstfeld and Kenneth Rogoff point out that the typical Canadian province trades 20 times as much with other provinces as it does with the typical US state – far more than can be explained by size or distance[24]. And James Anderson and Eric van Wincoop have estimated that the mere existence of national borders – with no formal barriers to trade – reduces trade between industrialized countries by between 20 and 50 per cent.[25]

Levels of trade in goods and services do not, then, suggest we are living in a fully globalized economy.

Perhaps, however, we are looking for globalization in the wrong place. Surely, common sense suggests we are more likely to find it in capital markets than in goods markets.

But we don't. A paper by Marianne Baxter and Urban Jermann explains why[26]. There is, they say, a close correlation between long-run returns on human capital and those on physical capital within any country. This means that a worker who wants to insure against risks to her human capital should have a short position in her domestic stock market, and a long one in overseas markets which are weakly correlated with the domestic one. In the 1990s, for example, Japanese investors would have been wise to invest heavily overseas, as a falling domestic stock market provided no protection against increased job insecurity.

Investors' actual portfolios are, of course, far removed from this ideal. They own too many domestic equities. "Investors appear to remain stubbornly loyal to domestic assets" say Obstfeld and Rogoff.[27]

There's other evidence that capital does not flow as freely across borders as globalization theorists pretend. It was first pointed out in 1980 by Martin Feldstein and Charles Horioka.[28] They began from the perspective that, if there is complete international capital mobility, there should be no correlation between domestic savings and domestic investment. That is because capital should flow to wherever it can earn the highest return, and savings should respond to world-wide incentives to save, not merely local ones. However, they estimated that between 1960 and 1974, correlations between savings and investment within 16 major economies were huge. Capital, they concluded, was immobile.

And this is still true. Alan Taylor estimated that correlations between national savings and investment for major countries were no different in the early 1990s than they were a century before.[29] Things haven't changed much since his research. If there were full capital mobility and little correlation between savings and investment within countries, we would see enormous current account deficits and surpluses, as some countries' savings hugely exceed investment, whilst others' investment exceeds savings. But in advanced countries at least, we just don't see this. As I write, the US has a deficit of a mere 6 per cent of GDP – and this is considered by many to be worryingly large.

This evidence against globalization has, of course, been challenged. The most plausible counter-argument is that there should be a correlation between savings and investment even in a world of perfect capital mobility, simply because both are determined by the same thing – supply shocks. A technological breakthrough that boosts labour and capital productivity would cause both a rise in investment as firms buy the new efficient equipment and a rise in savings as workers, at least in the near-term, save their additional income[30]. Savings and investment will appear closely correlated, even though international capital is perfectly mobile.

Although theoretically plausible, this idea runs into two factual obstacles. One comes from Taylor's research, which found that there have been times when savings-investment correlations were indeed low. The other was pointed out by Stefan Sinn[31]. He estimated savings-investment correlations for 48 US states. And he found these were negative. That suggests capital flows much more freely between US states than it does between countries. These findings raise the questions: what exactly are the supply shocks that have caused savings and investment to be highly correlated since the 1990s? And why were such shocks absent in the 19th century, and absent within national boundaries?

With such questions unanswered, it is probable that we do indeed live in a less globalized world than we would like to think. As Krugman has written: "Our grandfathers, armed with ledgerbooks and telegraphs, created a far more extensive capital market than we have managed to create with our computers and satellites."[32]

In this light, it's no surprise that some of the predictions made by globalization theorists have been strikingly wrong. Consider these from Noreena Hertz's *The Silent Takeover*, published in 2001:

"The shareholding class created in the Thatcher revolution has made a policy of renationalization unfeasible" (p28.)

In October 2001 Transport minister Stephen Byers renationalized Railtrack, with no compensation.

"Tony Blair and Gerhard Schroder almost certainly spend more time on promoting the sales of British and German companies than on foreign policy" (p67.)

Iraq.

"As capital and highly-paid labour are now able to move freely from high-tax countries to low-tax countries…a nation's ability to set tax rates higher than other nations is being put into question" (p53.)

However, there is little sign that taxes on profits are being forced down, or even becoming more equal, across countries. Two economists at the Institute for Fiscal Studies concluded: "None of the evidence…suggests that tax competition is driving tax rates or revenues to zero, or that there has been a significant erosion of the capital tax base."[33]

What's more, what capital mobility there is tends to occur within advanced economies. Table 1. overleaf shows that the vast bulk of the UK's outward direct investment goes to high-wage developed economies, and there is little sign of this changing. In the last five years, the UK has invested more in high-wage, high-regulated France than it has in the whole of the African continent.

Table 1. UK Net foreign direct investment

	Level (2004)		Flow (2000-04)	
	£bn	% of total	£bn	% of total
EU 25	348.3	53.0	191.3	60.1
Belgium/Luxembourg	88.9	13.5	-0.6	-0.2
France	30.9	4.7	20.5	6.4
Germany	11.9	1.8	124.1	39.0
Ireland	33.9	5.2	13.5	4.2
Netherlands	134.2	20.4	18.8	5.9
Other Europe	32.8	5.0	4.2	1.3
United States	148.6	22.6	71.3	22.3
Rest of World	127.1	19.4	51.7	16.2
Asia (inc. Middle East)	47.0	7.2	13.3	4.2
Caribbean, C. and S.America	40.0	6.1	19.9	6.2
Africa	17.3	2.6	14.0	4.4
Other	22.8	3.5	4.5	1.4
Total	656.8	100.0	318.5	100.0

Source: Office for National Statistics, Overseas Direct Investment 2004, 13 December 2005

This is powerful evidence against the notion that there is a form of Gresham's law, in which bad capitalisms drive out good, as capital flows to countries with the lowest wages and social protection. Whatever else globalization does, it does not cause a "race to the bottom" of low wages or low taxes on capital.

Obstacles to globalization

We do not, then, live in the globalized world of New Labour rhetoric. But, perhaps we soon will. "Maybe your wages were not set in Beijing yesterday or today, but tomorrow they will be" says Richard Freeman.[34]

Don't bet on it. For one thing, economists, as Freeman admits, are lousy forecasters. And for another, there are some powerful forces which prevent the economy becoming fully globalized. One lies in the very technical change which is often thought to be a cause of globalization. This can inhibit the rise in world trade in four different ways.

- The increasing speed with which technology is transferred across borders means that countries maintain a comparative advantage in the production of particular goods for a shorter and shorter time. That tends to limit the international division of labour and, with it, world trade growth.

- Rapid technical change might increase the demand for skilled labour. This reduces the attractiveness of many low-wage developing economies as locations for investment. If it is highly skilled technicians you want, you are better off investing in Germany than in Nigeria.

- The substitution of capital for labour reduces the share of wage costs in total costs. This in turn reduces the incentive for companies to relocate overseas to take advantage of cheap labour.

- Insofar as computer technology enables firms to minimize their holdings of inventories, it encourages them to maintain close geographical links with their suppliers. The benefits of "just-in-time" production methods disappear if one has to wait a month for components to be shipped from the other side of the world.[35]

There's more. One of the other powerful trends in the global economy – the shift away from manufacturing towards services – also acts as a brake on world trade growth. Your child's cuddly toys may be made in Beijing, and your software programmed in Bangalore – but you probably have your hair cut down the road.

Also, globalization can stop itself. In a fully globalized world, profit rates and expected (risk-adjusted) returns on financial assets would be equal across countries. But if this were the case, there would be little need for cross-border investment, except to arbitrage away those differences that do crop up.

It is, however, not only the equalization of prospective returns that might halt the growth of international capital flows. Alan Taylor's research has found two periods when savings-investment correlations were low and globalization therefore high – the 1880s and 1920s. Both were periods of rapidly rising stock markets, when an increased appetite for risk led to investment in increasingly exotic markets. But when stock markets fell and investors became more cautious, savings-investment correlations rose. Savings stayed at home. Economies became less globalized.

Perhaps, therefore, the rise in cross-border capital flows between the early 1980s and late 1990s reflected increasing appetite for risk – an appetite that also caused rapidly rising share prices. But there's little reason to suppose this will continue.

Finally, it must be remembered that the increasing integration of the global economy is, in large part, a political process. It is the result of the dismantling of trade barriers and capital controls.[36] And what the politician giveth, the politician can take away. In March 2002, the US government imposed stiff tariffs on imported steel, though it later removed them. In October 2006 the UK government imposed controls on the freedom of Bulgarians and Romanians to work in the UK. And barely a week passes without some call for increased protection from foreign competition, or for restraints to be placed on the free movement of capital or labour.

These protectionist or interventionist backlashes against globalization are nothing new. Jeffrey Williamson says globalization in the 19th century led to just such a reaction, and warns that a similar thing could happen again.[37] If there is a trend towards globalization, therefore, it is more precarious than one might think. "The present dominance of neoliberal globalization is not as secure as either many of its strongest proponents or its critics suggest" say David Held and his colleagues.[38]

The benefits of globalization

Economies, then, are far from fully globalized. And they may never be. But what if they were? Would it really spell the death of old-style social democracy? The answer, in some ways, is no. New Labour is guilty not only of propounding a false premise, but of drawing a false conclusion from it.

If we really did live in a global financial market, several of the longest standing problems social democrats have had would be solved at a stroke.

One of these was famously described by Will Hutton – that the UK's financial system retards investment by paying insufficient attention to long-term returns and demanding that loans be repaid too quickly.[39] In a truly global economy, however, this problem, if it is one at all, vanishes. If UK banks or financial markets deny a firm funding for a profitable project, it can simply borrow from overseas banks or capital markets. Globalization is, therefore, the solution to short-termism. There is evidence that this is really happening. The Bank of England estimates that, since 1997, UK companies have raised more venture capital from overseas investors than from domestic pension funds.[40]

Globalization would also solve another problem – the tendency for near-full employment to generate rising wage inflation.

To see how, imagine – which shouldn't be difficult – that the UK has fuller employment than other countries. Our labour is therefore relatively scarce. We will therefore import labour-intensive products. The prices of labour-intensive products made here should therefore fall because the supply of them has, in effect, increased. And if the price of labour-intensive goods falls, the marginal product of labour falls. So wages will fall.

Full employment, then, will not drive up wages. Globalization therefore reduces one of the things that has prevented the attainment of full employment for the last 25 years.

Of course, it only does this by replacing the trade-off between unemployment and inflation with a trade-off between unemployment and the trade balance. But this is no problem, because in a globalized world, it will be easy to finance trade deficits by attracting capital inflows.

And if it is possible to run large deficits, it will be equally possible to run large surpluses. In this case, there will be no necessary reason why commodity price shocks – such as the rise in north sea oil prices in 1979-80 – should crowd out manufacturing exports. Had we had a globalized economy 27 years ago, we might have suffered less de-industrialization.

We would also have suffered less during the deep recessions of 1980-81 and 1990-91. In a fully globalized world, we would invest more overseas. This would give us better insurance against domestic falls in production, and so protect us against home-grown economic risks.

One only has to mention all this to show just how far we really are from a truly global economy. But there is another way in which globalization may help social democrats.

In a truly global economy, government bonds would be very close substitutes for one another. It follows that any incipient rise in, say, UK bond yields due to increased government borrowing will cause international investors to sell their overseas bonds in order to buy UK ones. Governments can therefore borrow large amounts without seeing any rise in interest rates. Far from fiscal policy being "interdicted by global bond markets" as John Gray claims, therefore, it can be greatly facilitated.[41]

This is no mere textbook possibility. By a stroke of good luck, one of the few ways in which the current world economy is globalized is that bond markets often do permit more scope for fiscal expansion. Compare what happened in 2001-04 to 1975-76. Both were periods of high and rising government borrowing. In 1975-76, the borrowing drove up interest rates, as investors needed a big incentive to hold the extra debt. That led to talk of the "crowding out" of private investment by government spending. But in 2001-04, bond yields fell, thanks to favourable international markets.

There are other examples of how today's financial markets can help a government run a loose fiscal policy. In the late 1990s, it was economists working in financial markets who called on the Japanese government to use fiscal policy to reflate its economy – something the government was reluctant to do for fear of the high debt it will leave for future taxpayers. And the fact that European governments introduced a "stability pact" to limit government borrowing within the single currency – whilst Chancellor Gordon Brown proposed a "code for fiscal stability" to limit UK borrowing – shows that governments do not believe financial markets alone constrain state borrowing.

One of the key policies of old-style social democracy – fiscal policy – is, therefore, actually much more feasible in a global economy.

A Trojan Horse

All this suggests that it's odd that New Labour should try to justify its emergence in the 1990s by relying so heavily upon the idea of globalization. Not only is not obvious that globalization is a strong and irreversible force. But also, even if it were, its effects upon old-style social democratic policies would not be as disastrous as its advocates have suggested.

Why, then, does New Labour talk so much about globalization? There's a bad reason, and a good one.

The bad one is that globalization appeals to its managerialist ideology. Managers like to believe that the world is new and uniquely challenging.

But this is not true. Indeed, the current Labour government entered office freer from the pressures imposed by world markets than any of its predecessors. Not for it the acute dollar shortage that dominated the early years of the Attlee administration; nor the balance of payments constraint that hamstrung the 1964-70 government; nor even the oil and sterling crises that plagued the 1974-79 government. Gordon Brown has had a much easier job than any previous Labour chancellor.

What's more, pretty much every generation since the industrial revolution has believed it was living in a world of uncertainty, rapid technological change, and fierce foreign competition. As Marx and Engels put it in 1848:

> Constant revolutionizing of production, uninterrupted disturbance of all social conditions, everlasting uncertainty and agitation distinguish the bourgeois epoch from all earlier ones. All fixed, fast-frozen relations, with their train of ancient and venerable prejudices and opinions are swept away, all new-formed ones become antiquated before they can ossify. All that is solid melts into air....The need of a constantly expanding market for its products chases the bourgeoisie over the whole surface of the globe. It must nestle everywhere, settle everywhere, establish connections everywhere. The bourgeoisie has through its exploitation of the world market given a cosmopolitan character to production and consumption in every country.[42]

Even then, however, globalization was old hat. A generation earlier, in 1821, David Ricardo had warned that the mobility of capital and labour was a barrier to high taxes:

> It becomes the interest of every contributor to withdraw his shoulder from the burthen, and to shift this payment from himself to another; and the temptation to remove himself and his capital to another country, where he will be exempted from such burthens, becomes at last irresistible.[43]

What's more, he said, capital mobility means that one cannot stand in the way of technical change, even if such change makes some workers worse off:

> The employment of machinery could never be safely discouraged in a state, for if a capital is not allowed to get the greatest net revenue that the use of machinery will afford here, it will be carried abroad, and this must be a much more serious discouragement to the demand for labour than the most extensive employment of machinery.[44]

Even Ricardo, however, was saying nothing new. In 1776 Adam Smith had clearly warned of the difficulties of taxing capital because of its international mobility:

> The proprietor of stock is properly a citizen of the world, and is not necessarily attached to any particular country. He would be apt to abandon the country in which he was exposed to a vexatious inquisition, in order to be assessed to a burdensome tax, and would remove his stock to some other country where he could either carry on his business, or enjoy his fortune more at his ease. By removing his stock he would put an end to all the industry which it had maintained in the country which he left.[45]

Globalization, then, is as old as industrial society itself. Nor is there even anything new about its rediscovery. A 1956 White Paper, *Economic Implications of Full Employment,* spoke of the "increasingly competitive conditions which have developed in the last few years".[46] And in 1969

Charles Kindleberger claimed that "the nation state is just about through as an economic unit".[47]

So much for the bad reason for New Labour's fondness for the idea of globalization. What of the good reason?

Quite simply, talk of globalization is an effective rhetorical device. It's a Trojan horse, in which to smuggle in arguments against government intervention and for free markets. A good example of this is Kenichi Ohmae's influential book, *The End of the Nation State*. The factual evidence for globalization he presents is woeful. But his argument is not so much that nation states have lost their power to manage national economies, but that they deserve to lose that power:

> Because the global markets...work just fine on their own, nation states no longer have to play a market-making role. In fact, given their own troubles, which are considerable, they most often just get in the way. If allowed, global solutions will flow to where they are needed without the intervention of nation states. On current evidence, moreover, they flow better precisely because such intervention is absent.[48]

New Labour does the same thing. It uses globalization as a way of justifying policies that it considers desireable. For example:

> "In a global market place, traditional national economic policies – corporatism from the old left, isolationist ideology from the new right – no longer have any relevance" says Gordon Brown.[49]

> "The rapid globalization of the world economy has made achieving [macroeconomic policy] credibility more rather than less important" says Edward Balls.[50]

> "To compete in the new global market two things must be done. A country has to dismantle barriers to competition...a nation must also constantly be investing in new capacity and above all in the flexibility and aptitude of its people" says Tony Blair.[51]

These claims have one thing in common – their authors would believe them to be true even if they did not believe we lived in a global economy. Can you think of a world in which Mr Brown would think isolationist ideology relevant? Or in which Mr Balls would believe policy credibility unimportant? Or in which Mr Blair would think constant investment in capacity and training unnecessary? Of course not.

Nor should they. New Labour uses globalization as a justification for breaking with old Labour. It's an easy way of selling a change in Labour's thinking. It's far easier to say that "our policies were right for the time, but times have changed" than it is to admit that they were just wrong.

But supporters of old Labour *were* just wrong. Old-style social democracy was a lamentable failure, and not because of globalization. Mr Blair's claim that his revolution "was to do not with ideology but with the altered circumstances of the world economy" is, therefore, regrettable. It should have been to do with ideology. For it is here that the best case for Labour's changes lies.

But what exactly was wrong with old Labour, that required the emergence of a "new" "modernized" party? Let's have a look.

Notes

1. *New Britain: My Vision of A Young Country* p124.

2. *Has Globalisation Gone Too Far?* p79.

3. *False Dawn: The Delusions of Global Capitalism* p88.

4. *The Blair Revolution: Can New Labour Deliver?* p6.

5. *After Social Democracy: Politics, Capitalism and the Common Life*, p32, p26. See also Labour's 1995 economic policy document, *A New Economic Future for Britain* (p17): "the rapid integration of the global economy in recent years, combined with the reality of global capital markets, eliminates any lingering notion that economic policy can remain a matter solely for national governments."

6. "Open Macroeconomics in an Open Economy", *Centre for Economic Performance Occasional Paper no.13* p12.

7. *New Britain: My Vision of A Young Country* p123.

8. The relative roles of trade with emerging economies and technological change in causing this are strongly debated. See, for example, the symposium on the subject in the summer 1995 issue of the *Journal of Economic Perspectives* and September 1998 issue of the *Economic Journal*. One complication in this debate is that, if globalization causes companies to outsource some less-skilled production processes to low-wage countries, a fall in demand for unskilled workers will look as if it is due to technical change when in fact it is due to globalization. See Robert Feenstra, "Integration of trade and disintegration of production in the global economy", *Journal of Economic Perspectives*, 12, Fall 1998, p31-50. Another complication is that some question how far there has been a relative decline in demand for unskilled workers at all. Stephen Nickell and Brian Bell suggest that the decline may have begun to be reversed in the 1990s ("The collapse in demand for the unskilled and unemployment across the OECD, *Oxford Review of*

Economic Policy, 11, spring 1995 p40-62).

9. *New Britain: My Vision of A Young Country*, p66.

10. *New Britain: My Vision of A Young Country*, p123.

11. *New Britain: My Vision of A Young Country*, p120.

12. *False Dawn: The Delusions of Global Capitalism*, p70.

13. OECD *Employment Outlook* July 1997 p129. The report notes (p150) that "insecurity is significantly lower in countries where the unemployment benefit replacement rate is higher." Maybe, then, job insecurity nowadays reflects the greater costs of losing one's job, and not merely the higher probability of doing so. See also Simon Burgess and Hedley Rees ("Job tenure in Britain 1975-92", *Economic Journal*, 106, March 1996 p334-344), who estimate that job tenure fell only slightly between 1975 and 1992.

14. "Building a Recovery that Lasts", speech delivered on February 26 1997.

15. *Has Globalisation Gone Too Far?* p20. Note, however, that the extent to which this is true depends upon the wage-elasticity of labour supply. The more responsive labour supply decisions are to changes in wages, the greater will be the wage and employment changes in response to demand shocks. For prime-age males, however, labour supply may be relatively inelastic, so Rodrik's point, while valid, is less powerful.

16. *Has Globalisation Gone Too Far?* p53. This point was made earlier by David Cameron, in "The expansion of the public economy: a comparative analysis", *American Political Science Review*, December 1978 p1243-61.

17. *Has Globalisation Gone Too Far?* p55.

18. *Exchange Rate Instability* p3.

19. Insofar as we can tell. Given that the nature of our exports and GDP has changed so much in the last 100 years, it is extremely difficult to construct meaningful price indices for either series.

20. David Held, Anthony McGrew, David Goldblatt and Jonathan Perraton, *Global Transformations*, p173.

21. *Exchange Rate Instability* p10.

22. Speech in Winchester, Tuesday 10 October 2006.

23. Daniel Trefler, "The case of the missing trade and other mysteries", *American Economic Review*, 85, December 1995 p1029-46.

24 "Perspectives on OECD Economic Integration", p10, August 2000, available from www.kc.frb.org.

25. "Gravity with gravitas: a solution to the border puzzle", *American Economic Review*, 93, March 2003, p170-92.

26. "The international diversification puzzle is worse than you think", *American Economic Review*, 87, March 1997 p170-80.

27 "Perspectives on OECD Economic Integration", p7.

28. "Domestic saving and international capital flows", *Economic Journal*, 90, June 1980, p314-29.

29. "International Capital Mobility in History: The Saving-Investment Relationship", *National Bureau of Economic Research working paper no 5743* September 1996, p13.

30. Baxter and Crucini, "Explaining saving-investment correlations", *American Economic Review*, 83, June 1993 p416-36 and Ghosh, "International capital mobility amongst the major industrialised countries: too little or too much?", *Economic Journal*, 105, January 1995 p107-28.

31. "Saving-investment correlations and capital mobility", *Economic Journal*, 102, September 1992 p1162-70.

32. *Exchange Rate Instability* p78.

33. Lucy Chennells and Rachel Griffith, *Taxing Profits in a Changing World*, p10.

34. "Are your wages set in Beijing?", *Journal of Economic Perspectives*, 9, summer 1995, p15-32, p30.

35. This point, like the second one, is made by Hirst and Thompson, *Globalisation in Question* p118.

36. See Krugman, *Exchange Rate Instability* p7, Linda Weiss, "Globalisation and the myth of the powerless state", *New Left Review*, 225, September/October 1997, p3-27 and Held et al, *Global Transformations*, p215.

37. "Globalisation and the labour market" p193, in Philippe Aghion and Jeffrey Williamson, *Growth, Inequality and Globalisation*.

38. *Global Transformations*, p431.

39. *The State We're In*, especially chapter 6.

40. *Eighth Annual Report on Finance for Small Firms*, p50, March 2001.

41. This is the standard feature of the Mundell-Fleming model, described in any textbook of international macroeconomics. The caveat to it is that the capital inflow caused by the loose fiscal policy can drive up the exchange rate, with the result that the stimulus to activity given by the fiscal expansion is offset by the loss of exports caused by the rising exchange rate. In this case, fiscal policy becomes impotent – but for reasons utterly different from those generally described by the globalization school.

42. *Manifesto of the Communist Party.* In Lewis S.Feuer (ed) – *Marx and Engels: Basic Writings* p52.

43. *Principles of Political Economy and Taxation* (Everyman 1973) p163.

44. *Principles of Political Economy and Taxation*, p271.

45. *The Wealth of Nations Books IV-V*, (Penguin Classics 1999) p442.

46. Cmd 9725 p3.

47. Quoted in Alan Wolfe, *The Limits of Legitimacy* p240.

48. *The End of the Nation State* p4.

49. "Building a Recovery That Lasts", February 26 1997.

50. "Open Macroeconomics in an Open Economy", *Centre for Economic Performance Occasional Paper no.13* p8.

51. *New Britain: My Vision of A Young Country* p118.

3.

The Problem of Profits

The problem of profits is ... the central dilemma facing contemporary social democracy (Tony Crosland).[1]

There is a central contradiction in a capitalist universe between the Labour party's two goals – full employment and economic growth at one end, and a shift in power and wealth to working people and their families at the other (David Coates).[2]

Once upon a time, socialists believed capitalism would collapse under the weight of its own contradictions. They were wrong. What collapsed under the weight of its own contradictions was not capitalism, but post-war social democracy.

This matters for two reasons. First, the failure of the post-war settlement meant the Labour party had to rethink the goals and policies of social democracy. It really did have to put a "new" into New Labour. Those who complain that Labour has abandoned its roots miss the point. The party had to abandon some of its roots.

Secondly, post-war social democrats had one big thing in common with New Labour. Like New Labour, they believed it was possible to reconcile economic efficiency with equality. That their project failed should alert us to the fact that it is harder to reconcile these two ideals than is sometimes supposed.

So what was the contradiction that caused the collapse of the post-war settlement?

It is simply put. Its main aim – full employment – could only be maintained by ensuring a high level of corporate profits. That is because companies need profits if they are to invest, and investment is necessary for full employment. However, prolonged full employment inevitably squeezes profits. Investment therefore falters and unemployment rises. In this sense, full employment is unsustainable. The promise of the 1944 White Paper Employment Policy, on which post-war social democratic politics was founded – that "the government accepts as one of their primary aims...the maintenance of a high and stable level of employment" – was, therefore, a promise which could not be kept.[3]

This contradiction was exacerbated by the fact most social democrats thought that profits, though economically necessary, were socially unjust. The upshot was an ambivalent attitude towards them, even on the so-called right of the Labour party. In *The Future of Socialism*, Tony Crosland declared that the right of shareholders to profits "has no obvious moral or economic basis" and leads to unjustifiable inequalities of income[4]. But, he said, profits are "a pre-condition for rapid growth". "So long as we maintain a substantial private sector socialists must logically applaud the accumulation of private profits" he concluded.[5]

James Callaghan displayed a similar ambivalence. In his first Budget in 1964, he declared that his aim in reforming company taxation was to "provide an incentive to dynamic companies to develop at a rapid pace through the use of their ploughed-back profits".[6] Barely three years later, he had a different message: "In view of the very large increased profitability of industry that is likely to take place over the next 12 months, and in view of the fact that we are asking all sections of the community for a sacrifice, we should not put industry in a position where it can make very large, exceptionally large, profits."[7]

"The old dilemma of the social reformer"

Profits, then, were a problem for Old Labour. Equality required low profits, but full employment and economic growth required high profits.

However, this conflict between efficiency and equality was not supposed to happen. The architects of Old Labour, like New Labour, believed the two went hand in hand. "Redistributive measures commend themselves not merely on the grounds of social justice, but pre-eminently on the grounds of economic reason" said E.F. Schumacher in 1944. "The old dilemma of the social reformer has been solved."[8]

This thinking was based upon one interpretation of Keynes's *General Theory of Employment, Interest and Money*.

To Keynes, employment was determined by effective demand. "The propensity to consume and the rate of new investment determine between them the volume of employment" he said[9]. Unfortunately, investment depended upon "animal spirits" which were difficult to influence. Full employment therefore could best be achieved by raising the "propensity to consume" or reducing the propensity to save. And this could be done by shifting incomes away from profits, a high proportion of which were saved, and towards wages, the vast bulk of which were spent – and, for the same reasons, from high personal incomes towards low personal incomes. "The growth of wealth, so far from being dependent on the abstinence of the rich, as is commonly supposed, is more likely to be impeded by it" wrote Keynes.[10] "Any redistribution of incomes towards a smaller inequality is bound to reduce private savings and may thus contribute to the solution of the unemployment problem" said Schumacher.[11]

Now, you might think this is just incoherent. Surely, lower profits mean lower investment and therefore lower growth.

Not necessarily. We must distinguish between the profit share and the profit rate. If the propensity to spend out of wages is greater than the propensity to spend out of profits, demand will rise if incomes shift from profits to wages. If it rises sufficiently, the profit rate will rise. A low profit margin is no problem, if sales volumes are high enough to generate big profit rates.

If this is the case, high wages, high investment, full employment and high profit rates are all mutually compatible.

Unfortunately, this happy outcome – what Stephen Marglin and Amit Bhaduri call a "stagnationist-co-operation" regime – requires some rare conditions to be met.[12]

For one thing, it requires workers to spend their wages. If they start saving them, a shift in incomes from profits to wages could reduce aggregate demand and so raise unemployment.

Second, workers must not exploit too much the strong bargaining position that full employment gives them. If they do so, and demand big wage rises, companies will either raise prices – which means higher inflation and lost international competitiveness – or cut investment.

Third, companies must continue investing. This requires that they be confident about future demand and profits.

If these conditions are not met, we'll get what Marglin and Bhaduri call a "conflictual-stagnationist" regime. Conflictual, because a rising share of wages in GDP reduces profit rates as well as profit shares, thus generating class conflict. Stagnationist, because this shift reduces long-term growth. In this regime, equality – in the sense of a rising wage share – and economic growth become incompatible.

In what follows, we shall show how the "stagnationist-co-operation" regime crumbled, to be replaced by the "conflictual-stagnationist" one. The "old dilemma of the social reformer" therefore re-emerged. Equality and efficiency ceased to be compatible.

The collapse of profits

Two facts show that, by the 1960s, the UK economy was indeed in a "conflictual-stagnationist" regime. Fact one is that the fall in the share of profits in GDP during the 1960s and 1970s was accompanied by a fall in the profit rate. The share of profits in business sector incomes fell from 24.5 per cent in 1960 to 19.7 per cent in 1973. During this time the profit rate fell from 13.5 per cent to 7.8 per cent.[13] Fact two is that capacity usage did not increase as the profit share fell. Years of low profit shares, such as 1967 and 1975, were also years of large spare capacity. And years of high profit shares, such as 1960 and 1973, were also years of high utilisation.

But why did the profit share fall? Two explanations can be ruled out immediately.

It was not because of the oil price shocks of the 1970s. The pre-tax profit share and the profit rate were both falling from the 1950s onwards. The profit share was lower in 1973 – the peak of one of strongest post-war booms – than it was in the early 1950s. As Stephen Marglin has said: "There was....well before the oil shock, a general 'full employment profit squeeze' throughout the OECD countries."[14]

Nor was it merely because full employment caused wages to accelerate. Rising wages alone can never squeeze profits. This is because if workers spend all their incomes, what firms (in aggregate) lose through the back door because their wage costs rise, they get back through the front door in the form of higher consumer demand. This was why Michal Kalecki declared that it is "entirely wrong" to believe higher wages mean lower profits[15]. The link between wage militancy and the fall in the profit share is, as we shall see, more subtle than this.

So, why did profit rates and profit shares fall?

One explanation blames increasing international competition. Robert Brenner has written:

> The entry of lower-cost German and Japanese producers, and the subsequent failure of higher-cost US producers to leave their lines...brought about over-production and over-capacity and a falling rate of profit on an international scale, focused on the manufacturing sector.[16]

You might think this means post-war social democracy really did collapse because of globalization – albeit not in the way that is generally claimed by globalization theorists.

However, this is not so. For one thing, globalization was not an exogenous development. One reason why Japanese and German firms devoted so much effort to their export drives was precisely that they knew that the Keynesian commitment to full employment, in the US and UK, assured them of a big and growing market.

Also, increased competition per se – as Brenner recognises – is not the whole story. Two things tell us this. First, why was it that globalization caused profits to fall rather than wages? Secondly, increased competition predicts that inflation should fall. But it didn't. Inflation drifted upwards after the mid-1950s.

There is, therefore, more to the story than international competition alone.

To see what this is, consider a simple national accounts identity. It says that profits, by definition, are equal to: the excess of private consumption over wages; plus investment; plus the excess of government spending over taxes; plus net exports; minus other incomes.

Fluctuations in the share of profits in GDP can then be decomposed into just five components. Table 2 does this. The picture that emerges is clear. In a statistical sense, the fall in the profit share was entirely due to a fall in the gap between private consumption and wages.[17]

Table 2. Accounting for the falling profit share

	Profit share	Net consumption	Investment	Govt deficit	Trade deficit	Other income
1953	15.5	12.6	17.1	7.7	-1.0	20.8
1955	16.9	11.3	18.9	5.8	-1.8	17.3
1958	14.7	9.9	18.4	5.6	0.6	19.6
1960	16.1	8.5	20.8	5.9	-1.7	17.4
1962	13.9	7.0	19.2	6.4	-0.4	18.3
1967	12.8	5.2	22.7	6.3	-1.3	20.0
1973	15.3	3.6	24.7	7.9	-2.9	18.0
1975	12.3	-3.0	20.6	14.0	-2.0	17.2
1977	13.9	0.5	22.3	10.6	0.7	20.2

Source: author's calculations, based on tables 1.3 and 1.4 of Economic Trends annual supplement 1996. Relationship between columns: 1=2+3+4+5-6. Investment includes stockbuilding and other income includes stock appreciation.

Why did this happen? Conventional accounts blame the "wage explosion" after the mid-1960s. But this is wrong. The share of wages in GDP was quite stable between the late 50s and early 70s. It was the share of consumer spending in national income that declined, from around 77% of GDP in the mid-50s to under 70% by the mid-70s.

Kalecki and Schumacher were wrong. They assumed workers did not save. In the 1940s, that was true. But by the early 1970s, it was not. Between 1946 and 1950, the personal sector's saving ratio averaged just 2.1 per cent of post-tax income. Between 1971 and 1975 it averaged 9.8 per cent.

This is important. Because employees were starting to save, the shift in income from firms to workers did not significantly increase the propensity to consume. That meant effective demand did not rise much as the profit share fell, so profit rates fell as well as profit shares. Equality, in the sense of high wages and low profits, therefore began to conflict with efficiency, in the sense of high investment and growth.

But why did the savings ratio rise? Partly, it is because people got richer. As Keynes said:

A higher absolute level of income will tend, as a rule, to widen the gap between income and consumption. For the satisfaction of the immediate primary needs of a man and his family is usually a stronger motive than the motives toward accumulation, which only acquire effective sway when a margin of comfort has been attained. These reasons will lead, as a rule, to a greater proportion of income being saved as real income increases.[18]

This, however, is not the whole story. What also contributed to the rise in the savings ratio was a pick-up in inflation. This caused consumption to fall, relative to income, for two reasons. One is that inflation reduces the real value of financial assets. To restore real wealth, therefore, people need to save more.[19] Secondly, inflation creates uncertainty. And uncertainty increases savings.

All this means the rise in inflation from the 1960s onwards had even more grievous effects than thought. It was a key cause of the squeeze in profit margins and slowdown in growth.[20]

But why did inflation rise? It is here that the true importance of wage militancy lies. For inflation did not rise simply because of the pressure of demand. This much is clear from the simple fact that both inflation and unemployment were on a rising trend from the early 1960s onwards.

This is prima facie evidence of one thing – a rise in the so-called natural rate of unemployment (NRU), or the rate required to ensure stable wage and price inflation. To see why this happened, a simple diagram helps.[21]

Fig. 5

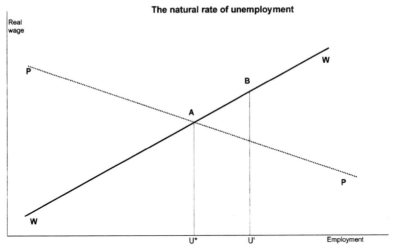

The natural rate of unemployment

Common sense suggests that, as the demand for labour rises, workers will demand higher real wages. The line WW, showing the target real wage, will therefore slope up. But firms will only hire workers if it is profitable to do so – that is, if there's a mark-up of prices over wages. This desired mark-up, shown by the PP line, represents the feasible real wage.[22]

The two lines intersect at point A, implying a NRU of U*. Now, imagine that – as a result, say, of the government expanding the economy – employment increases to U' and point B. Workers then demand higher real wages. But firms, seeking to protect their profit margins, simply raise prices in response to higher wages. But those price rises mean that wages have not risen in real terms. So, workers demand still higher wage rises. And firms react simply by raising prices still more. The upshot is that, when employment rises to the right of U*, inflation accelerates. This means U* is the maximum employment rate (or the minimum unemployment rate) consistent with inflation stability. It is that rate which "brings peace in the battle of the mark-ups."

Now, inflation and unemployment were both rising in the late 1960s. That must mean the NRU was rising. In our diagram, U* was shifting to the left. This can have been for only one of two reasons. Either the WW curve shifted left – because, say, workers demanded a higher real wage for any given level of unemployment. Or because the PP curve shifted down – because firms required a higher mark-up of prices over wages at any given level of activity.

The latter did happen after the 1973-74 commodity price shock. To pay for the higher cost of raw materials then, firms had to raise the mark-up of prices over wages. But it's unlikely that the PP curve shifted down in the UK much before then. Instead, the NRU rose – and profits were squeezed – mainly because wage militancy increased. The WW curve shifted left. "The main propulsive force behind the sharp acceleration in both wage and price inflation was a rise in worker militancy" say Flanaghan, Soskice and Ulman.[23]

The key fact to explain here is not simply that wage inflation rose because unemployment was low. In our diagram, this is a shift *along* the WW curve – not a shift *in* the WW curve. We must explain why the target real wage rose at any given level of unemployment.

One possible reason is that workers simply 'wised up' and finally recognised that inflation would eat away at the money wage rises they were negotiating. As a result, they demanded pay rises not only to compensate for past inflation, but to compensate for higher, future, inflation as well. In other words, 'money illusion' faded.[24]

A second reason lies with the rising tax burden on workers.[25] Higher marginal tax rates in the 1960s meant bigger pay rises were necessary to achieve a given rise in take-home pay. Allied to higher inflation expectations, the result was a rise in pay demands.

To all this, we must add another cause – that workers' aspirations rose. Sociologists such as John Goldthorpe have attributed this to "the decay of the status order".[26] As class inequalities came to be viewed as less defensible, he argued, workers became less inhibited about pushing forward their demands. Why this should have happened in the late 1960s, rather than before or after, is unclear. Explanations range from the meta-historical – the legacy of feudalism faded – through to political theory – the democratic ideal requires people to push their opinions forward – to the more parochial – episodes such as the Profumo affair exposed the ruling class as being unworthy of deference.[27]

There is another explanation. As Newell and Symons point out, "the wage explosion was in some measure due to the passing of a risk-averse cohort of workers".[28] The idea is simple. In the 1950s, the memory of the 1930s depression exacerbated workers' fear of unemployment. That meant they settled for low wage rises even though the reality was that they had little to fear. By the late 1960s, however, workers who remembered the depression were retiring, to be replaced by younger people who had known nothing but full employment. The upshot was that perceptions of the risk of job loss declined. As a result, workers grew more militant. Indeed, Newell and Symons estimate that all of the rise in the NRU between the 1960s and 1970s was due to this generational shift.[29]

Full employment, then, was inherently unsustainable. As the fear of the sack faded, wage inflation rose. This caused price inflation to rise. This, in turn, led to a rise in workers' savings. That meant that the shift in incomes from profits to wages did not increase demand and profit rates as economists had hoped in the 1940s. So investment, and hence economic growth, eventually faltered. Equality and efficiency therefore became incompatible, contrary to the desires and intentions of the architects of the post-war settlement. As Samuel Bowles and Robert Boyer said, "Full employment equilibrium is impossible except under highly restrictive conditions".[30]

You might wonder why, if full employment squeezed profits, investment stayed so strong, as table 2 shows. There are several reasons. Tax breaks for companies became increasingly generous. Firms were investing to catch up with "best practice" of high-productivity US firms. The same confidence in full employment that caused workers to demand pay rises also encouraged firms to invest in new capacity. And company managers might have become over-confident about their individual ability to grow; as the cliché says, everyone thinks they're a genius in a boom.

These causes of investment, though, were sticking plasters that disguised the underlying tensions in the post-war settlement. And not everyone was fooled by them. "The high post-war investment has essentially the nature of a gigantic cyclical boom" said R.C.O. Matthews in 1968.[31]

"Told You So" – The warnings of the 1940s

You might object here that I'm committing the fallacy of historicism – the notion that, just because history turned out a certain way, this course of events was inevitable.

I'm not. The problems unleashed by full employment – of rising workers' militancy, inflation and a profit squeeze – were widely anticipated in the 1940s.

Keynes' critics clearly foresaw the prospect of rising inflation[32]. What's more interesting, however, is that his sympathisers also anticipated problems.

Writing in 1943, Michal Kalecki warned: "Under a regime of permanent full employment, 'the sack' would cease to play its role as a disciplinary measure. The social position of the boss would be undermined and the self-assurance and class consciousness of the working class would grow. Strikes for wage increases and improvements in working conditions would create political tension."[33]

Such pessimism was by no means confined to those with a Marxist's scepticism about the viability of capitalism. A year later, William Beveridge said that "If trades unions under full employment press wage claims unreasonably, maintenance of a stable price level will become impossible".[34]

James Meade echoed these warnings. He said: "If the trade unions make a free and full use in each industry of the bargaining power which their monopoly power confers on them, there is the greatest danger that it will be impossible to maintain full employment without an inflationary upward movement of money wages, money costs and money prices"[35]. He thought an unemployment rate as high as 4% was necessary simply "to allow for the necessary turnover of jobs." But, he added, "the real danger... is that the unemployment percentage will have to be much higher than this technical minimum" in order to hold down inflation.[36]

All this was heeded by Aneurin Bevan. Writing in 1952 he noted that "the maintenance of full employment always carries with it the threat of inflation".[37]

That full employment was potentially inflationary was therefore widely acknowledged by the architects of post-war social democracy. But what was their solution?

It was certainly not to tolerate a little bit of inflation as the price of full employment. The 1940s creators of full employment were far more like "inflation nutters" than the Bank of England is now. Whereas the latter tolerates a little inflation, the former wanted price stability. "The level of prices and wages must be kept reasonably stable" proclaimed the 1944 White Paper, *Employment Policy*, adding that "we must enter the post-war period with a firm determination to keep stability in the general *level* of wages and prices"[38]. And in Labour's second Budget Hugh Dalton promised that "a stable cost-of-living *index* is a sheet anchor for us".[39]

One reason for this commitment to price stability was that few believed full employment would cause only a small amount of inflation. In a striking anticipation of Milton Friedman's rejection of the notion of a stable trade-off between inflation and unemployment, Beveridge had worried of the danger of "a *vicious spiral* of inflation".[40] The Phillips curve – the idea that there was a stable trade-off between inflation and unemployment that policy-makers would exploit – was an invention (in every sense) of the late 1950s.

With tolerance of inflation rejected, many economists in the 1940s saw only one solution to the "wage problem" – state control. "Wage bargaining in full employment is, in fact, a political problem and it will be settled on the political plane" said G.D.N. Worswick. in 1944.[41] "And", agreed Beveridge, "if wage militancy does become a problem, wage determination will perforce become a function of the state".[42] These points were not lost on Bevan. "A national wages policy is an inevitable corollary of full employment" he said.[43] Equality and efficiency, these men thought, might have been compatible – but only at the price of liberty, the freedom of workers to negotiate their own pay.

Attitudes towards the "wage problem" in the 1940s split roughly into two camps. In one were the optimists, such as William Beveridge and some in the Treasury, who thought a political solution could be found to the problem. They believed a combination of faster productivity growth – as full employment stimulated technical progress and reduced workers' opposition to new technology – and workers' willingness to accept wage restraint in exchange for full employment would hold down inflation.

In the other camp were pessimists such as Kalecki, who thought political solutions unlikely. He said: "the assumption that a government will maintain full employment in a capitalist economy if it only knows how to do it is fallacious"[44]. Meade, in his gloomier moments, agreed. Because of "uncontrolled inflation,...we might have to give up the employment policy" he said.[45]

One thing, then, is clear. As Russell Jones has pointed out, "policy-makers early in the Keynesian era did an acceptable job in warning future governments of the inflationary pitfalls" in a full employment policy[46]. That full employment – indeed, far fuller than anyone envisaged – would lead to wage militancy would have come as no surprise to intelligent thinkers in the 1940s. The collapse of the post-war boom was not only foreseeable – it was widely foreseen.

"A Middle Class Racket" – The role of the Welfare State

The welfare state as we know it has no rationale, no animating principle and no genuine justification. It is not an adequate safety net, nor an instrument whereby the underclass is re-integrated into civil life, nor yet an effective machinery for redistribution, but virtually the contrary of each of these distinct institutions. The welfare state does not relieve poverty, but institutionalises it. It does not emancipate the underclass but instead imprisons it in ghettos of dependency...It does not redistribute income from rich to poor but instead, for the most part, acts in accordance with Director's Law: it serves as a middle class racket whereby income transfers are effected from rich and the poor to the majority in the middle. (John Gray).[47]

Old Labour, then, failed to achieve economic efficiency, in the sense of full employment and sustained growth.

But it also failed to abolish poverty or create greater equality just as much as it failed to maintain full employment. If Labour governments really did choose equality over efficiency they did not get what they wanted[48].

The present-day notion that poverty is largely due to the combination of the emergence of an under-class, under-funding of the welfare state and a collapse in demand for unskilled workers distracts us from the fact that even the pre-Thatcherite welfare state had failed to abolish poverty, at least in the social democratic sense of a low income relative to others.

The earliest evidence of this came from Brian Abel-Smith and Peter Townsend in 1965. They estimated that the number of people living in relative poverty almost doubled between 1953-54 and 1960[49]. And this was a period of consistently full employment and strong economic growth. When Townsend returned to this issue later in the 1960s, he found that poverty had increased still further.[50]

The 1970s slowdown did not reverse this trend. Writing in 1979 Frank Field said: "The numbers of poor have grown in the post-war years...The years of affluence of have failed the poor."[51]

Indeed, in 1979 the Royal Commission on the Distribution of Income and Wealth found that the income distribution changed remarkably little during the post-war settlement:

> If the decline in the share of the top 1% is ignored, the shape of the distribution is not greatly different in 1976-77 from what it was in 1949. The major part of the fall in the share of the top 1% is balanced by an increase in the shares of the other groups in the top half of the distribution.[52]

One reason for this is that labour market trends did not greatly help the poorer worker. In 1938, the lowest-paid decile of male manual workers received wages which were 67.7% of the median. In 1970, that percentage had dropped slightly, to 67.3%. Indeed, Peter Townsend estimates that, in 1968-69, nearly half of all unskilled manual workers and their dependants were living on the margins of poverty.[53] "The rising prosperity of the 1950s and early 1960s failed to eradicate low pay" agreed Field.[54]

The conclusion is clear. Full employment, the welfare state and progressive taxation all failed to abolish relative poverty or significantly reduce inequality. As Anthony Giddens has said: "Attempts at the redistribution of wealth or income through fiscal measures and orthodox welfare systems on the whole have not worked."[55]

You might reply that inequalities of income are not the only ones with which the welfare state was concerned. Inequalities of health, housing and education are also important. The post-war welfare state also tackled these.

Table 3. Distribution of incomes after taxes and benefits, % of total

	1949	1959	1964	1970-71	1973-74	1976-77
Top 1%	6.4	5.3	5.3	4.5	4.5	3.5
2-5%	11.3	10.5	10.7	10.0	9.8	9.4
6-10%	9.4	9.4	9.9	9.4	9.3	9.5
Top 10%	27.1	25.2	25.9	23.9	23.6	22.4
11-20%	14.5	15.7	16.1	15.9	15.5	15.9
21-30%	11.9	12.9	12.9	13.3	13.2	13.4
31-40%	10.5	11.2	11.1	11.2	11.2	11.3
41-50%	9.5	9.9	8.8	9.5	9.5	9.4
51-60%		7.2	8.0	7.8	7.8	7.9
61-70%		6.6	5.6	6.5	6.4	6.8
71-80%	26.5#	5.2	5.1	5.2	5.4	5.2
81-90%		6.0*	6.5*	6.6*	4.2	4.6
91-100%					3.2	3.1
Gini coefficient	35.5	36.0	36.6	33.9	32.8	31.5

Source: Royal Commission on the Distribution of Income and Wealth, Report no.7 p15. *
81-100%, #= 51-100%

Indeed it did – by making them worse. "Almost all public expenditure on the social services in Britain benefits the better-off to a greater extent than the poor" said Julian Le Grand in 1982.[56] Table 4 on the next page quantifies this. With the exception of council housing and pre-16 education, the government spent more per person on those in the top fifth of the income distribution than it did on those in the bottom fifth.

Le Grand estimates that even the NHS benefited disproportionately the better-off. That he said was because: the well-off were more likely to visit their doctors for a given illness than the worse-off; because doctors spent longer with well-off patients than poorer ones; because hourly-paid and piece-rate workers were reluctant to lose pay in order to see their doctor; and because the middle class, being more confident, were more likely to make demands upon their doctors.

These factors, plus the fact that free health care was available to many of the worst-off before the NHS was formed, led, said Le Grand, to an alarming

Table 4. Spending on social services

	Ratio of spending per person in the top quintile to that per person in the bottom quintile, late 1970s
Council housing	0.3
Under-16 education	0.9
National Health Service	1.4
Higher education	3.5
Bus subsidies	3.7
Universities	5.4
Mortgage interest tax relief	6.8
Rail subsidies	9

Source: Le Grand – "The Middle Class Use of the British Social Services" p92 in Gooding and Le Grand – Not Only The Poor.

fact – that inequalities in health "may have become worse over time".[57] He found that, although unskilled workers were less likely to die in 1970-72 than in 1930-32 – because absolute mortality rates declined – their risk of death relative to the better-off actually deteriorated in the post-war period.

Inequalities in income and health were not the only ones which the post-war welfare state failed to address. Le Grand also found that inequalities of opportunity had not changed much either. "Not only are the chances of 'getting to the top' much greater for those with fathers already at the top, but they have not altered significantly over time" he said.[58]

His is not a lone opinion. "Post-war increases in social expenditure have been accompanied by little discernible reduction in social and economic inequality" says the Organisation for Economic Co-operation and Development[59]. Tony Blair himself has belatedly realized this. The post-war welfare state, he has said, "overwhelmingly benefited the middle class".[60] And James Bartholomew argues in *The Welfare State We're In* that the poor have "suffered the most" under the welfare state.[61]

So, why did Old Labour's welfare state fail to increase equality?

Because it wasn't trying to. The Beveridge Report – the foundation of post-war social security – reveals this. To Beveridge, the relief of poverty through the use of social security was a low priority. He said: "Income security, which is all that can be given by social insurance, is so inadequate a provision for human happiness that to put it forward by itself as a sole or principal measure of reconstruction hardly seems worth doing."[62]

One reason for this is that Beveridge, like New Labour, believed that work was the best route out of poverty. Another reason was that the social security system was in most regards already adequate. "Provision for most of the many varieties of need... has already been made in Britain on a scale not surpassed and hardly rivalled in any other country of the world" he wrote.[63]

The relief of poverty, then, was not the main aim of the Beveridge report. So what was? Partly, it was to simplify the prevailing complex system of benefits.[64] Also, Beveridge was as keen to increase the responsibilities of ordinary people as he was to expand their welfare rights. In a striking anticipation of New Labour rhetoric that rights and responsibilities go hand-in-hand, he wrote: "The plan is one to secure income for subsistence on condition of service and contribution and in order *to make and keep men fit for service.*"[65]

Beveridge also wanted to increase the population. The Report "starts from two facts" – the ageing population and a low birth rate. It continues: "Unless this rate is raised very materially in the near future, a rapid and continuous decline in the population cannot be prevented." It is, therefore, "imperative to give first place in social expenditure to the care of childhood and the safeguarding of maternity".[66]

There is another reason why the post-war welfare state failed to reduce inequality significantly – one that contains an important lesson for New Labour. This is that the rising tax burden meant that it was increasingly difficult for the tax system to act as a redistributive device. Big government and a redistributive tax system are mutually incompatible. As Gosta Esping-Andersen has written:

> As the incidence of taxation grows,...the tax system automatically loses its potential for progressive redistribution. Under conditions of heavy expenditure, the bulk of taxes must be collected among the largest income brackets, and that happens to be workers and middle-level white collar employees.[67]

Table 5 shows that although the tax burden rose for all income groups during the 1950s and 1960s, the biggest rises were endured by those outside the top 10% of income recipients. Between 1959 and 1976-77, the tax burden for the top 1% rose by just 5.3 percentage points. For those in the 41-60% range, however, it grew by 12 percentage points.

Because of this, the tax system played little role in increasing income equality during the years of post-war social democracy. What increase in equality there was during the post-war boom – and it consisted mainly in a redistribution from top to middle rather than top to bottom – was due to market forces, not the tax system.[68] It was the market that increased income equality, not the state.

The rise in government spending in the post-war period, therefore, failed to eliminate poverty or to reduce inequality. But it may have helped to undermine full employment, because it might have contributed to the profit squeeze in four different ways.

Table 5. Taxes as a % of income

	1959	1967	1973-74	1976-77
Top 1%	43.2	43.3	42.0	48.5
2-5%	19.1	20.6	21.9	28.7
6-10%	11.3	14.6	18.6	24.2
Top 10%	23.5	24.5	25.6	31.1
11-20%	7.8	13.3	15.8	21.7
21-40%	5.7	11.1	14.5	19.8
41-60%	4.9	9.1	12.1	16.9
61-80%	2.6	4.7	5.3	9.1
81-100%	0.1	0.8	0.4	2.1

Source: Royal Commission on the Distribution of Income and Wealth, Report no.7 p31

First, the increasing generosity of unemployment benefits, relative to post-tax wages, might have increased wage militancy by weakening the costs of a spell of unemployment. Richard Layard and Stephen Nickell estimate that a rising ratio of unemployment benefits to post-tax wages raised the natural rate of unemployment by 0.64 percentage points between 1956-66 and 1967-74.[69]

Secondly, as we have seen, it is possible that rising tax rates led to rising wage demands, as workers sought compensation from their employers for the cut in their effective incomes.[70]

Thirdly, rising government employment sustained full employment, even though private sector employment was declining from the mid-1960s onwards. That may have contributed to the sense of job security, which helped to fuel wage militancy.

Fourthly, government spending is subject to a "ratchet effect" – it is much easier to raise it than cut it. This meant that when tax revenues began to falter in the 1970s public borrowing exploded. In the early 1970s – when borrowing tended to exceed gilt issuance – this added to the money supply. That may have contributed to the rise in inflation and inflation expectations which bolstered pay demands. And in the later 1970s, when the borrowing was financed by gilt issuance, the higher interest rates may have contributed to lower investment.

None of this is to claim that the welfare state is always an insuperable obstacle to economic growth. As Angus Maddison has written, "there is no clear evidence that the growth of the welfare state has had adverse effects on economic performance".[71] What it does mean, however, is that, in conditions of full employment, rising government spending might have contributed in part to the profit squeeze. That might not have been so bad, had the welfare state been effective in preventing poverty. But it was not.

Conclusion

Much of the conventional history of Labour governments in the 1960s and 1970s invokes the words "if only". If only the Wilson government had devalued the pound upon taking office in 1964, instead of condemning the economy to three years of weak growth. If only a successful incomes policy had been found. If only the government had accurate forecasts of the public sector borrowing requirements in the mid-1970s, and so been able to avoid the humiliation of calling in the IMF. If only James Callaghan had called an election in October 1978.

These laments ignore the crucial fact. The collapse of post-war social democracy occurred not because of individual mistakes by policy-makers – though there were plenty of those – but because of its own deep-rooted structural failures.

Failure one was that full employment was inherently unsustainable. Full employment led to increasing wage militancy and hence inflation and a profit squeeze. That led to faltering investment and employment.

Failure two was that full employment and ever-increasing welfare spending did not abolish poverty or significantly increase equality. The "disappearance" of poverty at the peak of the boom owed less to the genuine elimination of hardship than to the fact that no-one was looking for it – an example of what Richard Titmuss called the "irresponsible society".[72]

Post-war Labour governments, therefore, failed to achieve both of the main aims of social democracy. They delivered neither economic success nor greater equality. Those who accuse New Labour of breaking with Labour traditions are guilty of hopelessly romanticizing Labour's past.

In light of all these failures, one vital but now over-looked fact acquires greater resonance. This is that the 1974-79 Labour government was booted out of office by precisely those on whom it had traditionally relied for support. In the 1979 general election, there was a swing towards Labour of 5% amongst the social class AB – professionals and managers – and a swing towards it of 5% amongst the white-collar C1s.[73] What cost Labour the 1979 election was the 10% swing against it among skilled manual workers and a 9% swing against it among lesser-skilled manual workers.

Thatcherism may have been sustained in office by middle-class greed. But it was put in office by working class disillusionment – a disillusionment that was well-founded.

The creation of "New Labour", therefore, should be seen not as a response to the new global economy, nor even as a lurch to the right. Instead, it is best seen as an attempt to find new policies to address the twin goals of "social justice" and economic efficiency. Such a search is necessary because the old policies failed – and failed miserably. If, in this enquiry, New Labour betrays Labour traditions, that betrayal is wholly justified.

So, how does New Labour hope to reconcile equality and efficiency? Let's take a look.

Notes

1. *The Future of Socialism* (1964 ed) p300.

2. *Labour in Power?* p263.

3. Cmd 6527 p3.

4. *The Future of Socialism* p282, 56.

5. *The Future of Socialism* p300.

6. *H.C.Debates* November 11 1964 c1042.

7. *H.C.Debates* November 20 1967 c944.

8. "Public Finance – Its Relation to Full Employment" in Oxford University Institute of Statistics, *The Economics of Full Employment* p90.

9. *The General Theory of Employment, Interest and Money* p30.

10. *The General Theory of Employment, Interest and Money* p373.

11. "Public Finance – Its Relation to Full Employment" p91.

12. "Profit Squeeze and Keynesian Theory" in Marglin and Schor (eds) – *The Golden Age of Capitalism*. Another account of how co-operation between capital and labour broke down can be found in Gavin Cameron and Chris Wallace, "Macroeconomic performance in the Bretton Woods period and after", *Oxford Review of Economic Policy*, 18, winter 2002, p479-94.

13. Armstrong, Glyn and Harrison, *Capitalism since World War II*, tables A2 and A4. Unfortunately, figures for the profit rate are subject to a wide margin of error. This is because the denominator – the capital stock – cannot be measured at all accurately. A particular problem is that, in measuring this stock, statisticians usually assume that machines and buildings last for a constant time – that their asset lives do not vary. In practice, however, a sharp downturn in the economy could cause accelerated scrapping of capital, whilst a boom might cause scrapping to be postponed. This might cause profit rates to be over-stated in a boom, and under-stated in a recession.

14. "Lessons of the Golden Age: An Overview" in Marglin and Schor (eds) – op. cit. p19.

15. *Selected Essays in the Dynamics of the Capitalist Economy* p163.

16. "The economics of global turbulence" p157, *New Left Review*, 229, May-June 1998.

17. This, it should be stressed, is a purely statistical exercise.

18. *The General Theory of Employment, Interest and Money* p97.

19. This is a standard finding in the empirical literature on consumer spending. See, for example, Speight – *Consumption, Rational Expectations and Liquidity* p135-7 or Dicks – "Interest Elasticity of Consumer Spending" in Henry and Patterson (eds) – *Economic Modelling at the Bank of England*.

20. This does not mean conventional wisdom believes inflation had no impact on profits. By 1974, it was widely appreciated that the soaring cost of replacing inventories and working capital was eating into cash flow. As a result, the decline in the profit share had by then become a full-blown liquidity crisis, with companies' retained cash plummeting and their borrowing soaring.

21 This is taken from Layard and Nickell – "Unemployment in Britain", *Economica*, 53, 1986 supplement, p121-69, p143. See also Bean – "Capital Shortages and Persistent Unemployment", *Economic Policy*, 8, 1989 p11-45, and Broadberry – "Employment and Unemployment" in Floud and McCloskey (ed) – *The Economic History of Britain since 1700* vol III, p206-7.

22. In the diagram, we show this as a downwardly sloping line, reflecting the possibility that the desired mark-up rises as capacity usage (and hence employment) rises. However, one can equally well think of it as a horizontal line – that is, a non-cyclical desired mark-up.

23. *Unionism, Economic Stabilisation and Incomes Policies*, p373.

24. We shouldn't, however, make too much of this. The fact that wage demands increased quickly in response to the higher price inflation caused by the 1950-53 Korean war suggests that money illusion was never complete. See *The Passing of the Golden Age* (Centre for Labour Economics Discussion Paper no.347, June 1989) p4-5.

25. For data on marginal tax rates, see Price – "Budgetary Policy" table 4.1 on p141 of Blackaby (ed) – *British Economic Policy 1960-74: Demand Management*. Note that my argument here applies only to the short run, which can last a few years. In the very long-run, a high tax burden does not raise the NRU. If it did, unemployment would be far higher now than it was a century ago – which is not the case.

26. "The Current Inflation: Towards a Sociological Account" in Hirsch and Goldthorpe (eds) – *The Political Economy of Inflation*.

27. See Brittan "The Economic Consequences of Democracy" in King et al – *Why is Britain Becomig Harder to Govern?*, Crozier, Huntingdon and Watanuki – *The Crisis of Democracy* and Wolfe – *The Limits of Legitimacy* for different interpretations of this problem. Joseph Schumpeter had warned of this in his *Capitalism, Socialism and Democracy* (chs 11-14), where he argued that capitalism broke down feudal habits of thinking that sustained deference towards authority.

28. *The Passing of the Golden Age* p10.

29. *The Passing of the Golden Age* p28.

30. "A Wage-led Employment Regime", in Marglin and Schor, *The Golden Age of Capitalism* p191. The key word here is "equilibrium. Nothing in this account rules out the possibility that full employment could be achieved for a while. The point is that it cannot be sustained for a lengthy period.

31. "Why has Britain had full employment since the war?", *Economic Journal*, 78, September 1968, p555-69, p561.

32. Richard Cockett, *Thinking the Unthinkable: Think-tanks and the Economic Counter-revolution*, p42-44.

33. *Selected Essays in the Dynamics of the Capitalist Economy* p140-1.

34. *Full Employment in a Free Society* p207.

35. *Planning and the Price Mechanism* p69.

36. *Planning and the Price Mechanism* p70.

37. *In Place of Fear* p182.

38. Cmd 6527 p16, p8, emphasis added.

39. *H.C. Debates* April 9 1946 c1809.

40. *Full Employment in a Free Society* p199, emphasis added.

41. "The Stability and Flexibility of Full Employment" p66, in Oxford University Institute of Statistics, *The Economics of Full Employment*.

42. *Full Employment in a Free Society* p207.

43. *In Place of Fear* p138.

44. *Selected Essays in the Dynamics of the Capitalist Economy* p138.

45. Quoted in Jones, *Wages and Employment Policy* 1936-85 p28.

46. *Wages and Employment Policy* 1936-85, p136.

47. "Limited Government: A Positive Agenda", in *Beyond the New Right*, p 24.

48. Not, of course, that Labour did make this choice. As Jim Tomlinson reminds us, economic efficiency loomed as large in Labour minds in the 1940s – and earlier – as the aim of greater equality; see *Democratic Socialism and Economic Policy: The Attlee Years 1945-51*, passim.

49. *The Poor and the Poorest* p28. I stress again that all this refers to "relative poverty" – that is, expenditure of less than 140 per cent of the basic National Assistance level – rather than absolute poverty. I'm not denying that absolute living standards rose considerably in the 50s and 60s.

50. *Poverty in the United Kingdom*, p272.

51. "Poverty, Growth and the Redistribution of Income" in Beckerman (ed) – *Slow Growth in Britain: Causes and Consequences* p85, 101.

52. *Report no.7: Report on the Standing Reference*, p17.

53. *Poverty in the United Kingdom* p293.

54. "Poverty, Growth and the Redistribution of Income" p93, 95. Official thinking agreed. A report from the Department of Employment and Productivity in 1969 admitted that "one of the weaknesses of the system of free collective bargaining has been its inability to solve the problem of the low paid" *(Productivity, Prices and Incomes Policy after 1969, Cmd 4237, December 1969)*.

55. *Beyond Left and Right: The Future of Radical Politics* p156.

56. *The Strategy of Equality* p3.

57. *The Strategy of Equality* p37.

58. *The Strategy of Equality* p68.

59. *Social Expenditure 1960-90: Problems of Growth and Control* p61.

60. Speech to Fabian Society, June 17 2003.

61. This particular claim is on p340.

62. *Social Insurance and Allied Services*, Cmd 6404 p163.

63. *Social Insurance and Allied Services* p5.

64. *Social Insurance and Allied Services* p6.

65. *Social Insurance and Allied Services* p 170.

66. *Social Insurance and Allied Services* p8. Only a cynic would note the juxtaposition of this eugenicist undertow with the fact that the post-war health service increased inequalities of mortality rates.

67. *Politics Against Markets: The Social Democratic Road to Power*, p35.

68. Between 1949 and 1976-77 the Gini coefficient – a measure of income inequality – fell from 41.1 to 36.5 for pre-tax incomes. That drop of 4.6 points suggests equality increased. For post-tax incomes, however, the Gini coefficient fell by only 4 points, from 35.5 to 31.5. (*Report no.7: Report on the Standing Reference* p14-15.)

69. "Unemployment in Britain", *Economica*, 53, 1986 pS121-169, pS159. For a contrary view, see P.N.Junankar, "An Econometric Analysis of Unemployment in Great Britain 1952-75", *Oxford Economic Papers* 1981 p387-400, p390, 398.

70. See, however, Carruth and Oswald, *Pay Determination and Industrial Prosperity* ch.7, for an econometric account of wage inflation in which income taxes are insignificant.

71. "Origins and Impact of the Welfare State 1883-1983" p77 in *Banca Nazionale del Lavoro Quarterly Review* March 1984 p55-87.

72. "The Irresponsible Society" p 226 in *Essays on the Welfare State*.

73. Figures cited in Ken Coates "What Went Wrong?" p30-31 in Coates (ed) – *What Went Wrong?*

4.

Making Work Pay

A good example of policies designed to increase both equality and efficiency are those intended to "make work pay." Tax credits, the introduction of a 10p starting rate of tax and reform of National Insurance contributions are all meant to raise both efficiency and equality.

The concern with efficiency arises from the fact that before New Labour came to power, low-wage earners faced very high effective marginal tax rates. For some, the combination of the withdrawal of Family Credit, Housing Benefit and Council Tax Benefit, plus income tax and National Insurance payments, meant an effective marginal tax rate of 97%.

Such high tax rates deterred some people from working long hours, and others from working at all. They therefore added to long-term unemployment, and caused some people to drop out of the labour market altogether. This created several costs.

- Inflation. Because some of the unemployed were not looking for work, they were not bidding down wages. As a result, in the 1980s, wage and price inflation rose whilst unemployment was high.

- High taxes, as the long-term unemployed claimed welfare benefits.

- Long-term disincentives to work. With vast numbers of children brought up to believe worklessness was natural, their inclination to look for work when they grow up might be impaired. The costs of worklessness could last for decades therefore.

Not only was all this economically inefficient, it also increased inequality. By creating large numbers of people with little experience of work, the benefit system helped breed poverty and alienation. And by removing benefits quickly as incomes rose, those in work were trapped in poverty. This contributed to a big rise in child poverty. Between 1970 and 1995, the proportion of children in households without a full-time employee rose from 16% to 33%.[1] When New Labour entered office in 1997, 2.2 million children – almost one-in-five of all children, and half those in poverty – lived in households where no adult was working.

Tax credits are a response to all this. By providing more generous in-work benefits, they make the working poor better off. And they increase the financial incentives to work. Work, the government believes "is the best long-term route out of poverty".[2]

What's more, New Labour's reforms also remove tax credits and benefits more slowly as income rises. Fewer people now face enormous effective marginal tax rates. That should increase incentives to work longer hours, or to find better jobs.

Tax credits, then, are good for efficiency, as well as equality.

This combination of concern for both the poor themselves, and for the wider economic benefits, was spelt out by Martin Taylor, the former chief executive of Barclays Bank appointed by Chancellor Gordon Brown in 1997 to advise on reforming the tax and benefit system. In launching the Working Families Tax Credit – the predecessor of the current tax credit arrangements – he wrote:

> Worklessness is damaging. People without work face reduced employment prospects in the future and risk low self-esteem. It results in lower economic growth, as well as worse public finances...Improving the effective supply of labour is a very important objective. Increases in the supply of labour help to maintain high and stable levels of employment, improvements in living standards, and economic growth.[3]

Tax credits and labour supply

But can policies of "making work pay" really increase the supply of labour?

Casual evidence suggests they can do so. In the 1980s and 1990s the UK experienced a big increase in the number of households containing no-one in work. The US did not. The obvious explanation for this is that incentives to work were greater in the US than UK, partly thanks to the US's Earned Income Tax Credit. It was this that provided the inspiration for New Labour's tax credits.

The thinking behind them is straightforward. Tax credits – originally the Working Families Tax Credit, now the working and child tax credits – are more generous than the family credit that preceded them. This means the returns to working, as opposed to living on benefits, are higher. And this should attract more people into work.

Table 6 shows one good measure of this – the replacement rate. It shows the ratio of net income out of work to the net income in work. The lower the percentage, the greater is the financial benefit from working. You can see that replacement rates have fallen for single parents, which mean they have bigger incentives to work. They've also fallen for those single–earner couples who faced very high replacement rates in 1997.

Table 6. Replacement rates 1997-2004

	1997	2004	Change
Lone parents			
Mean	67.9	65.0	-2.9
Median	71.9	65.9	-6.0
25th centile	55.8	52.3	-3.5
75th centile	81.9	80.4	-1.5
% with higher rate		21.3	
% with lower rate		56.7	
1-earner couples			
Mean	59.3	61.1	1.8
Median	62.6	65.5	2.9
25th centile	41.3	45.3	4.0
75th centile	80.6	79.5	-1.1
% with higher rate		52.7	
% with lower rate		26.6	

Source: Brewer and Shephard, Has Labour made work pay?, table 2.

With work more attractive for most single parents and for some couples who previously faced big disincentives to work, you'd expect the labour supply to have risen.

However, this fact does not show up in macroeconomic data. Between Q2 1997 and Q2 2005 the percentage of working age adults who were economically active was flat, at 78.6%[4]. On its own, though, this tells us nothing, because countless other things have affected economic activity.

To see the impact of New Labour's policies, we need microeconomic studies. One of the best of these has come from research at the Institute for Fiscal Studies commissioned by HM Revenue and Customs.[5] They estimate that, between 1999 and 2002 the Working Families Tax Credit raised the labour market participation rate of single parents by 5.1 percentage points. And it raised the participation rate among men in couples by 0.73 percentage points.

This is what you'd expect from Table 6. New Labour made work pay for single parents and for single-earners in couples who previously had low in-work incomes compared to out-of-work incomes.

However, the researchers found that New Labour's reforms reduced incentives for the second-earner in couples with children to work. As a result, their labour supply fell.

This is consistent with basic economic theory. In-work benefits such as tax credits have an ambiguous effect.

On the one hand, in raising in-work incomes relative to out-of-work incomes, they encourage people to move into work. This is the substitution effect.

But on the other hand, they boost the incomes of working couples. That means some couples can meet their needs with just one earner, freeing up the other to look after the children.

On balance, the researchers estimate that the WFTC raised labour supply by a net 22,000, and cut the number of workless households by 43,000 by 2002.

However, spending on tax credits then was £6.46bn[6]. That works out at £150,000 for each household moved out of worklessness. This doesn't seem very efficient. Which only goes to show that a big purpose of the tax credit system is simply to redistribute income, not merely to increase the labour supply. As Andrew Dilnot and Julian McCrae have said: "The distributional effects of the reform are likely to be more dramatic than the behavioural effects."[7]

What's more, this redistribution comes at a price – many workers face higher marginal tax rates than they did before 1997. Table 7 shows that although the numbers of people facing absurdly high marginal tax and benefit deduction rates – over 80% – have fallen since 1997, the numbers facing very high rates have risen. Over 2.2 million now face a deduction rate of over 50%.[8] This is because, as incomes rise, tax credits, and in some cases housing and council tax benefits are reduced.

Table 7. Numbers facing marginal deduction rates

Thousands	Before 1998 Budget	2005
100%+	5	40
90-100%	130	120
80-90%	300	240
70-80%	740	180
60-70%	760	1390

Source: HM Treasury:The Child and Working Tax Credits, April 2002, p16, and Adam, Brewer and Shephard, Financial work incentives in Britain, p11.

Table 8 gives some more concrete examples of how low income-earners can still face vicious effective tax rates.

Table 8. Examples of high deduction rates

	Gross weekly earnings (£)	Deduction rate (%)
Lone parent, 1 child, local authority tenant	150	89.5
Lone parent, 2 children, LA tenant	200	95.5
Married couple, no children, private tenants	200	90.0
Married couple, 1 child, LA tenants	180	76.0
Married couple, 2 children, LA tenants	160	95.5

Source: Department of Work and Pensions Tax benefit model tables, April 2005.

Economists and common sense agree – this reduces people's incentive to work harder or get better jobs. The Organisation for Economic Cooperation and Development concluded: "High benefit withdrawal rates may have induced those with higher earnings to reduce the number of hours worked"[9]. And Mike Brewer and Andrew Shephard say: "Overall, more working parents face reduced incentives to progress in the labour market through Labour's tax and benefit changes than face improved incentives."[10]

This, however, is not an accident, caused by New Labour's stupidity. It's an unavoidable trade-off. Say a government has a given sum with which to support low-wage workers. It can use this in one of two ways:

1. It can target help at the very low-paid, and withdraw help quickly as earnings rise. This focuses aid well upon the poorest workers, but it means some face horrifically high deduction rates and therefore big disincentives to work harder or get better jobs.
2. It can withdraw benefits more slowly. This means fewer people face huge deduction rates, but more face high deduction rates.

There is therefore a trade-off. As Holly Sutherland and David Piachaud say, governments have a choice. They can reduce the unemployment trap (whereby the incentive to get out of work is poor). Or they can reduce the poverty trap (the low incentive for the low-paid to earn more). It is hard to do both.[11]

The Treasury, to its credit, has acknowledged this:

> The trade-off between incentives and support for those without resources of their own cannot be avoided. The issue is how fast the safety net should be reduced. If withdrawn rapidly, it will mean a relatively small number of people face very high marginal rates. If withdrawn more slowly, a larger number of people will be affected by moderately high rates.[12]

New Labour has, then, made a choice. It's chosen to give greater in-work support, thus increasing incentives to work in the first place. But it's imposed higher marginal deduction rates on many people, thus reducing incentives for people to earn more. It has, in effect, chosen to reduce the unemployment trap, and the worst features of the poverty trap, whilst imposing a smaller poverty trap on more people.

Its reason for doing this, as we've seen, is that it regards worklessness as very damaging, as a cause of alienation and social exclusion, as well as material poverty. It hopes that even poorly-paid work can be a stepping stone to better things.

But is it? The case for believing so is that unemployment itself makes people unemployable. It demoralises them, causes their skills to become out-dated, and sends a signal to employers that they might be bad workers. This was the thinking behind the fashionable "hysteresis" theory of the 1980s and 90s. If this is right, getting people out of unemployment, and into any work, will improve their future employability.

It's a nice theory. But that's all it is – a theory. Research by Mark Stewart has found that whilst being unemployed in one year greatly increases your chances of being unemployed later – as hysteresis predicts – so too does low-wage work. He concludes:

> A low-wage job does not augment a person's human capital significantly more than unemployment. If unemployed individuals' prospects are to be permanently improved, they need to find jobs where they can augment their skills (for example through on the job training), raise their productivity and move up the pay distribution.[13]

But high marginal tax rates deter people from doing this.

It would be hasty to conclude from this that New Labour's preference for reducing worklessness rather than giving the low-paid incentives to earn more is mistaken. Maybe the fall in workless households mean fewer children will grow up to believe that worklessness is normal, and so will be more inclined to work themselves. And studies show (as we'll see in chapter 11) that people in work are happier than the unemployed. My point is merely that New Labour has made a policy choice. And this choice is questionable.

Does supply create demand?

There's another curious fact about the policy of "making work pay." New Labour's focus upon increasing labour supply assumes that workers who look for work will be able to find it. In other words, there are no significant demand constraints upon the labour market.

This is a remarkable assumption. It's a flat rejection of the long-standing Keynesian idea – which underpinned years of Labour party thinking – that the barrier to full employment is a lack of demand.

Now, there is something to commend this thinking. In the long run, demand for workers certainly increases to meet the supply. After all, the US has received 200 million immigrants in the last two centuries, and it has found work for even the most unemployable of these. Even the people who appear on the Jerry Springer Show have jobs[14]. And in good macroeconomic times, as we have enjoyed recently, demand for labour increases anyway.

There are, though, two problems here. One is that there may well be a mismatch between the areas where labour supply rises and the areas where jobs are available. Andrew Glyn and Stewart Wood write:

Many of those brought into the labour force...will have relatively poor qualifications and will live in an area where labour demand is already weak, especially for the unskilled...For the policy to work, either the less qualified would have to be encouraged to move to the high-employment southern part of the UK or jobs would have to be created deliberately in the areas where labour supply is most expanded.[15]

Secondly, we cannot rely upon good macroeconomic conditions continuing. This raises the question. If there is a fall in demand for labour, what then will be the merits of greater incentives to work? Is it really right to cause people to suffer a big fall in incomes – as they move from work to unemployment – through no fault of their own? And is it good for human happiness to give people incentives to look for something that doesn't exist?

Tax credits and managerialism

There's another question surrounding the introduction of tax credits. Why has the task of administering help to poor working families been transferred from the Benefits Agency to the HMRC, as we must now call the taxman?

Cynics will say it's a presentational move. Replacing Family Credit with tax credits looks like a cut in public spending and a cut in the tax burden. This allows the government to claim that the share of taxes in national income has fallen. At the stinkingly low level at which political debate occurs, this can pass for a serious point.

There is, though, a more respectable reason for the shift. HMRC already knows people's incomes. It can therefore, in theory, administer a means test less intrusively and less expensively than the Benefits Agency. And in removing the stigma and intrusiveness of a means tests, a barrier to taking up benefits has been removed.

Sadly, though, it's not obvious that these advantages have actually accrued. The replacement of benefits with tax credits did not increase take-up rates, as New Labour had hoped. Mike Brewer says the take-up rate for the working families tax credit, at 62 per cent, was lower than the 72 per cent take-up rate for Family Credit.[16] This, of course, automatically undermines New Labour's efforts to improve equality and efficiency.

Nor is it obvious that the system is better administered now. The problem here is not that tax credits are paid in error, with people getting too much or too little. This is not a design flaw, but an inevitability. The low-wage end of the labour market is volatile, with many moving in and out of work. And with people's circumstances changing often, their entitlements will change. The IFS's Mike Brewer estimates that one million families a year will be eligible for extra tax credits, and 750,000 subject to credit cutbacks, as a result of changes in their circumstances.[17]

No. The real problems with the administration of tax credits lie elsewhere. One problem has simply been the failure to process applications. Three months after the introduction of the child tax credit in April 2003, 220,000 claims had yet to be processed. And such is the complexity of the system that HMRC at one point received 2 million inquiries a day.[18]

Another problem is a form of fraud. If two mothers arrange to be childminders for each other's children, they become employed and entitled to tax credits – which is clearly absurd.

And then, of course, there's plain bad administration. HMRC itself has estimated that fraud, error and overpayment cost it £1.7bn a year[19]. And this is a longstanding problem. David Blunkett (admittedly not perhaps the most reliable commentator) wrote in his diaries in May 2002 that "the tax credit system is a shambles, a total mess".[20]

Now, it's as easy to overstate these problems as to understate them. Herein, though, lies a suspicion. Could it be that New Labour's managerialist ideology – its belief in the power of central agencies to administer society for the better – has led it to under-estimate these difficulties, and to over-estimate the likely success of tax credits?

The trade-offs behind tax credits

One reason for suspecting so is that New Labour's enthusiasm for tax credits betrays another symptom of managerialism – the failure to handle awkward trade-offs well.

We've already seen that it has at least recognised one trade-off – the one between steep deduction rates for a few versus shallow ones for the many. But there are others which New Labour is quieter about.

Simplicity versus targeting

There's a trade-off between administrative simplicity versus targeting needs.

The simplest benefit system of all would be a basic income – where the same sum is paid to everyone, regardless of circumstances. This would not respond to differences in people's needs, or to changes in needs over time.

But a system that targeted needs precisely would be astoundingly difficult to administer. It would require the government to have full knowledge of each individual's circumstances at every point in time. That would be prohibitively expensive, in terms of money and freedom. Worse still, its intrusiveness might deter people from claiming the benefit – as means tests have generally done.

If your managerialist ideology causes you to over-estimate administrators' skill, you'll choose a point on this trade-off closer to targeting needs than to administrative ease.

Incentives versus risk-spreading

In raising in-work benefits, New Labour has increased the cost of losing one's job. This could prove a big problem if or when macroeconomic conditions deteriorate and the demand for labour falls.

There's a trade-off between sharpening incentives on the one hand and spreading risk on the other. The greater is the incentive to work, the greater is the cost of losing your job.

Incentives versus redistribution

There's also a trade-off between relieving poverty and increasing incentives. Relieving poverty requires high benefits for those out of work. Improving incentives to work requires that out-of-work benefits be low.

Of course, if you believe people are masters of their own fate, your choice here will be easy. If poverty is the free choice of the unemployed, we can forget about relieving it. If on the other hand you believe people are merely passive victims of fate, your preference will be for greater redistribution.

Your choice on this trade-off therefore rests, at least in part, upon the tricky philosophical question of just how much free will, how much individual agency, we actually have.

Relieving poverty versus populism

Tax credits are withdrawn more slowly, and over a longer range of incomes, than the old Family Credit was. This is why, as we've seen, many people face higher marginal withdrawal rates.

The counterpart to this is that New Labour's tax and benefit reforms don't just redistribute to the poor. There's plenty of redistribution towards middle and higher earners, for example:

- The Treasury estimates that a family in the sixth decile of the income distribution – that is, just in the top half – will gain over £15 a week as a result of its new support for children.[21]

- Families earning up to £58,000 – more than twice average earnings – are eligible for the child tax credit.

- The working tax credit – paid to over-25s without children, in full-time work – does little to alleviate poverty, simply because few such people are poor. IFS economists estimate that only 2.5 per cent of such people are in poverty.[22]

New Labour describes these measures as "progressive universalism" – "supporting all families with children but offering the greatest help to those who need it most".[23]

But you could equally see it as the result of a choice. Relieving severe poverty means helping a minority. That doesn't win you elections. However, redistribution towards median voters – those in the middle of the income distribution – does win elections. New Labour has made this choice.

Conclusion

This chapter has had three aims. First, I've tried to show that one of New Labour's most distinctive and important policies – "making work pay" – has been motivated by a belief that equality and efficiency are compatible.

Second, I've tried to show that this belief is a reflection of a managerialist ideology. New Labour believes it has sufficient knowledge of the labour market to design policies that increase labour supply and employment, and that central government has the administrative skill to target benefits properly. Both ideas, however, are doubtful.

Thirdly, this managerialism disguises the fact that any tax and benefit system confronts awkward trade-offs. Sometimes New Labour has recognised these, sometimes not. Nevertheless, there are choices to be made, costs to be paid.

Let's, though, assume that New Labour has made the right choices. Let's imagine that the policy of making work pay does increase the supply of labour substantially. How do these extra workers find jobs?

Basic economics has an answer. An increase in supply leads to lower prices, which leads to increased demand.

This, of course means that when the labour supply increases, wages fall.

If this happens, though, the gains from tax and benefit reform pass from workers to employers. Efficiency – increased employment – will be achieved at the expense of equality, and a big bill for taxpayers who subsidize low-wage work.

This, of course, is where the minimum wage comes in. One of its main functions is to stop this happening – to ensure that tax credits do not become a wage subsidy, but instead genuinely make working families better off.

However, for decades the common sense among economists was that minimum wages destroy jobs. If this is right, another trade-off emerges. In raising the wages of the low-paid, we are reducing the chances of people finding work and so increasing poverty.

Or are we? This conclusion may be a little premature. Many doubt whether the minimum wage does in fact destroy jobs. Let's turn to this question.

Notes

1. H.M.Treasury, *The Modernisation of Britain's Tax and Benefit System 3: The Working Families Tax Credit* p6.

2. H.M.Treasury, *The child and working tax credits*, April 2002, p14.

3. *The Modernisation of Britain's Tax and Benefit System 2: Work Incentives* p25-6.

4. Table A.1 of October 2006 *Labour Market Trends*.

5. Mike Brewer, Alan Duncan, Andrew Shephard and Maria Jose Suarez, *Did Working Familes Tax Credit Work?*, HMRC 2005.

6. Mike Brewer and James Browne, *The Effect of WFTC on labour market participation*, p8.

11. *The Family Credit system and the Working Families Tax Credit in the United Kingdom,* p18.

8. Stuart Adam, Mike Brewer and Andrew Shephard, *Financial work incentives in Britain,* p11.

9. "Making work pay", *OECD Economic Outlook 66,* December 1999, p151-159, p157.

10. Mike Brewer and Andrew Shephard, *Has Labour Made Work Pay?* Pviii.

11. "Reducing child poverty in Britain", p96, *Economic Journal 111,* February 2001, p85-101.

12. H.M.Treasury, *Work Incentives: A Report by Martin Taylor. The Modernisation of Britain's tax and benefit system 2,* para 1.13.

13. "The inter-related dynamics of unemployment and low-wage employment", December 2005, p22.

14. Richard Jackman, Richard Layard and Stephen Nickell – *Combating Unemployment: Is Flexibility Enough?,* Centre for Economic Performance discussion paper 293, March 1996, p7.

15. "New Labour's economic policy", *University of Oxford Department of Economics discussion paper 49,* December 2000, p9.

16. "The new tax credits", p12.

17. "The new tax credits", p8.

18. *The Times,* July 24 2003, p2.

19. *The Regsiter,* July 13 2006.

20. *The Guardian,* October 12 2006.

21. *The child and working tax credits,* chart 3.3, p13.

22. 8. Brewer, Clark and Myck, "Credit where it's due: an assessment of the new tax credits", *IFS working paper,* October 2001, p18.

23. "The child and working tax credits", p4.

5.

The First Rule of Economics

A national minimum wage... is both just and efficient. A minimum wage will stop the taxpayer having to subsidize low pay through the ballooning Family Credit bill. It will decrease employee turnover, encourage investment in training, and help motivate employees (Tony Blair)[1].

If you raise the price of something, people will buy less of it. This is the first rule of economics. For years, this was sufficient to cause many to believe a National Minimum Wage (NMW) would be both unjust and inefficient. Unjust, because it would throw some of the most vulnerable people in the labour market out of work. And inefficient, because it would destroy jobs unnecessarily.[2]

For this reason, support for a minimum wage until the 1990s was largely confined to the "hard left", who demanded it in order to demonstrate that decent wages and capitalism were incompatible.

Then things changed. New Labour adopted a minimum wage as one of its most distinctive policies.

But how could a policy which was once regarded as revolutionary come into the mainstream?

To a large extent, it was because there was growing evidence that the first rule of economics might be false. And if a NMW would not destroy jobs, the thinking went, maybe it could tackle successfully the problem of low pay.

One piece of evidence that state-mandated wage rises did not cost jobs was the Equal Pay Act in the 1970s. It raised women's pay without raising female unemployment[3]. Also, the abolition of Wages Councils in the 1990s did not raise employment in the sectors covered by the councils.[4]

In themselves, these episodes were unconvincing. After all, it was easy to imagine that there were other factors which could account for these trends.

The New Jersey devil

There was, however, one piece of evidence that was more influential in convincing New Labour of the merits of a minimum wage. This was a study of fast food outlets in New Jersey and eastern Pennsylvania in 1992.[5]

In April of that year, the minimum wage in New Jersey rose from $4.25 an hour to $5.05. Elementary economics says this should have priced some workers in New Jersey's fast food sector out of jobs. The fact that the minimum wage in neighbouring Pennsylvania stayed at $4.25 provided what seemed to be an ideal control group with which to test this prediction.

David Card and Alan Krueger did just this. They surveyed 410 fast food outlets in both states just before New Jersey's rise, and again the following winter. Their results, summarised in table 9, suggest that "the rise in the New Jersey minimum wage seems to have *increased* employment at restaurants that were forced to raise pay".[6]

Table 9. Employment impact of New Jersey's Minimum Wage Rise

	Pennsylvania	*New Jersey*	*Difference*
Before MW rise	23.33	20.44	-2.89
After MW rise	21.17	21.03	-0.14
Difference	-2.16	0.59	2.76
t-statistic	1.73	1.09	2.03

Numbers are for full-time equivalent employees, where part-time workers count as half a full-timer. Source: Card and Krueger table 2.2, p34

This is a remarkably radical finding. If it is true, it means the first thing we learn in economics is false. And it means a NMW might be able to remove poverty wages without imposing large costs.

But is it true? Years after Card and Krueger published their findings, they are still the subject of fierce debate.[7]

There are, however, three things we can say with confidence.

First, their findings are entirely consistent with the possibility that minimum wages really do destroy jobs. This survey only covered restaurants in the Burger King, KFC, Wendy's and Roy Rogers chains.[8] But these, compete with many other food-sellers, such as McDonalds, Chinese takeaways and hot dog stalls. New Jersey's minimum wage rise might have increased costs for the latter outlets by more than those in the former. If so, the prices of (say) Chinese takeaways will have risen relative to the prices of (say) KFC food. And if that happened, consumers would have substituted away from Chinese food and towards KFC. Employment in KFC might therefore have risen as employment in Chinese takeaways fell. In this scenario, Card and Krueger's research would show that the minimum wage increased jobs. But this would be an illusion. The minimum wage would have destroyed jobs across the fast food industry as a whole. As Finis Welch has said: "Nothing, repeat nothing, in ordinary competitive theory predicts that employment in any given industry or in any given restaurant will decline in response to an increase in the minimum wage."[9]

Secondly, employment figures do not suffice to refute the common sense view that higher minimum wages cut demand for labour. We measure demand for labour by measuring hours worked, not employment. It's possible that higher minimum wages don't lead to cuts in jobs, but to cuts in hours instead.

Thirdly, Card and Krueger's findings are only a teeny fraction of the total empirical research on the impact of minimum wages in the US. And most of this shows that the first law of economics is right. For example, Stephen Bazen and Velayoudom Marimoutou conclude: "The effect of a rise in the minimum wage of 10% in real terms with real average wages constant is to reduce teenage employment by 2 to 3%."[10] David Neumark summarises the research: "The evidence from the national studies of state minimum wage increases, using both time series and across-state variation in minimum wages quite unambiguously points to disemployment effects of minimum wages upon teens and young adults."[11]

The British evidence – so far

Card and Krueger's evidence, then, is not as decisive as its publicity might suggest. One of the main foundations for support for a UK minimum wage is therefore rather insecure.

But what impact did the introduction of the minimum wage have upon jobs here in the UK?

Superficially, it seems not to have had the adverse effects claimed by its critics. Before the 1997 election, some Conservatives claimed the NMW would destroy hundreds of thousands of jobs. With unemployment having fallen since the NMW was introduced, this view seems refuted.

So it should be, because it was stupid. Forecasts of massive job losses were based on the assumption that workers paid more than the minimum wage would get wage rises comparable to the low-paid, to preserve their differentials. But we don't live in a Fred Kite world in which workers are obsessed by preserving differentials. The effect of the NMW on wages seems to have been confined to the very lowest paid. One study found that its introduction had no effect outside the bottom 10 per cent of wages.[12]

With the effect on wages confined to the very low paid, any macroeconomic study of the impact on jobs of the NMW is plain useless. There are three reasons for this.

First, orthodox theory predicts that the job losses will be too small to show up in the macroeconomic data. A quick calculation shows this. The Low Pay Commission's 2006 report estimated that the NMW raised the wages of just over 20% for roughly one million workers, 3.1% of total employment[13]. That's a rise in the aggregate wage bill of 0.6%. A reasonable estimate of the wage elasticity of demand for labour would be around 0.6.[14] This implies a fall in employment of just under 0.4%. With employment of just over 28 million, this is just over 100,000 workers. This is less than three week's inflow into unemployment, or less than one quarter's rise in employment in a good quarter. Spread over a few years, such a number would be undetectable in macroeconomic data.

Secondly, aggregate estimates of the numbers of low paid are wildly inaccurate. The Low Pay Commission originally estimated that around 2 million employees would have had their pay raised by the NMW. It's now thought that only 1.3 million would have been entitled to a rise.[15] If we don't know how many low-paid there are in the first place, we haven't much hope of measuring how many, if any, lost their jobs.

Thirdly, there's a problem of establishing a counterfactual. Let's say there was clear evidence that the number of low-paid jobs fell after the introduction of the NMW. Would this mean the NMW destroyed jobs? Not necessarily. "After it" does not mean "because of it." Maybe globalization and technical change would have destroyed low-wage jobs anyway, and the NMW contributed nothing extra to the job destruction.

To assess the true effect of the NMW on jobs, we therefore need specialist microeconomic studies.

The first of these was the Low Pay Commission's first report after the introduction of the NMW. Tucked away in appendix 5 of the report were the results of a survey of firms affected by the NMW. This found that 50 per cent said the NMW had led to some reduction in staffing levels, with 51 per cent saying it led to a cut in working hours.[16] And in 2005, the Commission conducted a survey into the effects of the 2003 rise in the NMW[17]. It found that, among firms in low-wage sectors, 37% cut staffing levels and 31% cut basic hours. This is what the first rule of economics would have predicted.

But this is not good enough. It doesn't tell us what the counterfactual was. For all we know, these employers might have cut jobs and hours anyway, and were only too willing to erroneously blame the cuts upon the NMW.

Mark Stewart conducted a neat study intended to solve this problem.[18] He compared the employment prospects of workers directly covered by the NMW – those earning less than £3.60 before April 1999 – with those of workers earning slightly more than the NMW. The idea here is that workers earning a little more than £3.60 an hour provide a control group. If, in the absence of the NMW, demand for low-wage workers would have fallen anyway, then employment in this control group would have fallen. By comparing employment growth of workers covered by the NMW to this control group, we can isolate the impact of the NMW.

Table 10 shows Stewart's results. Row 3 shows that employment of workers covered by the NMW did indeed fall after the introduction of the NMW. The chances of an adult male being in work fell from 90.8 per cent to 89.2 per cent, for example.

Table 10. Impact of the NMW on probabilities of employment

	Adult men	Young men	Adult women	Young women
Wages below NMW				
1. After NMW	89.2	87.0	88.2	85.5
2. Before NMW	90.8	88.7	88.5	89.0
3. Difference	-1.6	-1.7	-0.3	-3.5
Wages up to 10% above NMW				
4. After NMW	91.3	91.3	92.3	91.3
5. Before NMW	94.4	92.2	90.7	97.0
6. Difference	-3.1	-0.9	1.6	-5.7
7. Difference in differences	1.5	-0.8	-1.9	2.2

Source: Mark Stewart, "The impact of the introduction of the UK minimum wage on the employment probabilities of low wage workers", Warwick Economic Research Papers no 630, Jan 2002, table 1. Probabilities are the chances of being in work, given that one was in work the year previously. The period after the introduction of the NMW is Sept-Nov 1999.

However, row 6 shows that the employment prospects for workers earning slightly more than the NMW also deteriorated. This is consistent with the idea that demand for low-wage workers fell after the introduction of the NMW, but it did not fall because of the introduction of the NMW. The "difference in differences" for the two groups, shown in row 7, suggests, says Stewart, that the effects of the NMW were "insignificantly different from zero". In short, the NMW didn't destroy jobs.

These findings are strikingly similar to Card and Krueger's. In both, the minimum wage appears to have no effect on employment only because employment fell in the control group. This is odd. It's like a drug trial in which the medicine has no effect, but the placebo makes people ill.

So what's going on here? Maybe the minimum wage in both countries is simply too low to affect employment much. There is, though, another possibility – that both studies share similar flaws.

The first problem is one of timing. Some employers might have cut jobs in anticipation of rises in the minimum wage. If they did so, one would not expect to see any difference in employment after the increase. And if they cut jobs of low-paid workers too much, one would expect to see employment recover. Others on the verge of closure might soldier on for a few months before shutting down. In both cases, the minimum wage would cost jobs, without showing up in the figures.

Secondly, there's the problem of non-compliance. Perhaps workers earning less than £3.60 an hour in 1999 did not lose their jobs in large numbers because, for some, their wages didn't rise. In December 1999 the Low Pay Commission reported that "there are clearly still substantial numbers of workers being paid less than the minimum wage"[19]. On one estimate, there were 250,000 adults in April 2001 still earning less than it[20]. This matters enormously. It's a reasonable assumption that the firms most likely to cut jobs if wages rise are those most likely not to comply with the minimum wage law. If this is so, it's no surprise that the NMW doesn't cut jobs – because it doesn't raise wages.

Thirdly, remember that it is labour demand, measured by aggregate hours, that is supposed to fall when the minimum wage rises. And other research by Mark Stewart has found that average working hours did fall after the introduction of the NMW, by 1-2 hours per worker per week.[21]

Another study corroborates the view that the NMW cut labour demand. Stephen Machin, Alan Manning and Lupin Rahman studied the impact of the NMW on employment in residential care homes, a notoriously badly paid industry.[22]

They found that "employers cut employment and hours in response to the minimum wage." They estimated that each percentage point rise in hourly wages as a result of the introduction of the NMW led to a cut in hours worked of between 0.15 per cent and 0.4 per cent, and to a fall of 0.35 to 0.55 per cent in employment.

This is sufficiently small that those who kept their jobs enjoyed a rise in weekly earnings, on average. But it is consistent with what ordinary economic theory would predict – that the NMW does come at a price. And the price is job losses for some of the low paid.

Most of the evidence, then – not all, but most – suggests that the first rule of economics is right. Higher minimum wages do cause cuts in jobs and hours. That makes some of the low paid worst-off.

However, facts are never sufficient to defeat a theory. It takes another theory to do that. So let's have a quick look at the theory that the NMW won't destroy jobs. How could the first law of economics possibly be wrong in theory? The answer lies in what was, until Card and Krueger's work, merely a textbook curiosity – the theory of monopsony.

Monopsony and all that

A monopsonistic firm is one which must raise wages for all workers if it is to hire a single extra worker. The marginal cost of the extra worker therefore consists of two components; the wage paid to him, plus the additional wages that have to be paid to all workers in order to set wages high enough to attract the extra worker.

In Fig. 6 overleaf, this means the marginal cost of labour, MCl, is above the supply curve of labour, Sl. Such a firm will maximise its profits at the point where the marginal cost of an extra worker is equal to that worker's marginal product (which is shown by the labour demand curve). Employment is therefore L_m. The wage level is read off the supply curve, which shows the lowest wage the firm can get away with paying. So wages are W_m. This means workers are paid less than their marginal product – by an amount equal to AC.

This firm would like to hire more workers at the wage W_m. Ideally, it would employ $L_m{}^*$. However, because the supply of workers is limited, it could only attract that many workers by raising wages for everyone – and that is unprofitable. The upshot is that vacancies go unfilled; these are equal to the gap between L_m and $L_m{}^*$.

Fig. 6

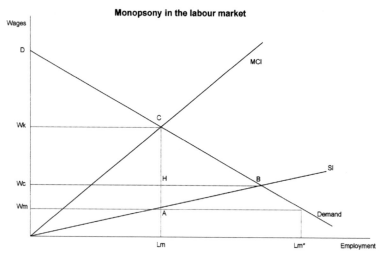

In this context, a minimum wage can raise employment. Imagine it is set a little above W_m. Higher wages will tempt workers into the labour force; there will be a move along the supply curve. The firm can now fill some of its vacancies. Employment will rise. What's more, the gap between each worker's wage and his or her marginal product will fall. Workers will be less exploited. Social justice will therefore be promoted. Equality and efficiency will go hand in hand.

Or will they? Does monopsony really exist in low-wage labour markets?[23]

Of course, there's plenty of evidence that many workers are paid less than their marginal product. One study of private residential nursing homes found that workers are on average paid 15 per cent less than their marginal product[24]. But this does not suffice to prove the existence of monopsony. As Deepak Lal has pointed out, wages can be below marginal product for a number of reasons: because workers are getting on-the-job training; because firms want wages to rise with experience in order to reduce staff turnover; or simply because, at any point in time, workers or employers lack full information.[25]

Indeed, even supporters of the NMW have found convincing evidence against monopsony in low-wage labour markets. Monopsony implies that product prices should fall in those industries affected by a minimum wage rise. That's because increased employment raises production, and firms must cut prices in order to sell this extra output. However, Card and Krueger could find no evidence of this after New Jersey's minimum wage rise[26]. And the Low Pay Commission's survey found that 57 per cent of firms affected by the NMW said they raised prices, not cut them.[27]

This shouldn't be too surprising, once we consider what might cause monopsony to exist in the first place. William Boal and Michael Ransom give five possible sources of monopsony power[28]:

- *Outright collusion amongst firms.* The classic instance of monopsony is where one company employs most of the workers in a town. By colluding, firms can approach this ideal.

- *Differences in non-wage attractions.* A company may be able to pay a worker less than her marginal product if it makes up for doing so by offering job security or attractive working conditions. Such a company may want to hire more workers at its low wage, but be unable to do so as potential applicants choose higher-paying employers.

- *Costs of moving jobs.* If these (such as the costs of moving house, or of losing job-specific skills or employment protection) are significant, a firm may enjoy monopsony power once it has hired workers, as these may not leave the company, even if its wages are a little below those of rival employers.

- *Efficiency wages.* As employment rises, an employer finds it harder to supervise workers. As a result, he may have to pay higher wages to everyone (to deter them from shirking) if employment expands. The marginal cost of an extra worker will therefore be greater than the cost of that worker's wage alone.

- *Ignorance.* People may simply not know the range of job offers available to them. So they may take a job at a wage below their marginal product, simply because they don't know where to get a better one, or because the costs of waiting for a better one to come up are prohibitively high.

These conditions do exist in many occupations.[29] But they are more common at the top end of the labour market, not the bottom end. The conditions that generate monopsony power are more likely to be found in law firms and investment banks than in fast food restaurants. In the latter, non-wage job attractions vary little from firm to another; the costs of moving from one to another are small; and direct supervision (the alternative to efficiency wages) is often much stricter than in other industries.

Monopsony theory, then, doesn't give us a good reason to reject the idea that minimum wages destroy jobs.

Unsurprisingly, therefore, many economists believe the first rule of economics really is right. As Gary Becker has said: "Even a wizard would have a great deal of difficulty repealing the economic law that higher minimum wages reduce employment. Since politicians are not wizards, they should not try."[30]

Efficiency, equality and the minimum wage

The evidence that minimum wages don't destroy jobs is, therefore, to say the least, highly contentious, at both the theoretical and practical level.

However, their advocates say that increased employment is not the only way in which the NMW may raise efficiency. They cite three others.

- *Lower labour turnover.* In raising wages, the NMW may reduce the incentive to leave the labour force. The costs of replacing workers – of hiring and training new staff – would therefore fall. These costs are significant, says Donna Brown.[31] With average job tenure in both industries less than a year, "reducing labour turnover could have a significant effect on business costs".[32]

- *Incentives.* The NMW is "essential to...help provide new incentives for the unemployed to take jobs" says the Labour party.[33] It may also encourage the least productive workers – those whose marginal product is less than the NMW – to gain more education and training, in order to avoid the risk of losing their jobs.

- *Higher productivity.* Higher wage costs might force firms to become more efficient. Increased wages might motivate existing employees to work harder. Or they might attract better workers to the firm. For these reasons, the NMW "might potentially provide a spur to increased productivity" says the Low Pay Commission.[34]

All this, however, is doubtful. Take the impact on turnover costs. In theory, firms should set wages to maximise their profits. If wages are so low as to cause high rates of turnover, it can only be because the losses caused by this are offset by the savings from having a low wage bill. To argue that firms will benefit from higher wages and lower turnover costs, one must therefore argue that they are not currently maximising profits. The Low Pay Commission claims just this. "Firms may simply be unaware of their turnover rates and the costs imposed on their business" it says.[35]

This is feeble. It's a crass manifestation of one aspect of the managerialist ideology – the presumption that so-called experts know better than tens of thousands of people. If turnover costs are as large as claimed, it would be a remarkably stupid business that was unaware of them. Such a company would be unlikely to last long in the competitive markets in which low-wage firms operate. It is only where turnover costs are small that firms are likely to be unaware of them. But in this case, the gains from eliminating them would also be small.

But would it be so good to reduce job turnover anyway? At a given level of employment, the counterpart of some people spending longer in jobs is that others spend longer out of work. And, as the Commission on Social Justice once pointed out, it may be worse to have a few people face long spells of unemployment than to have many face short spells.[36] Only if business costs are reduced so much that firms want to take on extra workers would a lower rate of job turnover be good for the unemployed.

Turn now to the impact on incentives. It would not only be the long-term unemployed who might be attracted into the labour market by a minimum wage. So too might more students, or the semi-retired, or housewives. All of these may be more attractive to employers than the young, semi-educated workers available to them before the NMW was introduced. Even if the NMW leaves the overall level of employment unchanged, therefore, it could still have regressive effects, by forcing the least skilled, poorest, workers out of jobs, to be replaced by more affluent ones.[37]

Also, although the NMW might increase the incentive for the very least skilled to get training, it might reduce incentives for others to gain skills. Deepak Lal points out that, because the NMW reduces wage inequality, it gives workers less incentive to go to the trouble of acquiring the training that would equip them for better-paid jobs. "Support for the minimum wage is at odds with another valid desire, to promote skill accumulation by unskilled workers – particularly the young and females" he says.[38]

What's more, US research suggests minimum wages cause some teenagers to leave school to find work. These could displace other workers, who drop out of the labour market altogether to enter the black economy or careers in crime. David Neumark and William Wascher say: "Although minimum wage increases had only small negative net effects on overall teen employment, such increases reduced the proportion of teenagers enrolled in school, and increased the proportion of teenagers neither enrolled nor employed."[39]

These last two points hint at a worrying possibility. Maybe minimum wages have adverse long-run effects on the wages of the low-paid. If they deter low-wage workers from getting training, or if they encourage young people to leave school early, they reduce human capital formation and hence wages later in life. Naturally, there's no UK evidence on this point yet. But there is American evidence. David Neumark and Olena Nizalova show that teenagers who were exposed to high minimum wages had lower wages in their late 20s.[40]

It is not only in its impact on job turnover and incentives that the benefit of the NMW may be exaggerated. So too might be its impact on productivity. Economists have long been sceptical of the idea that minimum wages can raise this. As long ago as 1946, George Stigler, in a paper that for decades represented the conventional wisdom on minimum wages, described the notion as "lacking in empirical evidence but not in popularity".[41]

The empirical evidence is still lacking. LSE economists, in their study of care homes cited earlier, found no evidence of increased productivity as a result of the introduction of the NMW.[42]

To see why productivity doesn't rise, bear in mind that the impact of the NMW will be much greater on small firms than large ones; the Low Pay Commission has estimated that the effect on wage costs will be six times larger for firms with less than 9 employees than for firms with more than 100 workers[43]. These, however, are often the firms which are: most subject to product market competition; least likely to suffer from managers pursuing their private objectives at the expense of efficiency (because owners and managers are the same people); and most likely to have close supervision of the workforce. In other words, they should already be working at close to maximum efficiency – because if they were not, competition would have forced them out of business. They just can't increase productivity, therefore.

Indeed, there's one way in which a minimum wage might reduce productivity. To see it, consider an interesting fact about employment. It is often an exchange of gifts; employers pay higher wages than they strictly need to, and, in exchange, workers put in more effort than the bare minimum.

Now, in introducing a minimum wage the government alters this gift exchange. Workers might now regard their wages as less generous than they previously thought – because they compare them to the legal minimum rather than to some lower amount. If they do this, they could decide to put in less effort. Productivity will then fall. And knowing this, employers paying a little better than the minimum wage might cut wages back. In this way, a minimum wage can reduce pay and productivity. Laboratory experiments by Jordi Brandts and Gary Charness have found that effort can fall very sharply through this route.[44]

If you're unconvinced by all this, just recall what productivity is. It's defined as output per person. A rise in it must therefore mean either more output or fewer workers. Supporters of a NMW are loath to admit the latter. And as we've seen, the former implies that prices should fall – but there's no evidence they do.

But even if productivity does rise, there is no free lunch. As Walter Oi has pointed out, high productivity can reduce job satisfaction (as people are forced to work harder), or reduce consumers' welfare by compelling them to wait longer to be served.[45] Someone loses.

To all this it may be replied that a NMW minimum wage might raise productivity in another way – by compelling firms to compete on the basis of high quality, rather than low prices.

The problem with this, however, is that many customers may want low-quality, low-price goods – because that is all they can afford. This is all the more likely if the customers of low-wage businesses happen to be poor themselves. In this case, "a higher minimum wage essentially takes money from the people in front of the counter at McDonalds and gives it to the people behind the counter".[46]

The minimum wage and poverty

Herein lies a crucial feature of the minimum wage. Even its intelligent advocates agree that its effect on adult poverty is "statistically undetectable".[47] Table 3 shows estimates by the Institute for Fiscal Studies of the percentage of households which gain from the minimum wage. It is clear that more people in middle-income groups gain than in the poorest 10%.

The reason for this is simple. The very worst-off are out of work altogether, so gain nothing from the minimum wage. And many of the winners from a minimum wage are the second or third earners in comfortable households. Indeed, some estimates show that half of the low-paid are in households with above-average household incomes.[48] IFS economists say: "the overlap between low pay and low income is weak."[49]

Table 3. Percentage of households gaining from NMW by income decile

	% who gain
Poorest	3.5
2nd	6.6
3rd	7.4
4th	8.4
5th	9.0
6th	9.5
7th	7.7
8th	6.7
9th	3.1
10th	1.9

Source: IFS press release, 5 June 1998.
Assumes no impact on employment.

IFS findings have been supported by more recent research. "84 per cent of families affected by the NMW are not poor" says Holly Sutherland.[50] She estimates that of the 23 per cent fall in the numbers in poverty as a result of New Labour's policy changes, only 1.2 percentage points are due to the NMW even assuming no change in employment as a result of it. The rest is due to changes in the tax and benefit system.

You might think there's an obvious reply to this – it merely shows that the NMW is too low. If we had a higher minimum, it would make more serious inroads into reducing poverty.

No. The level of the NMW, says Ms Sutherland, "has a very small impact on the poverty rate".[51]

This is because, as the NMW rises, entitlement to means-tested benefits and tax credits falls. As we saw in chapter 4, minimum-wage workers receiving tax credits see over half the rise in their wages snatched away as tax credits and benefits are withdrawn

There is, however, one caveat to all this. These figures are a snapshot, showing who would benefit from the NMW at any point in time. However, millions of people alternate between spells of low pay and spells of unemployment. It follows that many of the unemployed would, over time, benefit from a NMW because it would raise their incomes during the periods when they are in work. Research by IFS economists has found that a NMW set at half median male earnings would, at any point in time, benefit 7% of employed men and 28% of employed women. However, at some point during the 1991-94 period, 12.5% of men and 42% of women would have benefited from the NMW. So, they conclude, "churning between low pay and unemployment means that a minimum wage will appear to be more redistributive in terms of income measured over a few years than in terms of income measured at one point in time".[52]

This, however, is little comfort. First, it assumes a NMW will not affect job turnover. But as we've seen, many of its advocates believe it will, with the result that some of the unemployed could be frozen out of jobs for longer periods.

Secondly, all the above assumes the NMW does not affect employment. But it might. Even if the level of employment is unaffected, the composition might be, as workers from more affluent backgrounds might displace worse-off ones. If that happens, table 3 would understate the gains enjoyed by middle income households, and overstate the gains of poorer ones. Worse still, IFS research has found that the probability of escaping low pay rises sharply as experience and job tenure rise.[53] Anything that jeopardises job attachments, therefore could increase the problem of low pay.

The problem of profits revisited

Minimum wages, then, may not raise the incomes of the worst-off.

But they do reduce employers' profits. One paper concludes that "profitability was significantly reduced by the introduction of the minimum wage".[54]

The Low Pay Commission was relaxed about this. It said in its first report: "In competitive product markets...businesses may have less scope to pass on higher costs to customers and there may be a greater cut in profits, at least initially."[55]

But should the commission have been so sanguine? Perhaps instead New Labour is making the mistake we saw that Old Labour made – of ignoring the consequences of lower profits. There are three:

- *Business closures,* especially amongst the smallest firms, which will be most affected by the NMW. As Stephen Davies has pointed out: "As long as firms are free to enter and exit an industry, the marginal firms in that industry should be earning only just enough to survive. Even a small increase in wages will mean that marginal firms are no longer sufficiently able to go on."[56] The Low Pay Commission was blind to this point. It claimed that the NMW was set at a rate which "sound businesses can afford to pay" – oblivious to the fact that many people, through no fault of their own, work for unsound businesses.[57] Granted, even the paper that found a big fall in profits as a result of the minimum wage found no evidence of increased business closures. But it could be just a matter of time.

- *Fewer business start-ups.* With profits lower, the incentive to start up new businesses may be lower. "Minimum wage increases may slow the rate of small business formation, a possibility that has not received much attention in the literature" says Madeline Zavodny.[58]

- *Increased concentration.* If small businesses close, and fewer take their place, you might think the result, in the long run, would be higher unemployment. Not necessarily. Jobs could instead be transferred to larger, more profitable businesses.[59] Even this is not without its costs. The loss of small firms, and increased concentration amongst larger ones, implies an increase in monopoly power – and therefore in prices for ordinary consumers.[60]

In this context, the naivete of the Low Pay Commission is striking. "We were struck by the extent to which businesses welcomed the general principle of the NMW" they say.[61] But of course, businesses might welcome it precisely because they hope it will drive their rivals out of business, and thus give themselves greater monopoly power.

A case for minimum wages?

In short, the minimum wage is far from a free lunch. As David Metcalf wrote before he joined the Low Pay Commission: "someone has to pay for a NMW – via lower profits for firms, lower wages for those above the low pay threshold, higher consumer prices, or displaced workers."[62]

This does not mean a case cannot be made for a minimum wage. You might argue that the costs of a minimum wage are outweighed by the benefits. After all, the evidence from care homes suggests that those workers who keep their jobs do enjoy higher wages. Maybe the gains to them exceed the losses suffered by the workers who lose their jobs.[63]

What's more, the NMW stops employers driving down wages in the knowledge that workers' incomes will be topped up by tax credits and in-work benefits. In limiting the costs of such benefits and tax credits, the NMW either saves taxpayers money or allows these benefits to be more generous. In this indirect sense, the NMW does help raise the incomes of the low paid.

There's a more subtle way in which the NMW can reduce poverty and improve aggregate economic welfare, as a paper by Robin Boadway and Katherine Cuff points out.[64]

The theory here is that it may be efficient for the lowest ability workers to be unemployed and to give them welfare benefits. This is because the value of their output is tiny, and the psychological costs of them working are large, to themselves and perhaps their colleagues. However, the welfare benefits they get on the dole are low, because taxpayers, not wanting to give money to lazy but able people, are reluctant to finance decent unemployment benefits.

This can be both unjust and inefficient. It's unjust because people who, through no fault of their own, have low ability do not get sufficient compensation for their misfortune. And it's inefficient because it encourages these people to look for work, when they – and us – might be better off if they stayed at home.

A minimum wage can solve this problem. It gives higher-ability but lazy workers an incentive to work. This means the unemployed are more likely to be the genuinely unlucky or unskilled. taxpayers' reluctance to pay unemployment benefits – for fear these will go to shirkers rather than the genuinely deserving – will therefore be lower. Benefits should therefore rise. Poverty is therefore cut and efficiency enhanced.

This, of course, is a long way from what most supporters of the NMW intend – which only goes to show that, very often, the political arguments you hear most are merely the crudest ones.

There is, though, another case for the minimum wage, which its supporters might find more congenial. This is that selling one's labour-power for a low wage should be what Michael Walzer has called a "blocked exchange"[65]. Some trades, the argument goes – such as selling oneself into slavery, or selling honours – are so morally abhorrent that we should outlaw them. Maybe poverty wages fall into this category. However, even blocked exchanges can be mutually beneficial for those who engage in them. To outlaw them, one must show that the costs of the exchange to the rest of the community outweigh the benefits to the participants. Perhaps this can be done. One should not, however, fool oneself into thinking it can be done so at no cost – even to the worst-off.

Notes

1. *New Britain: My Vision of a Young Country* p133.

2. This was not the only reason for opposition to a NMW. In 1969 the Department of Employment and Productivity published a study rejecting the idea. (*A National Minimum Wage: Report of an Inter-departmental Working Party*). It did so on the grounds that the overlap between low wages and poverty was small – because many of the low-paid were wives of well-paid men – and because it would lead to higher inflation, as trades unions demanded pay rises to maintain differentials with the low-paid. One reason for renewed interest in the NMW is that these premises are much less valid these days.

3. Fernie and Metcalf – *Low Pay and Minimum Wages: The British Evidence* (Centre for Economic Performance 1996), p14.

4. Gregg, Machin and Manning – "High pay, low pay and labour market efficiency" p108 in Glyn and Miliband (eds) – *Paying for Inequality: The Economic Costs of Social Injustice*.

5. *Myth and Measurement: The New Economics of the Minimum Wage,* ch.2.

6. *Myth and Measurement* p21, emphasis added. This was not the only evidence they found for the notion that minimum wages did not destroy jobs. When the federal minimum wage was raised in April 1990, employment in low-wage firms in Texas also rose (*Myth and Measurement* p59) However, most attention has focused on the "natural experiment" in New Jersey, so we will concentrate on this.

7. See David Neumark and William Wascher, "Minimum wages and employment: a case study of the fast food industry in New Jersey and

Pennsylvania: comment", *American Economic Review,* 90, December 2000, p1362-96, and Card and Krueger, "Reply", *American Economic Review,* 90, December 2000, p1397-1420.

8. *Myth and Measurement,* p28.

9. Finis Welch, "Comment", p847, *Industrial and Labour Relations Review,* 48, July 1995 p827-49.

10. "Looking for a needle in a haystack?" January 2000, p16.

11. "The economic effects of minimum wages", *Show-Me Institute Policy Study no.2,* October 2006.

12. Richard Dickens and Alan Manning, "Spikes and spill-overs: the impact of the national minimum wage on the wage distribution in a low-wage sector", *Economic Journal,* 114, March 2004, pC95-C101.

13. http://www.lowpay.gov.uk/lowpay/lowpay2006/

14. This estimate comes Stephen Bazen, "On the employment effects of introducing a national minimum wage in the UK", *British Journal of Industrial Relations,* 28, July 1990, p215-26, p216.

15. *The National Minimum Wage: First Report of the Low Pay Commission,* p5, and "Improved estimates of low pay 1998-2001, National Statistics press release, October 3 2002.

16. *The National Minimum Wage: The Story So Far,* p168.

17. http://www.lowpay.gov.uk/lowpay/lowpay2005/appendix3.shtml

18. "The impact of the introduction of the UK minimum wage on the employment probabilities of low wage workers", *Warwick Economic Research Papers no 630,* January 2002.

19. *The National Minimum Wage: The Story So Far* p113.

20. "Improved estimates of low pay", National Statistics press release, October 3 2002. Note that a wage below the NMW is not in itself proof of non-compliance; workers getting free housing or training are not entitled to the NMW.

21. Mark Stewart and Joanna Swaffield, "The other margin: do minimum wages cause working hours adjustments for low-wage workers?", February 2006.

22. "Where the minimum wage bites hard: the introduction of the UK national minimum wage to a low wage sector", November 2002.

23. What seems to be the most obvious problem with monopsony – that it implies, absurdly, that everyone who wants a job can find one (because monopsonistic firms have unfilled vacancies) – is not actually a serious

difficulty. Alan Manning has shown that monopsony can be consistent with involuntary unemployment ("How do we know that real wages are too high?", *Quarterly Journal of Economics*, 110, November 1995 p1111-26).

24. Gregg, Machin and Manning – "High pay, low pay and labour market efficiency" p107.

25. *The Minimum Wage: No Way to Help the Poor* p23-25.

26. *Myth and Measurement: The New Economics of the Minimum Wage,* p383.

27. *The National Minimum Wage: The Story So Far,* p168.

28. "Monopsony in the labour market", *Journal of Economic Literature*, 35, March 1997 p86-112.

29. Alan Manning, "The real thin theory: monopsony in modern labour markets", *Centre for Economic Performance*, May 2003.

30. Gary Becker and Guity Nashat Becker, *The Economics of Life*, p38.

31. "What do I get? How some employers might benefit from a minimum wage", *Centrepiece*, spring 1998, p21.

32. *The National Minimum Wage: First Report of the Low Pay Commission* (Cmd 3976) p105.

33. *A New Economic Future for Britain*, p41.

34. *The National Minimum Wage: First Report of the Low Pay Commission* (Cmd 3976) p110.

35. *The National Minimum Wage: First Report of the Low Pay Commission* (Cmd 3976) p250.

36. *Social Justice: Strategies for National Renewal,* p170.

37. Richard Freeman – "The minimum wage as a redistributive tool", *Economic Journal*, 106, May 1996 p639-49, p642. Note that this process need not involve anyone being directly sacked. The replacement of disadvantaged workers by more advantaged ones could happen as a result of natural job turnover.

38. *The Minimum Wage: No Way to Help the Poor* p27.

39. "Minimum wage effects on school and work transitions of teenagers", *American Economic Review Papers and Proceedings*, 85, May 1995, p244-49, p244.

40. "Minimum wage effects in the long run", *NBER working paper 10656*, August 2004.

41. "The economics of minimum wage legislation", *American Economic Review*, 36, June 1946, p358-65, p359.

42. "Where the minimum wage bites hard: the introduction of the UK national minimum wage to a low wage sector", p25.

43. *The National Minimum Wage: First Report of the Low Pay Commission* p105.

44. "Do labour market conditions affect gift exchange? Some experimental evidence", *Economic Journal,* 114, July 2004, p684-708.

45. "Consequences of minimum wage legislation", *Economic Affairs,* 17, June 1997 p5-14, p13.

46. Donald Deere, Kevin Murphy and Finis Welch – "Examining the evidence on minimum wages and employment" p36, in Marvin H. Kosters (ed) – *The Effects of the Minimum Wage on Employment,* ch 3.

47. *Myth and Measurement* p280.

48. Sloane and Theodossiou – "Earnings mobility, family income and low pay", *Economic Journal,* 106, May 1996 p657-666, p661.

49. IFS press release, 6 June 1998.

50. "The national minimum wage and in-work poverty", *University of Cambridge Department of Applied Economics Working Paper 0111,* July 2001, p8.

51. "The national minimum wage and in-work poverty", p9.

52. Gosling, Johnson, Macrae and Paull – *The Dynamics of Low Pay and Unemployment in Early 1990s Britain,* p3.

53. *The Dynamics of Low Pay and Unemployment in Early 1990s Britain,* p98.

54. Mirko Draca, Stephen Machin and John van Reenan, "Minimum wages and firm profitability", December 2005.

55. *The National Minimum Wage: First Report of the Low Pay Commission* p119.

56. *The Minimum Wage: No Case for Complacency, IoD Discussion paper,* 1996 p4.

57. *The National Minimum Wage: First Report of the Low Pay Commission* p102.

58. "Why minimum wage hikes may not reduce employment", *Federal Reserve Bank of Atlanta Economic Review, Q2 1998* p18-28, p26.

59. *The National Minimum Wage: First Report of the Low Pay Commission* p119.

60. *Employers and a National Minimum Wage,* EPI Report July 1996.

61. *The National Minimum Wage: First Report of the Low Pay Commission* px.

62. Fernie and Metcalf – *Low Pay and Minimum Wages: The British Evidence (Centre for Economic Performance 1996)*, p4.

63. Is it possible or morally right to make such inter-personal comparisons of well-being? I'll examine this question in chapter 11.

64. "A minimum wage can be welfare-improving and employment enhancing", *European Economic Review*, 45, March 2001, p553-76.

65. *Spheres of Justice* p100-103.

6.

"The Best Economic Policy There Is"

Education is the best economic policy there is, and it is in the marriage of education and technology that the future lies. The arms race may be over; the knowledge race has begun...Britain has neglected the impact on economic growth of investment in human capital (Tony Blair).[1]

One of New Labour's most radical and controversial commitments is to ensure that half of all young people enter higher education. What should we make of this pledge?

Cynics say it reflects a peculiar combination of historical continuity and managerialism.

Continuity, because a common complaint about the UK economy for decades has been that we lack skilled workers. This complaint dates back at least as far as 1835, when Richard Cobden complained that poor education was hampering Britain's economic performance[2]. What's more there is a great tradition in the Labour party – embodied in organizations such as the Workers Education Association – which prizes education highly. Not only has it been regarded as a force for social change, but also as a route out of poverty.

Continuity is now accompanied by managerialism. The "new times" and modernity rhetoric of New Labour tells us that we live in an age of unprecedented technical progress and globalization. This means we'll need more and more skilled workers to use new technology and fight off competition from low-wage economies. From this background, New Labour's interest in education reflects several managerialist strands: a belief that the future is predictable; the idea that governments should act as a human resources department for companies; and a confidence that governments can mould individuals to fit the unquestioned needs of the economy.

All this may be an explanation for New Labour's interest in education, but it is not a full justification for it. This lies elsewhere – in the fact that there's increasing evidence that education is an important influence on both inequality and economic performance.

Education, equality and efficiency

One reason for this is that your chances of being in work depend increasingly upon your qualifications. Table 11 shows that, during the 1980s and 1990s, the proportion of unskilled men out of work rose sharply. In 2000 two-fifths of men without qualifications were out of work. But 2000 was a year of generally low unemployment. That so many unskilled men were out of work even when macroeconomic conditions were favourable shows that macroeconomic policy alone won't create full employment. Some other policy is needed.

Table 11. Percentage of men out of work by qualification

	1979	1990	1995	2000
Higher	2.4	6.8	11.4	8.5
Intermediate	3.6	12.1	17.9	14.4
Lower	4.9	12.8	19.5	21.4
None	10.8	30.6	43.4	42.4

Out of work is defined as unemployed or economically inactive. Source: Steve Nickell and Glenda Quintini, "The recent performance of the UK labour market" tables 10 and 11, *Oxford Review of Economic Policy*,[18] summer 2002.

What's more, even if you get a job, your education now has a bigger influence on your pay than it did a few years ago. Table 12 shows that the gap between the wages of the highly qualified and unqualified rose during the 1980s and 1990s. In 1980 graduates earned 48 per cent more than non-graduates. By 2004, they earned 64 per cent more.

Dramatic as these figures seem, they actually understate the importance of education. One reason for this is that, as Alan Krueger and Mikael Lindahl say, "the pay-off to investments in education are higher for more disadvantaged individuals".[3] Young people from middle-class homes often have the contacts and self-confidence to prosper without formal education, and the capital with which to set up their own businesses. For poorer ones, there are only two roads to riches – education or crime.

The fact that education is an increasingly important determinant of both employment prospects and wages shows that there is a pressing egalitarian case for improving educational standards and access to higher education –

because those without education are losing out in the labour market. In the words of the great Brown – James Brown – "without an education you might as well be dead." As Blair said, "social justice can only be achieved through education".[4]

Table 12. How education raises wages

	Graduates as % of total employment	Relative wages of graduates
1980	5.0	1.48
1985	9.8	1.50
1990	10.2	1.60
1995	14.0	1.60
2000	17.2	1.64
2004	21.0	1.64

Source: Machin and Vignoles, "Education policy in the UK", Centre for the Economics of Education discussion paper March 2006.

There's more. The gap between graduate and non-graduate pay has risen at the same time as the numbers of university graduates rose sharply. Other things being equal, this increased supply should have depressed graduate wages. That this did not happen can only mean that the demand for graduates rose so much as to more than offset their increased supply.

This has increased suspicions that a combination of globalization and technical change have raised the demand for educated workers. If these trends continue, it will be important for the economy to have a rising supply of skilled workers.

You don't, however, have to indulge in futurology to believe education is important. In the last 20 years, economists have come to believe that it matters more for economic growth than they previously thought.

Back in 1989, Robert Barro pointed out a depressing fact – that poor countries did not generally grow faster than rich ones.[5] This, he said, was because many poor countries couldn't learn from rich countries' more productive techniques because their people weren't educated enough. A country needs education if it is to catch up with wealthy nations.

Consider sub-Saharan Africa and South East Asia. In 1960, incomes in these two regions were similar. But many South East Asian countries subsequently boomed, whilst many African ones stagnated. The reason for the difference, said Barro, was that the Asian countries had high school enrolment rates in 1960 whilst the African ones had low enrolment rates. Raising the school enrolment rate from 50 to 100%, he estimated, would raise GDP growth by 1.5 percentage points a year. Over 30 years, this would raise national income by more than 50 per cent – the difference between life and death for millions in the poorest economies.

Soon afterwards, Greg Mankiw, David Romer and David Weil pointed out another fact about long-run growth[6]. Population growth, they found, was more damaging to economic growth than previously thought, whilst increased savings were more effective in raising growth. This, they said, was because education – more human capital – was very important. Higher savings and investment raise incomes, which raises the stock of human capital, which in turn gives another kick to incomes. But if the population grows quickly, human capital is spread more thinly, so economic growth falls.

More recently, economists have found other ways in which education can cause a permanent increase in the rate of growth. There are at least four ways in which this is possible:

- A more skilled workforce can attract foreign direct investment. It therefore encourages the transfer of foreign technology, and increases the chances of that technology being adopted by indigenous firms.

- Better trained workers can encourage firms to introduce new equipment and technology, in the confidence that employees will be able to understand how to use them. And higher capital spending means higher growth.

- Some abilities become more valuable if others have them as well. Skills in programming software, for example, are more useful if there are more people who know how to use that software. Such network externalities mean that additional training and education can raise the value of the pre-existing skills of other workers.

- Education can encourage investment in research and development, by providing research staff. That, in turn, improves technological innovation, and therefore growth.[7]

It seems, therefore, that Blair's famous mantra,"education, education, education", is no mere soundbite. It really is the key to both reducing inequality and improving economic performance.

Or is it? This account raises a lot of problems. Does education really raise incomes, and if so by how much, and why? What exactly is the link between education and inequality? And is it possible to have too much of a good thing, and to over-invest in education?

Human capital, attitude and signalling

Let's take the first question first. There is no doubt that educated people, on average, earn much more than uneducated ones. Table 13 shows that people with degrees have hourly wages around a quarter higher than those with just A levels.

Table 13. Returns to qualifications in 2002 (%)

	Men	*Women*
Post-graduate degree	12.6	16.2
Degree	25.3	23.5
2+ A levels	13.8	14.4
5+ GCSEs (C grade or better)	24.6	21.9

Numbers show returns to the qualification relative to the qualification below. Source: Steven McIntosh, Further Analysis of the Returns to Academic and Vocational Qualifications, CEE Discussion paper January 2004.

In themselves, these figures don't prove that education causes higher earnings. Graduates tend to have higher innate ability than others. Such ability might well cause them to earn more, whether they have degrees or not.

In theory, this point could be important. If all the correlation between earnings and education were due to the contribution of unteachable cognitive skills to earnings, increased spending on education would be a waste of money, because it would not raise either the earning power of the poor or the economy's productive capacity.

In practice, though, the point seems less significant. A vast literature has tried to examine the returns to education whilst controlling for innate ability[8]. Generally, it's found that these are high. Education, then, really does add to an individual's earnings.

But why? The answer's not as obvious as you might think.

Traditionally, there have been two competing explanations (there is in fact a third, as we'll see soon.)

The dominant one is human capital theory. This says that education makes us cleverer and so more productive. It raises our human capital. And high levels of human capital, just like high levels of physical capital, lead to higher output.

For years, though, there has been a challenge to this idea – the signalling and screening hypotheses. These say that employers use education to select employees and reject undesirable applicants. Knowing this, potential employees go to university not to acquire skills, but to signal to employers that they are valuable recruits.

The debate between human capital and the signalling/screening theories matters enormously. If human capital theory is right, expanding higher education is a great idea. It'll increase the economy's stock of human capital, which will make the nation richer. And if everyone has lots of skills, wage inequalities should narrow. New Labour will then be right – education will be good for efficiency and equality.

However, if the signalling and screening hypothesis is right, expanding education could be downright dangerous. If everyone has a degree, employers won't be able to select the right employees so easily. This will increase the chance of hiring the wrong applicants, thus raising companies' costs. And it will encourage people to invest in technically unnecessary and costly qualifications merely to signal their skills. All this would be inefficient.

It might be unjust too. If employers cannot distinguish applicants on the basis of qualifications, they might revert to using social connections or asking for "good interpersonal and communication skills", which are euphemisms for being middle class. Inequalities of opportunity would then increase.

So, what's the evidence for human capital theory?

Some of it comes from the earnings of the self-employed. If screening and signalling were significant one would expect graduates who work for others to earn more than graduates who work for themselves. But they don't.[9] This suggests signalling isn't an important influence on earnings.

More evidence comes from a paper by Alan Carruth and his colleagues[10]. They found that the majority of differences in wages across industries were in fact due to differences in workers' observed and unobserved abilities. Wages in the chemicals industry, for example, are higher than those in the textiles industry largely because chemicals workers have higher ability than textiles workers. This is evidence for human capital theory.

Unfortunately, there is also strong evidence against human capital theory:

- IFS research found that men (though, oddly, not women) who drop out of degree courses earn less than those who do not even start such courses[11]. This contradicts human capital theory simply because even part of a degree course should increase ability a little, and so raise productivity and earnings. But it's entirely consistent with signalling theory, which suggests that failure to complete a course sends a negative signal – that someone lacks application and determination.

- Jeremy Smith and colleagues have found that the probability of a graduate getting a job for which he or she is fully qualified is higher for people from higher social classes.[12] This is not just British snobbery. US research has also found that success in the labour market is partly inherited.[13] This is hard to reconcile with human capital theory, but easily consistent with signalling theory: employers believe posh people are more likely to have the right attitude.

- A lot of training and education doesn't add to earnings. Research on twins has found that the returns to many post-A-level vocational qualifications are virtually zero.[14] And graduates working in jobs where their degree is directly relevant to the job don't generally earn more than those whose degree isn't so relevant. All this is hard to reconcile with human capital theory, but consistent with signalling. Only some types of qualifications signal high ability.

- Not all degrees do raise wages. Men with arts degrees earn less than those with A levels only. This is not because such men have low ability; entry requirements for many arts degrees are higher than for many science degrees which do pay a good return. The signalling hypothesis provides a natural explanation for this. Arts degrees signal that their holders prefer to spend their time indulging their tastes rather than in hard self-sacrifice. They also signal that a candidate is ill-equipped for the philistine and anti-intellectual world of business. Both should carry a wage penalty.

- Being in a professional or managerial occupation raises graduates' wages.[15] This sounds trivially true – except that human capital theory predicts that individuals of the same ability should earn the same, regardless of their occupation.

- Evidence from elsewhere in the labour market shows that low pay is much more persistent than theory suggests it should be. IFS research suggests that a better predictor of low pay than any personal characteristic, such as age or education, is the fact that one was low paid in the previous year.[16] Being low-paid may, therefore, signal to potential employers that one is a poor worker, even if one is not. If signalling is important at the low-wage end of the labour market, why should it be less important for higher-wage jobs where employers are usually more choosy?

Table 14. Returns to a degree by subject (%), 1999

	Men	*Women*
Languages	4.7	17.0
Health	26.0	45.0
Science	13.8	24.7
Maths	25.3	32.5
Economics	29.0	41.6
Law	27.3	43.6
Social sciences	7.4	27.9
Arts	-9.4	15.4

Source: Ian Walker and Yu Zhu, "The returns to education: evidence from the Labour Force Surveys", DfES research report 313.

Of course, human capital theorists have answers to all this. Many of these anomalies might reflect one common phenomenon. Male arts graduates, university drop-outs or people from lower social classes might lack unobserved attributes which employers require. If so, they should earn less, just as human capital theory predicts.

But what are these attributes?

The right attitude, that's what. And this raises an idea beloved of the old left – that education indoctrinates people into the ways of capitalism. 30 years ago, Harry Braverman wrote:

It is...not so much what the child learns that is important as what he or she becomes wise to. In school the child or adolescent practice what they will later be called upon to do as adults: the conformity to routines, the manner in which they will be expected to snatch from the fast-moving machinery their needs and wants.[17]

This notion has recently been revived by Samuel Bowles and Herbert Gintis. Education, they say, creates or improves "incentive-enhancing preferences".[18]

The idea here is straightforward. It's well-known that employers value a good "attitude" as much as formal skills. This is no mere prejudice. Because labour contracts are incomplete, and bosses cannot continuously supervise workers, employers need workers they can trust. And educated workers are often more trustworthy. They have a high marginal utility of income, a propensity for hard work, low time preference rates, a tendency to tell the truth and an ability to identify with managers rather than workers. Employers want workers with all these characteristics, and so pay more to get them. And education either produces these or demonstrates that graduates have them. As Bowles, Gintis and Osborne put it: "A substantial portion of the returns to schooling are generated by effects or correlates of schooling substantially unrelated to the cognitive capacities measured on the available tests."[19]

This idea is consistent with most of the facts we've described. It's consistent with the fact that arts graduates and drop-outs earn less, because these don't have incentive-enhancing attitudes. It's consistent with the fact that people don't earn more if their degrees are job-relevant – because a degree in ancient history is as likely to inculcate the right attitudes as one in science.

It's also consistent with an otherwise curious fact – that male mature graduates have a higher probability of unemployment and lower wages than men who went to college straight from school.[20] This is hard to reconcile with human capital theory – because mature graduates have as much of this as less mature ones. It's also hard to reconcile with signalling theory – a man who has given up a job to complete a degree, rather than trodden the natural path from school to university – is displaying more than usual self-discipline and determination. That should make him stand out to potential employers. It is, though, easily consistent with Bowles and Gintis' theory. Mature students are harder to socialise into the right set of preferences than their younger, more malleable, counterparts, so they should be less attractive to employers.

If the "incentive-enhancing preferences" theory is right, New Labour's desire for more education might at least be economically sensible. Education will create a "better" workforce insofar as it inculcates the right attitudes. And it might also increase equality by converting the poor into people who are more attractive to employers.

This, though, is probably not what New Labour supporters intend. If education works by changing our characters, and by straightening the crooked timber of humanity into something useful to bosses, prosperity is achieved by sacrificing liberty and diversity to managerialism.

Education and economic growth

So far, we've considered the link between individual education and individual incomes. But what about the link between aggregate education and aggregate incomes?

This is not merely the individual relationship writ large. In theory, my education might be good or bad for the economy in general. It'll be bad if it merely gets me a job that would otherwise go to someone else of equal ability, or if it merely increases my ability to exploit others. But it'll be good, if others learn from my skills and become more productive.

So, we need some macroeconomic studies. There are plenty of these – of the sort pioneered by Barro and Mankiw, Romer and Weil – that show education to be an important source of rising aggregate incomes.

Sadly, though, there are lots of problems with them.

- They often cannot answer the question: does education raise the level of income (as standard neoclassical theory implies) or the growth rate, as new growth theories imply? The distinction matters. Neoclassical theory says that there will come a time when the effect of education on growth will stop – to get ever-increasing incomes we need ever-increasing levels of human capital. New growth theory, by contrast, is more optimistic. It says a one-off rise in education will have permanent effects on growth.

- It's hard to measure accurately the stock of human capital. Early studies, such as Barro's and Mankiw, Romer and Weil's used secondary school enrolment rates. However, these are subject to error – because students can enrol without turning up to class – and are of course no measure of the quality of education. More sophisticated attempts to measure the stock of human capital have found a smaller impact of human capital on growth.[21]

- It's hard to identify the pure effect of education on growth. Countries that invest a lot in education will often possess other qualities and institutions that are favourable for growth – such as scientific attitudes, a willingness to prepare for the future and political stability. It's often hard to see how much education contributes to growth on top of these qualities. Unless we know precisely what these are and how to measure them, we cannot control for their influence upon growth.

- Some research on cross-country growth differences has found no role for education. This is true of the nearly two million regressions run by Xavier Sala-i-Martin.[22] And Kristin Forbes has estimated that it is only female education that affects growth, not male.[23] There are two competing explanations for these findings. At face value, they suggest the benefits of education are overstated. Alternatively, they might merely be victims of the problem of measuring the level of human capital. It's a rule of statistics that if an input is subject to measurement error, estimates of the link between the input and the output will be biased towards zero.

- Cross-country studies are typically silent on the crucial question: what exactly is the mechanism whereby education raises growth? As we've seen, new growth theory has several ideas. Unfortunately, the hard evidence that these mechanisms are actually important is "quite weak".[24]

- Casual empiricism suggests increases in education might not boost growth. Ken Mayhew and Ewart Keep point out that in the UK the proportion of 18-year-olds entering higher education has risen from 4 per cent to 40 per cent since 1945. But economic growth has stuck around 2.5 per cent a year.[25]

- Even if there is a strong correlation between human capital and subsequent economic growth, it may not be that schooling causes growth. Quite the opposite. Economic growth – and expectations of economic growth – will increase education. If people expect their economy to grow strongly, they will get more education. It will then look as though education has caused economic growth, when in fact it is expected growth that has caused education. Mark Bils and Peter Klenow have estimated that this mechanism might be important.[26]

Problems such as these mean that our knowledge of the link between education and aggregate economic performance is smaller than New Labour's managerialist hubris would have us believe. As one survey of the literature put it: "It is difficult to be left completely satisfied by the wide range of studies looking at the effects of education on economic growth."[27]

Education and rising inequality

Increasing education, therefore, might not increase economic growth. But would it reduce inequality?

Perhaps not. A ubiquitous result in research on the private returns to education is that education and observed ability can explain only a small proportion of the variation in earnings from individual to individual – typically, less than half. Gary Becker, the doyen of human capital theorists has written:

> Gains from college education vary not only between groups, like men and women, but also substantially within given groups...A large dispersion in the rate of return to college education makes it difficult for any individual to anticipate his gain from education.[28]

This is because there are some very strange things that affect our earnings, aside from skill and luck:

- *Monopsony.* This can lead to wage differences from firm-to-firm even for identical workers, as each individual firm sets a different profit-maximising wage, to exploit its individual degree of monopsony power.

- *Appearances.* Everyone knows wages differ according to gender or race. They also differ according to physical attractiveness. Daniel Hamermesh and Jeff Biddle have estimated that good-looking people earn significantly more than ugly ones[29]. For men, the penalty for being ugly – 9% lower wages than the average – is higher than many estimates of the penalty for one year less of education.

- *Clean homes.* Americans who keep their homes clean and tidy earn more than those who don't. According to one estimate (this is not a very active research field) the correlation between cleanliness and earnings is half as great as that between education and earnings.[30]

- *Height.* Tall people earn more than stumpy ones. Controlling for education, a six-foot American man earns, on average, almost 7 per cent more than one who is five foot six. That's almost equal to the wage premium associated with a year's extra schooling.[31]

- *Left-handedness.* Left-handed men earn around 5% more than right-handers. But southpaw women earn around 3% less.[32]

- *Gap years.* Ian Walker and Yu Zhu have found that men who take a gap year between school and university earn 25 per cent more than men who don't, other things being equal.[33] This means the return to postponing going to university is as great as the three years spent at university. Someone who goes to India for a gap year is either signalling or acquiring skills that employers' value: Giles Wemmbley-Hogg may be an idiot, but he's an employable idiot.

- *Sorting and risk aversion.* Imagine two industries. One is old and stable, with a low variance in incomes. The other is new, with a high variance of incomes. Risk-averse people with high ability who have invested human capital in the old industry will want to stay in it, as they believe they have a good chance of success. However, less able people, though also risk-averse, will choose the new economy, where experience and track record count for less. Some of these will, thanks to the greater importance of luck in this sector, end up earning more money than more able workers in the old economy. There will therefore be little link between ability and earnings.

- *Labour market institutions.* Dan Devroye and Richard Freeman have found that there is greater inequality in wages among Americans with similar levels of measured skills than there is among all workers in Germany or Sweden.[34] This suggests that most of the differences in inequality between Germany and the US reflect the fact that luck and greater returns to ability play a much bigger role in the US than in Germany. This may be because of greater individual wage bargaining. Or it might be because of a more pronounced "winner-take-all" effect, whereby tiny differences in ability cause huge differences in pay. Whatever the explanation, the implication is important. Wage inequalities aren't due merely to differences in individual ability. They are also due to political and economic institutions.

- *Employer size.* Workers in smaller firms earn less than those in bigger ones.[35] This could reflect the fact that wages often contain an element of monopoly rents in product markets – as more profitable firms pay better wages – and small firms have fewer such rents to share.

- *Job changes.* Workers who become unemployed often find that their next job pays much less than their previous one. Amongst men who experienced a spell of unemployment between 1991 and 1994, 43.8% saw their wages fall by 10% or more. Amongst continuously employed men, only 18.3% suffered such a cut.[36]

For all these reasons, wage inequality is only partly related to educational differences. And if it is hard to relate the level of inequality to differences in qualifications, it will be difficult to relate changes in inequality to those qualifications. This is especially true as earnings' inequality has risen even among workers of similar age and qualifications. "A significant portion of the overall rise in inequality remains unexplained by rising returns to age and education" says Stephen Machin.[37]

All this suggests that attempts to increase the supply of educated workers might not be sufficient to significantly reduce wage inequality.

Indeed, some evidence suggests that increases in the supply of graduates may not reduce inequality at all – because what seems to be a rise in the return on education might instead be a rise in the return on skills which are correlated with education, but which may not actually be enhanced by more education.[38]

Three papers point to this. One comes from Richard J. Murnane and two colleagues[39]. They estimated the return on US college education for 24-year-olds in 1978 and 1986. The returns had increased between the two years. If, however, returns were adjusted to allow for scores on a maths test at the age of 18, the increase in the return to college education was much smaller. Indeed, for women, the return did not rise at all. This, they infer, suggests the rise in wages earned by college graduates is due not just to an increased return to college education, but also to an increased return to cognitive skills.

The second study is of US white male college graduates by McKinley Blackburn and David Neumark. They measured ability by the Armed Services Vocational Aptitude Battery Tests, a series of ten different tests of cognitive ability. They found that increased returns to college education were only enjoyed by graduates who scored highly on these tests. "Most workers with below average academic ability experienced a decline in the return to schooling" they concluded.[40]

Thirdly, Ian Walker and Yu Zhu found that, in the UK, the effect of education on wages grew more for high wage earners than for low wage earners in the 1980s and 1990s.[41] If we assume that high wage earners are more able than lower wage earners, this implies that education does more to raise the earnings of the able than the less able. It also suggests that the complementarities between education and ability rose in the 1980s and 1990s.

These papers suggest increasing education would just add to the earnings of able people who'd do well anyway. Although this might be good for economic growth, it would increase inequality.

There are other ways in which expanding higher education would increase inequality. The expansion of higher education seems to have increased the opportunities of people from richer backgrounds more than people from poorer backgrounds. Table 15 shows that the proportion of people from rich families who have degrees more than doubled in the 1980s and 90s, whilst the proportion from poorer families rose much less. What's more, the probability of a talented girl getting a degree if she comes from a poor family actually fell, despite rising numbers of graduates.[42] Fernando Galindo-Rueda and Anna Vignoles say: "It is not the most able who have benefited from the expansion of the UK education system but rather the most privileged."[43]

Of course, this happened before New Labour took office, so it's not their fault. But it shows an important point – that expanding higher education in itself is not sufficient to increase equality of opportunity.

There's another way in which mass higher education could reduce social mobility. If many people have degrees, employers will use factors other than education in their hiring decisions. This may favour middle-class people with social connections and "interpersonal skills", who are more likely to "fit in." In the 1970s and 1980s, graduates were so rare that a good degree signalled

Table 15. Percentage of 23-year-olds with degree, by parental income

	Lowest 20%	*Middle 60%*	*Highest 20%*
1981	6	8	20
1999	9	23	46
Change	3	15	26

Source: Stephen Machin and Anna Vignoles, "Educational inequality: the widening socio-economic gap", Fiscal Studies June 2004, p107-28.

high ability. So someone from a poor home who did get a degree stood a good chance of getting a good job. Today, that person faces competition from more graduates, so his chance of indicating high ability has fallen. And employers might prefer the middle-class graduate with the nice accent who'll fit in.

This might be one reason why earnings mobility has fallen. In 1958, a man born to parents in the lowest quartile of incomes had a 17% chance of getting himself into the top quartile. A man born in 1970 had only a 14% chance.[44]

The lesson of all this is simple. Increasing the supply of graduates, or increasing education generally, might not reduce inequality significantly. It might even increase it.

Does education have a future?

Four final problems deserve mention.

One – and this is just a conjecture – is that formal education might crowd out or inhibit other valuable forms of knowledge. There are four ways in which this might happen.

- The emphasis on explicit, codified information distracts us from the importance of what Michael Polanyi called "tacit knowledge", such as knowledge of local business opportunities or of precise details of production processes, or simply a gut feel for what might prove profitable. If this is the case, academic knowledge might displace entrepreneurial skills. Is it really an accident that so many successful businessmen – such as Alan Sugar, Richard Branson, Bill Gates and John Hargreaves – never completed university?[45]

- Traditional education has, complains Diane Coyle, put too much emphasis upon "whats?" and not enough upon "how tos".[46] Learning facts alone is pretty pointless. These are quickly forgotten, and can anyway be looked up quickly in reference books or on the internet. Instead, what matters is learning how to learn – how to analyse and communicate information. Good schooling will leave students with two things – a confidence to learn new things after they leave formal education, and a humility to recognise that their knowledge is inadequate and that their skills will need constant revision. Keeping the balance between these two things is a tricky job.

- The concentration upon the transmission of facts and formal logical reasoning ignores an equally important task – the teaching of how to think clearly under conditions of uncertainty and imperfect information. As we shall see in chapter 13, people are prone to all sorts of cognitive errors in such circumstances. Education does not prepare us to recognise these.

- Education may impart a subtle and unintended but nevertheless pernicious bias into our beliefs. Throughout school and university, we identify those in power with truth and wisdom. This can lead us to respect those in authority in later life, even where such people don't possess superior knowledge or wisdom. A professor is generally wiser than his students, but a chief executive will not so often be wiser than his workers. We often forget this distinction. And the better our teachers are, the more likely we are to do so.

Secondly, expanding higher education might lead to an expensive but futile inflation in credentials. The problem is this. If the "top half" of 18 year olds enter higher education, not having a degree will signal to employers that you have low ability. Employers will therefore want graduate workers not because they have acquired skills at university, but simply because these are the most able employees. Demand for non-graduates will therefore fall. Knowing this, youngsters will go to university not because they are suited to it, but simply to avoid sending the adverse signal to future employers. Higher education will then become like a lottery ticket. Having one doesn't guarantee you a prize – but you have no hope of winning if you don't have one.[47]

Thirdly, we have so far taken for granted the conventional wisdom, that technical change is raising the demand for graduates, and hence the return to degrees.

But this is not necessarily so. Frederick Guy and Peter Skott say that what happened in the UK and US in the 1980s and 1990s was not skill-biased technical change, but rather power-biased technical change[48]. Technical change, they said, allowed unskilled workers to be more closely monitored;

think of bar-codes in retailing or the rise of call centres. That meant unskilled wages could fall, as there was less need to pay such workers good money to motivate them. However, technical change also gave senior managers more discretion. Hence it was more "necessary" to pay them higher wages to attract and motivate them.

It is, as Guy and Skott acknowledge, difficult to distinguish between their theory and the orthodox view of skill-biased technical change. But there's one factoid that supports it. Ian Walker and Yu Zhu report that the rising return to education seems to have been confined to the US and UK in the early 1980s and 1990s – that is, to countries where labour market institutions and the ideology of managerialism permitted rising inequality.[49] By contrast, if technical change really determined rising inequality, you'd expect inequality to have risen in Europe too.

There's one final problem – it's impossible to forecast the demand for educated workers. This is one lesson from Gary Becker's classic text, *Human Capital.* Writing in 1973, he said: "Perhaps the current weak market for highly skilled manpower is the beginning of a resumption of the earlier 1900-40 decline."[50] But since then returns to education have risen sharply. That even someone of Becker's expertise should have been so wholly wrong shows the dangers of trying to forecast future demand for skills.

These dangers arise from the fact that the relative demand for skills depends, in large part, upon technical change. And forecasting this is a logical impossibility. As Humphrey Lyttleton once said, "If I knew where jazz was going, I'd be there already".[51]

New Labour's ideology prevents it from recognizing this possibility. Part of its rhetoric, as we saw in chapter 1, is that modernity and the future are clear and knowable.

Let's, however, assume that technical progress and globalization will indeed continue at a rapid pace. Even then, it doesn't follow that demand for unskilled workers in the UK will fall and that for graduates will rise. There are several reasons for this:

- Technology can displace skilled workers. Sophisticated software, such as that developed by Sage and more recently Microsoft, could eventually make accountants and tax lawyers redundant (oh happy day!). But it's hard to imagine how technology will make care workers, handymen or gardeners redundant. The notion that technical change must inevitably reduce demand for uneducated workers owes more to the "Star Trek fallacy" – the tendency to extrapolate recent trends into to the future – than to hard economics.

- Globalization can lead to a fall in demand for skilled workers. Philip Brown and Hugh Lauder point out that Indian universities produce over 60,000 computer science graduates a year, and these earn only around one-tenth of their UK equivalents.[52] They say: "A number of less developed countries including India, China and Malaysia are increasingly competing for high skilled work that could reduce the bargaining power of university graduates in the west."

- Forecasts of rising numbers of graduate jobs ignore the possibility that there will be a big replacement demand for non-graduates simply to replace retiring workers, most of whom do not have degrees. This demand, say Ken Mayhew and Ewart Keep, means we should be expanding vocational education and training, not higher education.[53]

- The high price of graduate skills might cause employers to seek ways of reducing graduate employment, by deskilling jobs. Those who forecast rising demand for graduates focus too much upon technology, and not enough upon employers' strenuous efforts to de-skill jobs in an attempt to maintain control of the workplace and reduce dependence upon employees.

Indeed, it may be that the return to a degree is already falling. Ian Walker and Yu Zhu estimate that for 25-29 year-olds, the average graduate mark-up was 21% for men and 25% for women in 1996-99. But in 2000-03, this fell to 15% and 21% respectively.[54] This, they say, is because increasing numbers of graduates are in non-graduate jobs, where the mark-up is small or non-existent.

The falling mark-up seems especially big for less able graduates. Nigel O'Leary and Peter Sloane estimate that between 1994 and 2002 the graduate mark-up for both men and women at the lower quartile of earnings fell by around 10 percentage points.[55] This suggests the supply of graduates with poorer cognitive skills has risen faster than demand. Which in turn means the rewards to expanding the education of such people are declining.

Perhaps, then, we are approaching the point where diminishing returns to education start to set in. This is good news if you're worried about rising wage inequality, but bad news if you're spending money increasing the supply of graduates.

This shouldn't be too surprising. Returns to education in continental Europe, where mass higher education has been the norm for years, are low. Perhaps the Atlanticist bias in New Labour's thinking – there was an unusual rise in returns to education in the 1980s and 1990s in the US – might bias the party against fully recognizing this possibility. Secondly, even before New

Labour took office, there was substantial over-qualification among graduates; Arnaud Chevalier estimates that around 18% were over-qualified in 1996.[56] Thirdly, even scholars sympathetic to the economic importance of education have found that its effects on growth are weak in richer, more educated nations. Alan Krueger and Mikael Lindahl say: "The positive effect of the initial level of education on growth seems to be a phenomenon that is confined to low productivity countries."[57]

Diminishing returns are, of course, exactly what ordinary neoclassical economics would predict – you can have too much of a good thing.

None of this, of course, means more and better education is a waste of money. That would be a silly hyperbole. But it might not be very much sillier than the claim that education is "the best economic policy there is."

Notes

1. *New Britain: My Vision of a Young Country,* p66, 78.

2. Cited in Correlli Barnett, *The Audit of War,* p205.

3. "Education for growth: why and for whom?" p1107, *Journal of Economic Literature, 39,* December 2001, p1101-36.

4. Speech to News Corporation, July 30 2006.

5. "Economic growth in a cross-section of countries", *NBER working paper 3120,* September 1989.

6. "A contribution to the empirics of economic growth", *NBER working paper 3541,* December 1990.

7. The pay-offs to higher research and development can be very large. Gavin Cameron has estimated that the social rate of return to R&D may be as high as 50% (*Innovation and Economic Growth,* Centre for Economic Performance discussion paper 277, February 1996, p17).

8. See, among others, Jonathan Haskel et al, "Estimating returns to education using a new sample of UK twins", paper presented to 2000 Royal Economic Society annual conference, Blundell, Dearden, Goodman, and Reed, *Higher Education, Employment and Earnings in Britain,* Ian Walker and Yu Zhu, "The returns to education: evidence from the Labour Force Surveys", *DfES research report 313,* Orley Ashenfelter and Cecilia Rouse, "Schooling, intelligence and income in America", in Kenneth Arrow, Samuel Bowles and Steven Durlauf (eds), *Meritocracy and Economic Inequality,* and Joshua Angrist and Alan Krueger, "Estimating the return to schooling using the Vietnam-era draft lottery", *NBER working paper 4067,* May 1992.

9. Chevalier, Harmon, Walker and Zhu, "Does education raise productivity or just reflect it?" *Centre for Economic Policy Research discussion paper 3993,* July 2003, p17.

10. "Inter-industry wage differences and individual heterogeneity", December 1999, www.ukc.ac.uk.

11. Richard Blundell, Lorraine Dearden, Alissa Goodman and Howard Reed, "The returns to higher education in Britain: evidence from a British cohort", *Economic Journal, 110,* February 2000, p82-99, table 4.

12. "Graduate employability: policy and performance in higher education in the UK", *Economic Journal, 110, June 2000,* p382-411, p401.

13. "The determinants of earnings: a behavioural approach", p1138, *Journal of Economic Literature, 39, December 2001,* p1137-76.

14. "Estimating returns to education using a new sample of UK twins" table 9.

15. *Higher Education, Employment and Earnings in Britain,* p60.

16. Gosling, Johnson, Macrae and Paull – *The Dynamics of Low Pay and Unemployment in early 1990s Britain,* p80-81.

17. *Labor and Monopoly Capital,* p287.

18. "Does schooling raise earnings by making people smarter?" p118 in Arrow, Bowles and Durlauf (eds), *Meritocracy and Economic Inequality.*

19. "The determinants of earnings: a behavioural approach", p1149.

20. "The returns to higher education in Britain: evidence from a British cohort" p93 and Jeremy Smith, Abigail McKnight and Robin Naylor, "Graduate employability: policy and performance in higher education in the UK", p390.

21. Ruth Judson, "Do low human capital coefficients make sense?" *FEDS discussion paper* June 1995.

22. "I just ran two million regressions", *American Economic Review Papers and Proceedings, 87,* May 1997, p178-183.

23. "A reassessment of the relationship between inequality and growth," *American Economic Review, 90,* September 2000, p869-887, p878).

24. Barbara Sienesi and John van Reenan, "The returns to education: a review of the empirical macroeconomic literature", *IFS working paper 02/05,* p4.

25. "The economic and distributional implications of current policies on higher education", p299, *Oxford Review of Economic Policy, 20,* summer 2004, p 298-314.

26. "Does schooling cause growth?", *American Economic Review*, 90, December 2000, p1160-83.

27. Philip Stevens and Martin Weale, "Education and economic growth", *NIESR discussion paper*, August 2003, p25.

28. *Human Capital* (3rd edition), p247.

29. "Beauty and the labour market", *American Economic Review*, 84, December 1994, p1174-94.

30. "The determinants of earnings: a behavioural approach", p1139.

31. T. Paul Schultz, "Wage gains associated with height as a form of health human capital", *American Economic Review papers and proceedings*, 92, May 2002, p349-353.

32. Kevin Denny and Vincent O'Sullivan, "The economic consequences of being left-handed", *IFS working paper WP06/07*.

33. "The returns to education: evidence from the Labour Force Surveys", p27.

34. "Does inequality in skills explain inequality of earnings across countries?" *NBER working paper 8140*, February 2001.

35. Gosling, Johnson, Macrae and Paull, *The Dynamics of Low Pay and Unemployment in early 1990s Britain*, p23.

36. *The Dynamics of Low Pay and Unemployment in early 1990s Britain*, p2.

37. "Wage inequality in the UK", p55, *Oxford Review of Economic Policy*, 12, spring 1996, p47-64.

38. It is important to note here that this is a subtly different point from the education-ability distinction I mentioned earlier. That focused on the link between the levels of education, ability and earnings at a point in time. This is about changes in those levels.

39. Murnane, Willett and Levy, "The growing importance of cognitive skills in wage determination", *Review of Economics and Statistics*, 77, 1995, p251-66.

40. "Omitted ability bias and the increase in the return to schooling", *Journal of Labour Economics*, 11, July 1993, p521-44, p538.

41. "The returns to education: evidence from the Labour Force Surveys", p40.

42. Stephen Machin and Anna Vignoles, "Educational inequality: the widening socio-economic gap", *Fiscal Studies* June 2004, p107-28.

43. "Class-ridden or meritocratic: an economic analysis of recent changes in Britain", *IZA discussion paper 677*, December 2002.

44. "Educational inequality: the widening socio-economic gap", table 6a. The odds for women fell from 17% to 13%.

45. The importance of entrepreneurship may also help explain why so many people believe the link between education and earnings must be causal, rather than the result of ability. Because education is often the only way to get a "good job" we assume that it causes high incomes. But we forget that a vitally important way in which able people can make money is by setting up their own businesses.

46. *Paradoxes of Prosperity*, p207

47. Ken Mayhew and Ewart Keep, The economic and distributional implications of current policies on higher education", *Oxford Review of Economic Policy*, summer 2004, p310.

48. "Power-biased technological change and the rise in earnings inequality", *ECINEQ working paper 2005-06*, November 2005.

49. "The returns to education: evidence from the Labour Force Surveys", p14.

50. *Human Capital* (3rd edition), p9.

51. quoted in Jon Elster – *Explaining Technical Change*, p9

52. "Globalization and the knowledge economy", p11, Cardiff University *School of Social Sciences working paper 43*, November 2003.

53. "The economic and distributional implications of current policies on higher education", p301.

54. "The college wage premium, overeducation, and the expansion of higher education in the UK", *IZA discussion paper 1627*, June 2005.

55. "The changing wage return to an undergraduate education" *IZA discussion paper 1549*, March 2005. By "at the bottom quartile" they mean someone who earns less than 75% of graduates.

56. "Graduate over-education in the UK", *Centre for the Economics of Education discussion paper*, December 2000.

57. "Education for growth: why and for whom?", p1130.

7.

"The Best Thing That Any Government Can Do"

Getting the overall framework of fiscal and monetary policy right, and ending the series of booms and busts that have characterised the British economy, is probably the best thing that any government can do to encourage investment (Alastair Darling)[1].

Labour came to power in 1964 firmly believing that it could improve on the Conservatives' growth record. Ministers had a clear picture of the "stop-go" cycle, which they intended to replace by steady expansion (Frank Blackaby)[2].

"Stability, stability, stability" has been as much a mantra of Gordon Brown's as "education, education, education" was for Blair.

There are some low motives for this. In the mid-90s, New Labour was desperate to convince the City (well actually the media) that it was economically "prudent", and the rhetoric of stability is one way of establishing a reputation for prudence. And talk of "stability" gives the impression that one is in control of affairs – an impression that might be mistaken, for reasons we'll discuss in chapter.[13]

There are, however, some higher motives behind New Labour's desire for a more stable economy. Stability, it believes, is another way of achieving both greater equality and economic efficiency.

There's increasing evidence that boom-bust cycles can be especially bad for the worst-off. One study has found a close positive correlation across 80 countries between the standard deviation of GDP growth between 1960 and 1990 and the level in inequality in 1990.[3] Economic instability leads to inequality.

One reason for this is that poorer workers suffer most in recessions. In one study of the 1980 recession, the costs to unskilled manual workers were found to be 8 times greater than those of professional workers.[4]

Also, the poor don't have the assets with which to protect themselves from economic downturns. The poorest 10 per cent of the population have no savings at all[5]. And only the very wealthiest invest in assets, such as government bonds, which offer higher returns during recessions. As Tony Blair said: "A wealthy family can afford a recession. A family trying to plan ahead, with all the pressures of everyday life, can't afford violent swings of the economic cycle."[6]

Not only would macroeconomic stability increase equality, it would also be economically efficient, New Labour believes.

Tony Blair has said that macroeconomic policy failures can "swamp" successful microeconomic policies.[7] Nicholas Oulton has described how the UK's industrial relations reforms of the 1980s genuinely raised labour productivity, but that this benefit was masked by an inability of macroeconomic policy to ensure steady growth[8]. And Peter Robinson has shown how the collapse of the Swedish model of social democracy in the early 1990s was due largely to macroeconomic policy errors.[9]

What's more, there is now evidence that boom-bust cycles can depress long-run economic growth.

Two papers point to this. One is by Garey and Valerie Ramey.[10] They found that countries with the most stable growth between 1960 and 1985 tended to have faster growth as well. Controlling for some of the standard causes of economic growth, they estimated, a one percentage point difference in the standard deviation of growth (roughly the difference between West Germany and Spain) was associated with a 0.36 percentage point difference in average annual GDP growth.[11] Over 20 years, this compounds to 7.5 per cent – equivalent to around £1500 for every person in the UK.

The second paper is by Nicholas Oulton. He found that, for 13 countries between 1977 and 1994, two-thirds of the variation in trend growth rates could be explained solely by the skewness of economic growth and initial per capita GDP. "A cyclical pattern like the UK's – short, sharp booms followed by long, shallow recessions – is associated with a lower trend growth rate" he concluded.[12]

But what, exactly, is the mechanism whereby instability causes slower growth? Oulton says instability reduces investment. Ed Balls agrees: "There is nothing so damaging for the animal spirits of business investors than repeated cycles of boom then bust."[13]

There are three ways in which this can be true. Volatility can make planning decisions harder, and leave firms with either inadequate or excess capacity. Either way, profits are low, which depresses subsequent investment. Secondly, volatility increases the chances of recession, which can do more harm to profits than booms do good[14]. And thirdly, volatile output means volatile interest rates, which can slow down investment.

This last point needs expanding, because it shows how more recent thinking suggests that instability can badly affect capital spending.

Consider a firm contemplating an investment decision. Orthodox theory says it should invest whenever the net present value (NPV) of the project –

that is, future profits minus capital costs – is positive.

But orthodox theory can be wrong. Firms sometimes have a choice – to invest now or invest later. When this choice exists, it will be wrong for them to invest whenever the NPV is positive – simply because it may become more positive later.

Anyone familiar with financial markets will recognise this. If you are holding a call option, you do not exercise it the moment it is in the money – because it may become even more in the money later. And, says Robert Pindyck, "an irreversible investment opportunity is much like a call option".[15]

An important feature of a call option is that it is more valuable, the greater the volatility of the underlying asset price. This is because high volatility increases the chances of the option being more in the money later. Your incentive to hold onto a call option, rather than exercise it, is therefore greater, the greater the volatility.

Similarly, if NPV is volatile, a firm has an incentive to hang onto its investment options rather than exercise them. Any volatility that affects NPV will, therefore, delay investment. So, volatile output, prices or interest rates will cause firms to delay investing. At any point in time, then, capital spending will be lower, the more economic volatility there is.

This account is simplistic[16]. In the real world, firms may be able to sell capital equipment if an investment project looks like going wrong. So the deterrent against capital spending may be smaller. Or it may not be able to wait, because a patent may expire, or because a rival may nip into its market. Or it may be that the gains from waiting are offset by the loss of near-term cashflow. And in some cases investment can reduce uncertainty – for example, one way of finding whether oil is under a particular part of a sea-bed is to invest in a test drilling.

Despite all these qualifications, and despite the difficulties in identifying volatility at the level of the individual firm, there is some evidence that the "real options" theory of investment really can explain actual capital spending decisions. A study of US manufacturing firms found that high variance in a firm's share price (a proxy for many types of volatility) was associated with low investment[17]. And Italian research has found that demand uncertainty is associated with low investment intentions.[18]

Whatever the merits or significance of real options theory, though, we mustn't believe that it is only by depressing capital spending that instability depresses growth. Indeed, Ramey and Ramey found that it does so, even controlling for capital spending.

This can be because of factor immobility. In a volatile economy, relative demand will be rapidly shifting from one industry or region to another. However, workers and capital cannot move so quickly. The upshot will be production bottlenecks. Not only do these depress growth directly, but – by causing inflation – they can depress it indirectly, by prompting central banks to raise interest rates.

Or it might be because recessions cause people to lose on-the-job skills and hence cuts productivity. This was the foundation of hysteresis theories of unemployment in the 1980s, which claimed that the natural rate of unemployment had risen as a result of the early 1980s' recession, as spells of unemployment made workers less employable.

The case against macroeconomic stability

All this sounds like an overwhelming case for putting an end to the cycle of boom and bust. Brown's talk of stability is much more than mere posturing.

Or is it? The truth is, output stability might not, after all, lead to faster growth.

One suggestion that this may be the case comes from casual empiricism. From the mid-50s to the mid-1970s, the UK economy was, by international standards, remarkably stable. And yet our growth performance lagged far behind others[19]. Between the mid-1970s and the early 1990s, the UK economy became relatively unstable – at the same time as our relative growth performance improved. As with the link between education and growth, therefore, the time series evidence conflicts with the cross-country evidence. As Oulton said: "Much about the growth process remains mysterious and few empirical regularities are robust."[20]

Indeed, troublingly for New Labour is that there may be ways in which volatility can actually cause faster growth:

- *Uncertainty can raise investment.* If there are economies of scale (for example, if a 400-room hotel is cheaper than two 200-room hotels), uncertainty about demand can lead to larger investment. This is because uncertainty makes big peaks in demand more likely, so firms are more willing to build the capacity to anticipate such peaks. Or if firms can rapidly adjust their labour-capital ratios, they may invest in the confidence that they can adapt to future volatility by adjusting employment.

- *Opportunity cost theories.* In a boom, firms are often working so hard on meeting current orders that they don't get the chance to think about how to boost efficiency or future growth. In recessions, however, they can afford to spend time thinking about how to raise productivity or invest in research. "Recessions, when expected to be followed by a more expansionary phase, are times when firms tend to invest more into productivity growth, either by reorganising their production activities or by investing in technical progress...to the extent that recessions induce firms to invest a higher share of inputs into research activities, an increase in their frequency has a direct positive effect on growth" say Philippe Aghion and Gilles Saint-Paul.[21]

- *Liquidation cycles.* Depressions, said Joseph Schumpeter, "are the means to reconstruct each time the economic system on a more efficient plan. But they inflict losses whilst they last, drive firms into the bankuptcy court, throw people out of employment, before the ground is clear and the way paved for new achievement of the kind which has created modern civilization...they are forms of something which has to be done, namely adjustment to previous economic change".[22] Brad De Long has shown that this might be a good description of many economic cycles[23].

- *Removing lame ducks.* Recessions can be ways of cleansing the economy. In forcing inefficient firms to shut down, resources are released which more efficient firms can employ, in the long run, therefore, productivity may rise. This view gains plausibility from a curious fact – that the rate of job destruction seems much more cyclical than the rate of job creation.[24] This is odd because, in theory, a firm need only cover its marginal costs in order to remain in business, whereas a firm thinking of opening up must cover its average costs. That, despite this, job destruction should be so cyclical suggests inefficient firms are indeed penalised by recession.

- *Encouraging innovation.* If innovation carries a heavy fixed cost (such as the cost of maintaining a research and development department) and if a firm can only take advantage of an innovation for a short while – say, because competitors will enter the market – a boom may be necessary to ensure that any innovation happens at all. That's because it will only be in a boom – when demand is high – that a firm can hope to cover its costs of innovating. As a result says Andrei Schleifer, "an attempt to eliminate the cycle with aggregate demand management at best will be wasteful and at worst will steer the economy into the stone-age equilibrium where there is no innovation and therefore no growth".[25]

- *Learning asymmetries.* It is easier to learn something than to unlearn it – at least if one is trying. As a result, says Keith Blackburn, the additional learning during expansions more than compensates for the loss of learning during recessions, so that, on average, the rate of technological progress increases when there is an increase in volatility.[26]

If all this is right, it means the promise to end the cycle of boom and bust – even if it could be delivered – would be very costly, There is, says Blackburn, "an inevitable policy conflict between short-term stabilisation and long-term growth".[27]

But is it right? There is some evidence it may be. Gilles Saint-Paul cites several cases where temporary rises in demand lead to lower long-run growth by reducing firms' incentives to raise productivity.[28]

This is, as one can imagine, controversial. A strong challenge to it comes from a survey by Paul Gregg and Paul Geroski of how the recession of the early 1990s affected companies. They make three germane points: that recessions do not necessarily weed out the weakest firms; that they do not boost innovative activity; and that by far the most common response to recession was simply to cut costs, rather than reorganise. Recessions, they conclude, "are useful for social scientists interested in finding 'natural experiments' which help them analyse what happens to firms in crisis, but they are probably not good for much else".[29]

This is not, however, conclusive. For one thing, it is anticipations of a boom that encourage innovation, not the fact of a slump. And for another, the distinction between cutting employment (an action undertaken by 82% of firms severely affected by recession) and re-organising production is one that is almost impossible to make. Firms often justify job cuts as part of re-organisation plans, and occasionally are right to do so. If so, job cuts may indeed help contribute to stronger post-recession growth.

It is, therefore, an open question whether macroeconomic stability is a good or bad thing for long-run growth.

But we should be about to find out. In recent years, the UK economy has been remarkably stable. In the nine years in which Brown has been chancellor (at the time of writing) the standard deviation of quarterly GDP growth has been just 0.27 percentage points. That's a record low. It's half the volatility we saw in the nine years to 1997, for example.

If New Labour is right, this should lead to faster growth. Now, the time lags are such that you wouldn't expect to see growth having been faster in recent years. But this stability should be associated with higher growth expectations.

But it isn't. At the time of writing (January 2007), the price-earnings ratio on UK shares is quite low. This suggests equity investors aren't looking forward to faster growth.

Of course, the stock market might be irrational. But there's another organization which doesn't believe that the UK's macroeconomic stability will lead to faster growth – the Treasury itself.

It estimates that the UK's trend growth rate in GDP per hour worked in 1986-97 was 2.22% a year. The stability of GDP growth has doubled since then. So, the Treasury's estimate for future trend growth should have risen, shouldn't it?

It hasn't. The Treasury estimates that trend productivity growth will be 2.25% a year[30]. Sure, it thinks total GDP growth will be higher – but only because the labour force will grow more quickly, and no-one attributes this to stability.

So, by New Labour's own reckoning, stability won't lead to faster growth.

Two stabilities

There's another question. What exactly does stability mean?

There are two different meanings. So far, we've considered only one – low volatility. But Gordon Brown often means something else. To him, stability means stable rules for economic policy. The rule for monetary policy is that interest rates should be set to keep inflation at 2%. And the rule for fiscal policy is that the debt-GDP ratio be kept stable, and that "over the cycle" the government borrows only to finance "investment."

The thing is, these two conceptions can conflict. Imagine there is an economic slowdown caused by a slower rate of technical progress[31]. The Bank of England cannot cut interest rates, because inflation expectations might rise. And nor can the government greatly increase borrowing, because this is ruled out by its golden rule. In this case, stable policy rules might increase the instability of output growth.

Which raises the question. Why haven't we seen this trade-off? Why has the adoption of policy rules, and the move away from discretionary ad hoc interventions, led to greater output stability.

It might be just luck. Greater macroeconomic stability is not merely a UK phenomenon. We've seen it around the developed western world. And James Stock and Mark Watson estimate that around half of the increased stability in the US has been due to simply to smaller shocks – better luck.[32]

Another possibility is that before 1997, discretionary policy interventions – changes in interest rates and government policy – actually increased economic volatility, as governments, possibly through simple error, loosened policy in booms and tightened it in slowdowns.

But there's a third explanation.[33] It starts from the premise that inflation targeting – especially after the Bank of England was given independence in 1997 – has led to inflation becoming less persistent. In the 1970s and 80s, people feared that higher inflation would feed on itself. To protect themselves from this, workers demanded, and got, higher pay rises, and firms raised prices. So, inflation fed on itself. Today, though, people see inflation more as a temporary blip. So they don't raise wages and prices in response. So their belief that inflation is only temporary proves self-fulfilling. Inflation, then, doesn't feed on itself.

This in turn means it doesn't require big rises in interest rates to cut inflation. Small ones will do. And if interest rates don't have to move so much, output will be more stable.

Here, though, lies a quirk. Let's say these second and third explanations are correct. They imply that the government has achieved stability – in the sense of low volatility – by intervening less, by following rules and delegating interest rate-setting to the Bank of England.

If you think low volatility is desirable, this contains an important lesson. Sometimes, governments can achieve their objectives by doing less. This, surely, is an argument against managerialism. And if this is true of the macroeconomy, are there not other areas of policy where it might also be true?

The red herring of macroeconomic stability

But is stability desirable? As we've seen, it doesn't necessarily increase economic growth.

And it might not be so good for equality either.

This is not because macroeconomic stability would increase inequality – there is no evidence for that. Instead, it is because talk of stability avoids a vitally important fact – that, even in good macroeconomic times, huge numbers of people lose their jobs.

Researchers at the Centre for Economic Performance have estimated that during the economic upswing of 1992-96 – a time of stable growth – an average of 6.1% of employees lost their jobs every year.[34]

In manufacturing, job insecurity may be even greater. Matthew Barnes and Jonathan Haskel have estimated that between 1980 and 1991 an average of one in seven jobs were destroyed every year[35]. This was partly offset by the creation of one in ten of all jobs every year. They estimate that job creation and destruction rates in the UK are comparable to those of Colombia or Chile – economies which are typically regarded as highly unstable.

Not only is there a good chance you'll lose your job in a boom, there's also a good chance you might keep it in recession.

This is because job losses tend to be highly concentrated. Geroski and Gregg found that only 18% of firms in 1993 claimed to be "extremely severely" affected by the recession of the early 1990s[36] And table 16 shows that 20% of firms accounted for 94% of all job losses between 1989 and 1991, whilst almost half of firms actually raised employment.

Table 16. Employment in 1989-1990/91

	Change in employment (000s)
Bottom decile	-725
2nd	-77
3rd	-31
4th	-12
5th	-3
6th	1
7th	7
8th	20
9th	60
Top decile	400
Total net change	-361
Total change of declining firms	-849

Source: Geroski and Gregg – Coping with Recession, table 3.1

The early 1990s recession was not unusual in this regard. David Blanchflower and Simon Burgess have estimated that, taking the average of the three years 1980, 1984 and 1990, some 4% of all firms accounted for half of all the jobs destroyed.[37] And even between 1980 and 1984 – a bad time for industry in general – a quarter of manufacturing plants saw employment rise by 20% or more.[38]

One reason for this is that so much that happens in an economy is, in fact, the result of events which are idiosyncratic to firms. Geroski and Gregg say: "Describing what happens during recessions using simple macroeconomic aggregates and representative firm models of the economy produces a seriously distorted picture of events. Recessions are about what happens to differences between firms much more than they are about what happens to firms on average."[39]

Job insecurity, then, has little to do with macroeconomic instability, as it exists in booms as well as slumps. We have a good chance of losing our jobs even in booms, and a good chance of keeping them even in recessions. Booms and slumps alter the odds a little. But even in the best of times, many of those in work are living lives of fear and insecurity. Talk of macroeconomic stability carries an implicit, and utterly false, promise that this might change.

But the truth is that macroeconomic stability means diddly squat for any particular person. You can have a stable macroeconomy without economic security for any individual.[40]

How then, can we increase economic security for individuals? The answer needn't lie in macroeconomic policy at all.

Instead, we should find better ways of insuring ourselves against the risks of job loss or falling demand which are an inherent feature of a market economy. This will require abandoning the managerialist pretence that a central agency can smooth the economic cycle, and develop insurance markets that allow people to trade risks, as Robert Shiller shows in his superb book, *The New Financial Order*.

As Robert E. Lucas Jr put it: "policies that deal with the very real problems of society's less fortunate – wealth redistribution and social insurance – can be designed in total ignorance of the nature of business cycle dynamics...and the discovery of better business cycle theories will contribute little or nothing to improved design."[41]

Notes

1. "A Political Perspective" in Kelly, Kelly and Gamble (eds) – *Stakeholder Capitalism*, p14.

2. In Blackaby (ed) – *British Economic Policy 1960-74: Demand Management*, p29.

3. Richard Breen and Cecilia Garcia-Penalosa "Income Inequality and Macroeconomic Volatility: An Empirical Investigation", July 1999, www.nuf.ox.ac.uk.

4. Clark, Leslie and Symons – "The costs of recession", *Economic Journal*, 104, Jan 1994, p20-36, p32.

5. James Banks and Sarah Tanner, *Household Saving in the UK*, Institute for Fiscal Studies, 1999, p53-57.

6. Sedgefield adoption speech, May 13 2001, www.labour.org.uk.

7. *New Britain: My Vision of a Young Country*, p85.

8. "Supply-side reform and UK economic growth: what happened to the miracle?", *National Institute Economic Review*, 154, November 1995, p53-70.

9. "The Decline of the Swedish Model and the Limits to Active Labour Market Policy", *Centre for Economic Policy discussion paper no.259*, August 1995.

10. "Cross-country evidence on the link between volatility and growth", *American Economic Review*, 85, December 1995, p1138-51.

11. "Cross-country evidence on the link between volatility and growth" p1142.

12. "Supply-side reform and UK economic growth: what happened to the miracle?" p65.

13. "Open macroeconomics in an open economy", *Centre for Economic Performance Occasional Paper no. 13*, p14.

14. Ricardo Caballero – "On the sign of the investment-uncertainty relationship", *American Economic Review*, 81, March 1991, p279-88.

15. "Irreversibility, uncertainty and investment", *Journal of Economic Literature*, 29, 1991, p1110-48.

16. A full account is Dixt and Pindyck's *Investment Under Uncertainty*.

17. John Leahy and Toni Whited, "The effect of uncertainty on investment: some stylised facts", *Journal of Money, Credit and Banking*, 28, January 1996, p64-83.

18. Luigi Guiso and Guiseppe Parigi, "Investment and Demand Uncertainty", *Centre for Economic Policy Research discussion paper 1497*, November 1996.

19. See for example, G.D.N. Worswick – "The End of Demand Management?", *Lloyds Bank Review*, January 1977 p1-29 and A. Whiting – "An International Comparison of the Instability of Economic Growth", *Three Banks Review*, 109, March 1976, p26-47.

20. "Supply-side reform and UK economic growth: what happened to the miracle?" p67.

21. Philippe Aghion and Gilles Saint-Paul – *On the Virtue of Bad Times*, Centre for Economic Policy Research discussion paper 578, 1991.

22. "Depressions" in Richard V. Clemence (ed) – *Essays of Joseph Schumpeter*, p113, 115.

23. "Liquidation Cycles", *National Bureau of Economic Research working paper 3546*, December 1990.

24. Olivier Jean Blanchard and Peter Diamond — "The cyclical behaviour of the gross flows of US workers", *Brookings Papers on Economic Activity 2,* 1990, p85-143, p102.

25. "Implementation Cycles", *Journal of Political Economy,* 94, December 1996, p1163-90, p1166.

26. Keith Blackburn – "Can stabilisation policy reduce long-run growth", *Economic Journal,* 109, January 1999, p67-77, p75.

27. "Can stabilisation policy reduce long-run growth", p75.

28. "Business cycles and long-run growth", *Oxford Review of Economic Policy,* vol.13, autumn 1997, p145-53.

29. *Coping with Recession,* p153.

30. Pre-Budget Report 2006, table A2.

31. There's some evidence that such supply shocks can be important. See Alison Holland and Andrew Scott, "The determinants of UK business cycles", *Bank of England working paper no.58,* January 1997.

32. "Has the business cycle changed and why?" *NBER working paper 9127,* September 2002.

33. William Martin and Robert Rowthorn, "Will stability last?", *CESIFO working paper 1324,* November 2004.

34. Gregg, Knight and Wadsworth – "Down and out in Beverley, Yorks", *Employment Audit,* autumn 1998, p19.

35. "Job creation, job destruction and small firms: evidence for the UK", paper presented to Royal Economic Society annual conference, April 2001.

36. *Coping with Recession,* p32.

37. "Job Creation and Job Destruction in Great Britain in the 1980s", *Centre for Economic Performance discussion paper no.287,* April 1996, p12.

38. "Job Creation and Job Destruction in Great Britain in the 1980s", p9.

39. *Coping with Recession,* p70.

40. What matter here are the correlations between individuals' incomes. If these are negative – so good times for one person are bad for another – the aggregate economy might be stable, even though all individuals are living in enormous insecurity.

41. *Models of Business Cycles,* p105.

8.

A Free Lunch

Central bank independence offers a free lunch (Alex Cukierman)[1]

There's something odd, almost unique, about New Labour's decision immediately upon taking office in May 1997 to grant the Bank of England freedom to set interest rates. Whereas most of its other policies have been attempts to increase governmental influence upon the economy, this is a rare instance of it relinquishing control.

So why did it do so? Because the facts suggested it should. Our two charts show that although there is a clear negative relationship between the degree of central bank independence and a country's average inflation level, the link between independence and economic growth is much weaker.[2]

Fig. 7

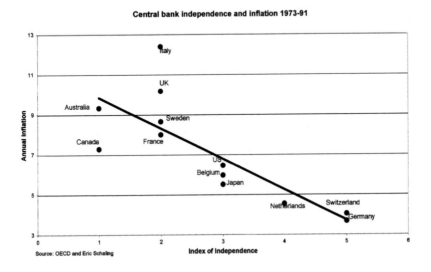

Central bank independence and inflation 1973-91

Fig. 8

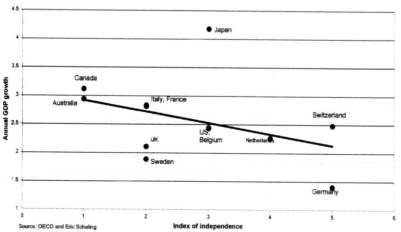

Central bank independence and GDP growth 1973-91

Source: OECD and Eric Schaling

This is not merely a modern phenomenon. Geoffrey Wood and colleagues have shown that the same was true before 1914[3]. What's more, they say, in four cases when a central bank changed status (the UK and Germany in 1946, New Zealand in 1935 and Canada in 1959), independence was associated was lower inflation, and subordination to government with higher inflation, in all instances.[4]

It's here that the free lunch described by Alex Cukierman can be found. Giving central banks independence can reduce inflation without affecting output.

This, like the other New Labour policies we have considered, is both just and efficient. It is efficient in the sense that lower inflation improves economic welfare. And it is just because the poor suffer more from inflation than the rich. This is not because inflation means faster price rises for the goods and services on which the poor spend most, but because the poor lack the assets with which to protect themselves from the uncertainties which often accompany inflation; holdings of index-linked gilts are concentrated among the wealthy.

But why does central bank independence reduce inflation but not growth?

There's one argument that won't wash. This is that the Bank of England's monetary policy committee has more knowledge and skill than the Chancellor, and so can conduct policy better. As the Chancellor said in October 1999:

Independent experts, skilled in judging often complex economic and financial information, and unencumbered by short-term political pressures, are best able to make forward-looking decisions in the long-term interests of the UK economy[5].

This view has not been confined to the Chancellor. Stephen Nickell, a former member of the MPC, has written that the case for an independent Bank:

Is not so much to take the politics out of interest rate setting, but to put the economics in. To have a group of knowledgeable individuals whose main job is to set rates enables the matter to be given the time and concentration it needs. Chancellors tend to be very busy people.[6]

This argument just won't do. First, we don't – in theory – need independent central banks for experts to conduct monetary policy. In principle, Chancellors before 1997 could have set interest rates according to the advice of experts, without heeding political considerations.

Secondly, as I'll show in chapters 13 and 14, even experts needn't make the correct decisions.

And thirdly, if the motive for granting independence to the Bank of England was merely to increase expert involvement, the government should have delegated other decisions to independent experts. Doctors know more about healthcare than government, teachers know more about education, and probation officers know more about crime. But the government hasn't devolved health policy to doctors, or education policy to teachers, or crime policy to probation officers.

What, then, is so special about monetary policy that justifies leaving it to the experts?

The "time inconsistency" problem

The answer has nothing to do with the monetary policy committee's greater knowledge or wisdom. It's because granting central banks independence to set interest rates changes the incentives policy makers have. And this – it is thought – is a good thing.

A conventional account runs something like this.[7]

Governments want to boost economic growth and create jobs, especially just before elections. One way of doing this is to keep interest rates low, which leads to higher inflation. Fearing this, the private sector will anticipate high inflation. And these anticipations will cause actual inflation, as companies raise prices in the belief that all their rivals will do so. The upshot, in the long run, will be high inflation but no extra growth.

A popular solution to this problem in the 1970s was the monetarist one, to ensure that the money stock grew at a constant rate. If there was a stable long-run relationship between inflation and the money supply, this could ensure that inflation could be held to zero, if only there was the political desire to do so. And if the private sector knew this, it would anticipate zero inflation. This would cause inflation to fall. Indeed, said monetarists, inflation would fall without any loss of output, as long as the government's commitment to zero inflation was credible.

Herein, however, lay a problem. To achieve this credibility, governments would have to stick to the money supply rule, come boom or bust. It would therefore be impossible to stabilise output.

This means there is a trade-off between credibility and flexibility. A credible policy gives us zero inflation on average, but is too inflexible to respond to booms and slumps. A flexible policy, on the other hand, stabilises output but will raise inflation, as people anticipate governments wanting to boost economic growth by keeping interest rates low.

This creates what economists call a "time inconsistency" problem. Initially, governments may try to keep inflation low by controlling the money supply. But such control might later cause a deep recession, which governments want to avoid. There will therefore be an inconsistency between what the government initially wants to do, and what it later wants.

Central bank independence is an attempt to solve this problem. Let's say we can appoint a "conservative" central banker – one whose aversion to inflation is greater than society's in general.[8] Because the private sector would know that the central banker hated inflation, its inflation expectations would fall. But because the central banker was not tied to any fixed monetary rule, he would have room to act to stabilise output fluctuations.

By appointing an independent central banker – whose conservatism can be forced upon him by the obloquy that would follow if he failed to hit the inflation target – we can therefore achieve low inflation and greater output stability than the monetarist rule offers. That's a free lunch. The expertise of the central banker, in this story, is secondary. What matters is his credible desire to hold inflation down.

Sadly, however, this theoretical case for central bank independence bears little relationship to reality.

One difficulty was pointed out by Alan Blinder.[9] The inflationary bias caused by discretionary policy has one origin – in the government's desire to raise employment above the level consistent with stable inflation. But, he says, governments rarely want to do this because voters hate inflation just as they hate unemployment[10]. When inflation rises, it is normally either because the government has over-estimated the stable-inflation level of employment (as Nigella's dad did in 1987-88) or because a shock such as rising oil prices has reduced it, rather than because the government has deliberately tried to raise employment above its natural rate.

Another problem is that this theory predicts that output will be more volatile under independent central banks than under pure discretionary policy. But it isn't. "Most empirical studies have failed to find any significant link between independence and the...variability of output growth" say some Bank of England economists.[11] The fact that output volatility has fallen since 1997 adds to this puzzle.

Why is this? Alberto Alesina and Roberta Gatti say it could be because independent central banks reduce the political business cycle, as policy-makers can no longer run a loose monetary policy in the run-up to elections.[12]

But this won't do. As Charles Goodhart has said, "there is relatively little evidence for any systematic political business cycle".[13] The Lawson boom of 1987-88 came immediately after a general election and the subsequent bust came immediately before one. The UK economy might have been more stable, if only we had had a political business cycle.

A more likely reason why output is no more variable under an independent central bank than under a dependent one is simply that no-one really knows how to stabilise output, because shocks to the economy are frequent and because economic forecasts are subject to such a wide margin of error. This provides a ready justification for central bank independence – because in making the Bank of England independent, we are not really losing any power to stabilise output growth.

Unfortunately, if we accept this argument, we cannot at the same time promise to put an end to the boom-bust cycle.

Credibility and its critics

The most common theory in the economic literature for why independent central banks deliver low inflation is, therefore, irrelevant to the real world.

Worse still, so too is the second most common theory. This is the notion that independent central banks have more anti-inflationary "credibility"[14]. As a result, when they announce an intention to reduce inflation, wage and price-setters take them seriously, and reduce the rate at which they raise wages and prices. Thanks to this, inflation can fall without the central bank having to cause a recession. The "sacrifice ratio" – the rise in unemployment necessary to achieve a given fall in inflation – should therefore be smaller when central banks are independent.

But it is not. Adam Posen looked at 56 episodes of disinflation between 1950 and 1989 and found that central bank independence increases the costs of disinflation. There is, he says, "no evidence to support the hypothesis that the mechanism by which central bank independence leads to low inflation is the enhancement of credibility of commitments to price stability".[15]

His is not a lone voice. Stanley Fischer says: "The more independent central banks, on average, pay a *higher* output price per percentage point of inflation to reduce the inflation rate."[16] For example, he says, the German disinflations of 1965, 1973 and 1980 saw bigger output falls, relative to the reduction in inflation, than the Italian disinflations of 1977 and 1980. There is, he concluded, "no credibility bonus in the labour markets for more independent central banks".[17]

Exactly why this should be so is unclear. Perhaps, because independent central banks have low inflation anyway, prices and wages are changed less often, so it takes longer for a policy change to affect inflation[18]. Or perhaps inflation expectations depend more upon the past history of inflation than upon policy changes, so credibility simply does not affect price-setting behaviour.[19]

Whatever the reason, the fact that independent central banks have higher sacrifice ratios than dependent ones creates some severe problems for supporters of central bank independence.

The first is that the free lunch disappears. Granted, the unemployment caused by the central bank's efforts to reduce inflation is only temporary. And granted, low inflation, in the long run, is a good thing. Nevertheless, in raising unemployment in order to reduce inflation, a central bank is imposing losses – temporary unemployment – on some in order to give benefits to others. As we shall see in chapter 11, it is unclear what ethical justification this has.

The second problem is that, with the likeliest explanations flawed, it is difficult to see why exactly independent central banks should deliver low inflation. Maybe they don't. Gabriel Mangano has shown that measures of central bank independence – of which there are at least 10 – can be very subjective. As a result, he estimates, the correlations between measures of independence and inflation might be much weaker than generally thought.[20]

And even if the correlation exists, it does not mean central bank independence causes low inflation. Correlation is not causality. There are three alternative explanations for the correlation:

- *Public support.* The popular desire for low inflation, says Bernd Hayo, is a "significant precondition" of sustained low inflation.[21] Without popular support for price stability, even an independent central bank may not deliver low inflation. The correlation between low inflation and central bank independence may therefore result from people wanting low inflation, and establishing an independent central bank, as a way of binding themselves to that objective.

- *Wage bargaining systems.* Where wage bargaining is highly centralised – as in Germany or Sweden – it is easier to control inflation, as the risk of "leap-frogging" pay settlements is lower. Fisher believes it is this, and not just the Bundesbank's independence, that explains Germany's traditionally low inflation.[22]

- *The financial sector's opposition to inflation.* Banks are more opposed to inflation than stockbrokers – because inflation erodes the real value of loans by more than it erodes the real value of equities. Where banks are influential and the equity market not – such as in Germany and Switzerland – opposition to inflation will therefore be strong. Adam Posen has estimated that it is the strength of the financial system's opposition to inflation, rather than central bank independence, that explains low inflation. "An independent Bank of England cannot bring about noticeably lower inflation so long as the British financial system is securities-based" he says.[23]

If central bank independence does not cause low inflation, why have it? Well, there are some other reasons:

- *Credibility* with financial markets, if not with wage and price-setters. Independence is a way of assuring international financial markets that the government is serious about wanting low inflation. That should encourage overseas investment in UK financial assets. This seems to have worked. The yield spreads between gilts and overseas government bonds have generally been smaller since the Bank was made independent than before. This fall in the cost of capital might have raised capital spending.

- *Creating a scapegoat.* "The Fed enjoys a large amount of independence because it performs a scapegoat function for incumbent politicians. When things turn out right in the monetary area, they can take some of the credit. When things turn sour, they can dissociate themselves from the outcome and blame it on the Fed" says Alex Cukierman.[24]

- *Signalling a break from the "predict and control" mentality.* Attempts to improve the UK's economic performance by using macroeconomic policy have failed. In throwing away a key instrument of macroeconomic policy, the government is signalling a desire to get away from such efforts.

Two costs and a puzzle

There are, however, a couple of costs to Bank independence.

One is the possibility that the co-ordination between monetary and fiscal policy may break down.[25]

Governments sometimes have an incentive to keep taxes down and public spending up. This can sometimes be inflationary. Fearing this, independent central banks will keep interest rates high. So fiscal policy might sometimes be looser than it should be, and monetary policy tighter.

The most famous example of this happening was in the US in the early 1980s, when a Federal Reserve committed to tight money coincided with an administration determined to cut taxes. That caused a huge over-valuation of the US dollar, to the detriment of US manufacturing industry and the stability of global financial markets.

A second, perhaps more important, cost of central bank independence is that, in Rogoff's words, "inflation targeting works poorly when supply shocks are significant".[26] To see the problem, imagine the UK had had an independent Bank of England pursuing an inflation target in 1973-74, when oil prices quadrupled. Had the Bank stuck to its target in the face of this inflationary shock, interest rates would have soared and the subsequent recession would have been more severe than it actually was. Low inflation would only have been achieved at the price of a huge loss of output.

This illustrates an important fact – that after an adverse supply shock, there is a trade-off between supporting output and controlling inflation.

Now, in the case of a huge shock, such as the oil price rise, the solution is simple – to suspend the inflation target.[27] Large and easily identifiable shocks are however the exception, not the rule. More often, the economy is hit by countless tiny supply and demand shocks at the same time, and policy-makers simply cannot tell which dominate.[28] What we do know, however, is that supply shocks are, at least, quite possible. There is, therefore, a risk that central bank independence, at least when accompanied by an inflation target, might sometimes cause output to be more volatile than need be.

You may think this cost is small. After all, haven't we shown in chapter 7 that the impact of output volatility on long-run growth might be tiny. Maybe – but the fact re-emerges, that central bank independence is, in theory, inconsistent with the promise to end the cycle of boom and bust.

And herein lies the great puzzle of Bank of England independence. It's worked far better than it should. It seems to have led not only to more stable output than anyone expected, but also to more stable inflation too. In 1998

Charles Bean – now the Bank's chief economist – estimated that inflation would deviate by more than one percentage point away from its target rate on almost 40 per cent of occasions.[29] But in the first nine years of Bank independence, it has never yet strayed this far from the target.

What's even more amazing is that this is not obviously because the Bank has set interest rates with more skill since 1997.

Fig. 9

A UK Taylor rule

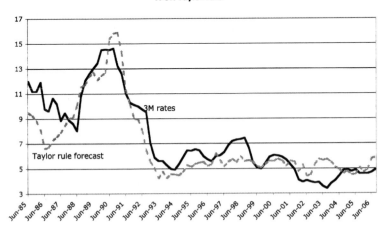

A handy way of predicting official interest rates is to use a Taylor rule. This says interest rates should depend simply upon inflation and the output gap, the deviation of output from its potential level.[30] Our chart shows how a very simple form of the rule has tracked actual base rates. It shows that actual rates were above the Taylor rule forecast in 1997-98 and below it in 2001-03, as the Bank cut rates as insurance against a severe downturn in the global economy after the attack on the World Trade Center in 2001.

It's far from obvious that this path of rates is much different from what a non-independent Bank might have done. Which just deepens the puzzle – of why Bank independence has worked so well.

But should we look this gift horse too closely in the mouth? Mightn't there be a big lesson here – that sometimes, the benefits to the government of relinquishing control can be much greater than anyone can foresee?

Notes

1. "Central bank independence and monetary control", *Economic Journal*, 104, November 1994, p1437-48, p1437.

2. The charts are based upon the Eijffinger-Schaling index of independence. There are many other indices, some of which show similar relationships. See Schaling, *Institutions and Monetary Policy* p84-87 and p123-27.

3. Wood, Mills and Capie – *Central Bank Independence: What Is It and What Will It Do For Us?* p20.

4. *Central Bank Independence: What Is It and What Will It Do For Us?* p21. One notable exception to this is that the German Reichsbank was made independent in May 1922, just before one of the worst hyper-inflations in history.

5. *The New Monetary Policy Framework,* October 1999, www.hm-treasury.gov.uk, p2.

6. "The assessment: the economic record of the Labour government since 1997", p110, *Oxford Review of Economic Policy*, 18, summer 2002, p107-120.

7. For a more mathematically formal account of the following argument, see Briault, Haldane and King, "Independence and Accountability", *Bank of England working paper 49,* April 1996, p12-16.

8. This idea comes from Kenneth Rogoff, "The optimal degree of commitment to an intermediate monetary target", *Quarterly Journal of Economics,* 100, November 1985, p1169-89.

9. *Central Banking in Theory and Practice,* p42

10. There are reasons why a government might want inflation to rise – because it brings in more tax revenue, or because it reduces the real value of government debt. But these have not applied in the UK for many years, if at all.

11. *Independence and Accountability,* p21.

12. "Independent central bankers: low inflation at no cost?", *American Economic Review Papers and Proceedings,* 85, 1995, p196-200.

13. "Game theory for central bankers", *Journal of Economic Literature,* 32, March 1994, p101-114, p111.

14. The distinction between the problems of time inconsistency and credibility is often blurred. However, as James Forder points out, the two are separate – because the problem of time inconsistency arises even when policy-makers have identical objectives as society, whereas the credibility problem

arises because agents suspect policy-makers may deceive them. See "Central bank independence: conceptual clarifications and interim assessment", *Oxford Economic Papers*, 50, July 1998, p307-334, p308.

15. Adam Posen, "Central bank independence and disinflationary credibility: a missing link?", *Oxford Economic Papers*, 50, July 1998, p335-359, p343.

16. "Modern central banking" in Capie et al, *The Future of Central Banking*, p262-308, p299, emphasis in original.

17. "Modern central banking", p300.

18. "Modern central banking", p269.

19. Brunila and Lahdenpera, "Inflation targets: principal issues and practical implementation" p124, in Haldane (ed), *Inflation Targeting*.

20. Gabriel Mangano, "Measuring central bank independence: a tale of subjectivity and its consequences", *Oxford Economic Papers*, 50, July 1998, p468-92

21. "Is central bank independence all we need to know about low inflation rates?", *University of Bamberg*, mimeo, p2.

22. "Modern central banking", p296.

23. "Why central bank independence does not cause low inflation" in Richard O'Brien (ed), *Finance and the International Economy*, 7, p4-65, p54.

24. Alex Cukierman, Central Bank Strategy, *Credibility and Independence: The Evidence*, p213.

25. The following draws heavily upon Christopher Doyle and Martin Weale, "Do we really want an independent central bank?", *Oxford Review of Economic Policy*, 10, Autumn 1994 p61-77, p71-73.

26 "The optimal degree of commitment to an intermediate monetary target", *Quarterly Journal of Economics*, 100, November 1985, p1169-89, p1186.

27. Suzanne Lohmann ("Optimal commitment in monetary policy: credibility versus flexibility", *American Economic Review*, 82, March 1992, p273-86) describes how this can be done as part of an optimal policy framework.

28. Indeed, the very word "shock" is misleading. It suggests disturbances to the economy are somehow exceptional, when in fact they are normal, frequent events.

29. "The new UK monetary arrangements: a view from the literature", *Economic Journal* 108, November 1998, p1795-1809, p1805.

30. The precise rule I use is R = (1.5 x RPIX) + (0.5 x output gap) +1.6. This implies that rates should be 5.4% per cent if output is at its trend level and RPIX inflation is 2.5%.

9.

What's Wrong with New Labour?

A reader of chapters 4 to 8 can be forgiven for thinking I have missed the point. Surely, you might think, New Labour's economic policies have been obviously good. Since it took office in 1997, unemployment has fallen, inflation has been low and stable, and output has grown steadily. The Chancellor has achieved a valuable goal that eluded his predecessors for decades – to make the economy sufficiently stable that businesses needn't waste much time worrying about the macroeconomic environment.

What's more, thanks to a combination of the Chancellor's prudence in his early years in office and decent growth, New Labour has been able to increase greatly spending on health and education. It's unclear that this has had an immediate impact in improving those services, but it might do so eventually.

New Labour's economic policies, therefore, have been a success.

Sadly, things are not so simple. There are big problems in judging New Labour's economic policies.

Problem one is to establish the proper counterfactual. It's possible that much of New Labour's success is due to luck and a benign global environment. Inflation might have been low because inflation around the world has been low. Technical progress in computing and telecommunications has increased the potential non-inflationary growth rate of the global economy – as evidenced in the US's remarkable productivity acceleration since the mid-1990s. Also, UK growth and employment has been helped by decent growth in overseas economies; the remarkable fact about the bursting of the US's "dot com bubble" was that it led to only the mildest recession in the country's history, from which it has since recovered strongly.

It would surely be wrong to give New Labour credit for what might have been due to just luck – just as it would be wrong to blame them if the global economy had been less healthy, or if technical progress had slowed down rather than accelerated, or if there hadn't been a consumer boom.

We don't know, therefore, how much of the UK's recent economic performance is due to New Labour's stewardship, and how much to factors beyond its control. The true test of New Labour's policies is not what happened whilst it was in office? Instead, it is: how did New Labour affect the economy in ways that alternative governments would not have done?

But we can't tell. We simply cannot run several different versions of post-1997 history, to see how New Labour would have fared in different economic climates, or how alternative governments would have done.

Faced with this problem, commentators commonly fall into two traps. One is to judge New Labour by the lowest possible standards. "We've done much better than the Tories did" proclaim their supporters.

I can only hope readers judge this book the same way: "It's fantastic – far better than an imbecile could have written."

The alternative is to judge them by impossibly high standards. To do this commits the managerialist fallacy I discussed in chapter one – it assumes that governments have unbounded knowledge and wisdom to manage society for the better.

From these perspectives, New Labour is either a brilliant success or a glaring failure. These views might dominate political "debate". But they are vacuous. They merely demonstrate the truth of Thomas Sowell's dictum: "Every policy is a success by sufficiently low standards, and a failure by sufficiently high standards."[1]

The second problem is that many of New Labour's policies could have long-run effects which are not yet known. New Labour supporters might, quite reasonably, argue for the following:

- Policies of "making work pay" will have beneficial effects upon labour supply in coming decades. In reducing the numbers of workless households, such policies might reduce the numbers of children who think it normal for adults to be out of work. This in turn might increase their willingness to look for work when they become adults.

- The improvements in primary school quality – as gauged by improvements in key stage two tests (for 11 year olds) – might enable a cohort of youngsters to acquire more education and skills in future years than they would otherwise have done. This will increase labour force quality and hence output in years to come.

- Macroeconomic stability will gradually encourage companies to increase investment; you wouldn't expect this to have happened yet, as it takes time to convince firms that the stability is here to stay. Because investment embodies new technology, it creates opportunities for further growth, as people learn how to use and further improve upon the technology.

- The apparent recent fall in returns to a degree might merely be the temporary result of increased mismatches between jobs and skills, perhaps caused by the increasing heterogeneity of skilled work. Perhaps in the long run these individual mismatches will be reduced, so the returns to a degree will rise.

With as much justification, New Labour's critics can argue instead that:

- The National Minimum Wage could weaken incentives for young workers to acquire the training and education that would equip them for better jobs. To people with low expectations and short time horizons, a wage of £150 a week can seem a handsome sum, especially if the egocentric attribution bias (the belief we are better than we really are) causes them to exaggerate their prospects of promotion. This problem could be magnified by the decision to extend the NMW to under-18s in 2004.

- Increasing regulation – and the statist culture it represents – might discourage people from setting up small businesses. This matters, because these are often important sources of economic growth.

- The high marginal tax rates we saw in chapter 4 could reduce incentives to work harder in the very long run. Assar Lindbeck has pointed out that our attitudes to work are determined not only by brute economic incentives, but also by social norms, which are slow to change.[2] An economy may benefit from a culture of hard work and entrepreneurship for years after economic incentives have undermined that culture. Likewise, it may suffer from a culture of indolence long after economic incentives have been put in place to change that culture.

These problems of establishing the right counterfactual by which to judge New Labour and of assessing its – potentially crucial – long-run effects are compounded by two others.

One is that it's unclear what economic efficiency actually is. Politicians often equate efficiency with economic growth. But as I'll show in chapters 10 and 11, there are strong reasons why this isn't a good idea, and there are instead five other conceptions of efficiency. Reasonable people can therefore differ about the proper standard for judging New Labour's policies.

Also, all our judgments under uncertainty are subject to numerous errors and biases. I'll return to these in chapter 13. Suffice to say here that these can infect our assessment of New Labour's policies.

It seems, therefore, that there is not much that can be said intelligently and decisively about New Labour's performance in office; the decisive points are not intelligent, and the intelligent points are not decisive.

Certainly, this is the impression one might have got during the 2001 and 2005 election campaigns. It is, however, not quite true.

New Labour and Equality

There is one thing we can say with some confidence – income inequality has not declined under New Labour. Table 17 shows that the income distribution now is almost identical to what it was in 1987, the peak of the yuppie, "greed is good" culture.

What's more, taxes and benefits don't equalize incomes, across the whole spectrum, any more than they did in 1987. The gap between the Gini coefficient for original incomes and post-tax incomes is the same – 15 percentage points.

Table 17. Trends in income equality

Gini coefficient (%)	Original income	Gross income	Disposable income	Post-tax income
1979	44	30	27	29
1985	49	32	29	32
1987	51	36	33	36
1990	52	38	36	40
1996-97	53	37	34	38
2004-05	51	36	32	36

Source: National Statistics, "The effects of taxes and benefits on household income", April 2006. The Gini coefficient is a measure of inequality which equals 100% if only one person gets all the nation's income and 0% if everyone gets the same. Original income is income before state benefits. Gross income adds benefits to this. Disposable income takes away direct taxes. Post-tax income takes away indirect taxes.

This suggests Blair has not delivered upon this promise:

We will create a tax system that is fair; where the abuses end, the perks stop, and where ordinary families are not squeezed to pay for the privileged. Tax should be related to ability to pay.[3]

Why has he failed to do so?

One reason is that income taxes aren't terribly progressive. New Labour is obeying Friedrich Hayek's rule for limiting redistributive taxation. He proposed that the top marginal rate of income tax be equal to the proportion of national income which the government takes in total taxes.[4] Under New Labour, the top tax rate has been 40 per cent, and taxation roughly 40 per cent of GDP.

Table 18 shows just how little direct taxes do to equalize incomes. This is shown by the difference between gross income and disposable income. This is small. It reduces the Gini coefficient by just 4 percentage points.

Secondly, indirect taxes are actually regressive. They add four percentage points to the Gini coefficient; this is the gap between disposable and post-tax incomes. The poorest fifth pay 29.6% of their gross income in indirect taxes, whilst the richest fifth pay just 14.4%. This is largely because the richest fifth save more, and spend proportionately less of their income on highly taxed alcohol and tobacco.[5]

Table 18. Income distribution 2004-05

Gini coefficient (%)	Original income	Gross income	Disposable income	Post-tax income
Bottom	3	7	8	7
2nd	8	11	13	12
3rd	15	16	17	16
4th	24	23	22	22
Top	50	43	41	43
Gini coefficient	51	36	32	36

Source: "The effects of taxes and benefits on household income 2004-05" table 2.

The message here is simple. Taxes, in themselves, don't redistribute income. It is state benefits that do that.

But why don't taxes equalize incomes? Herein lies an embarrassment. It's the problem we met in chapter 3. There is a trade-off between good public services and income redistribution. Good public services (it's thought) require lots of taxpayers' money. But the rich are not rich or numerous enough to provide this, so the tax burden must fall upon those on lower incomes. As it does so, taxes can no longer redistribute income.

There's another barrier to redistribution. It's that, in order to win the support of median voters, political parties must offer help to those on middle incomes, which limits the amount of help that can be offered to the genuinely poor.

In giving tax credits to families with incomes over £50,000, New Labour is merely doing what governments do. Table 19 shows that, on one estimate, the poorest fifth of the population has received a disproportionately low share of government transfers in many countries. Instead, redistribution is mostly towards middle-income groups.

Table 19. Share of government transfers received by income quintiles, mid-1980s

	Poorest	Middle	Richest
Australia	40.1	50.7	9.2
Norway	34.0	50.9	15.1
US	29.2	55.7	15.1
UK	26.7	61.4	11.9
Germany	21.8	59.9	18.3
France	17.5	57.8	24.7
Italy	15.6	56.8	27.6
Sweden	15.2	67.4	17.4

Source: Tanzi and Schuknecht, Public Spending in the 20th Century, p96.

Many social democrats believe this redistribution towards the median voter is the price we must pay to buy support for redistribution to the poor. As the cliché says, a service only for the poor soon becomes a poor service.

This argument, though, fails to ask: why do we want redistribution at all?

If our motive is mere charity – giving alms to the poor – there may be a case for this middle-class racket, as the poor do benefit. But what if we want redistribution to rectify some injustice? In this case, the racket may be positively counter-productive.

There are two problems here.

First, New Labour's efforts at reducing relative poverty – which have not been insignificant – have been directly mainly at those slightly below the poverty line, conventionally measured as 60% of median income. But support for the more extremely poor has been less. The upshot, as Conservatives have alleged, is that whilst the numbers of people with incomes of less than 60% of the median have fallen, the numbers in deep relative poverty – below 40% of median incomes – have risen.[6]

Secondly, these efforts have been directed towards pensioners and families with children, rather than single people. As a result, says the Institute for Fiscal Studies, "the poverty rate for the working age non-parent population – a group that has received little government attention – has actually risen since 1998."

Now, the thing is, the justice of these policies is dubious. If we wish to reduce inequality, surely we want to reduce the worst forms of it, which means helping the very worst-off, not merely the better-off of the worst-off.

Also, it's possible that the poverty of some pensioners and families with children is the consequence of freely made decisions – to have an extra child, or not to save during ones' working lifetimes. By contrast, the poverty of the single unemployed is often due to circumstances beyond their control – low skill or mental health problems that make it hard to hold down a job.

This might be deeply unjust. One common conception of justice says that inequalities are tolerable if they are the product of people's free choices, but intolerable if they are due to circumstances beyond an individual's control. This argues for giving less help to (some) families and pensioners, and more to the single unemployed – the exact opposite of New Labour's policies.

These policies are, of course, perfectly sensible from the point of winning votes – pensioners, parents and the slightly poor have more votes than the extremely poor. But they are much less sensible from the point of view of justice.

Which raises a nasty problem. There's not only a conflict between big government and redistribution, but there's also a conflict between justice and democracy. New Labour ignores these.

Trade-offs Revisited

These, though, are not the only trade-offs that governments face, and that New Labour is ignoring. There are many others, for example:

- Extraordinarily high levels of effective marginal tax rates on a few people, versus merely high ones on many others. As we saw in chapter 4, New Labour's tax and benefit reforms have replaced the former with the latter. One cost must be traded off against another.

- Reduced job turnover versus increased work incentives. Tax credits and the minimum wage increase the incentive for workers to stay in low-paid jobs. In reducing job turnover, however, there will be fewer new job openings. That could mean longer spells out of work for those who do become unemployed.

- Output stabilisation versus long-run growth. As we saw in chapter 7, it is possible, at least in theory and in some circumstances, that stabilizing output in the short term might reduce its growth in the long term.

- Risk-sharing versus incentives. One way to protect people from economic downturns – or from the irrational decisions of bosses – is to pay higher unemployment benefits. But "encouraging" people to look for work requires low benefits.

- Redistributive taxes versus efficient taxes. Taxes on cigarettes and alcohol are efficient, because they help ensure that private costs of drinking and smoking are aligned with the social costs of drunkenness and smelling bad. And in reducing the need to collect income tax, such duties reduce the disincentives to work that high income taxes would create. However, these taxes fall disproportionately upon the poor. There's a trade-off therefore between reducing inequality and efficiency.

- Higher output versus income equality. One way in which increased education might have powerful effects upon output is if "network externalities" are important – that is, if your education increases the productivity of others, say because your ability to use computers increases demand for Microsoft's software. In this case, the higher output caused by better education might also be inegalitarian, as it makes Bill Gates even richer.

- In-work benefits versus training. The National Minimum Wage and tax credits have the effect, other things being equal, of reducing wage inequality. However, this reduces the incentive for less skilled workers to train for better jobs, because the pay-off to doing so is smaller.

- Help for families versus long-run growth. A common finding of the literature on economic growth is that rapid population growth is bad for per capita output growth. Anything that gives people an incentive to have children could therefore reduce long-run growth.

The managerialist tendency

Isaiah Berlin, then, was right after all. There are trade-offs.

So, what does New Labour do about these?

In public – which is all that matters in democratic politics – it pretends they don't exist. Sure, Blair sometimes talks about "hard choices." But this is just managerialist rhetoric, used to give the impression that one is taking tough heroic decisions. It's not the starting point of serious analysis. You just don't hear New Labour figures talk seriously about trade-offs. They don't tell us which great goods they are sacrificing or why. Instead, the dominant idea is that "social justice is the partner of economic efficiency and not its enemy."

But how can New Labour sustain this illusion that Berlin was wrong?

One way in which it does so is by ignoring awkward facts. We've seen examples of this in chapters 4 to 8. For example, in the debate about the effect of minimum wages in the US, immense weight is placed upon Card and Krueger's research, whilst abundant contrary evidence has been ignored.

Similarly, New Labour seized upon research into cross-country differences in economic growth to justify its concern to raise education or achieve macroeconomic stability. But it ignores this research when it shows that big government spending or population growth are bad for growth.

New Labour also ignores a large body of evidence which suggests that valuable social goals can be achieved without big public spending. One recent study of public spending around the world by Ludger Schuknecht and Vito Tanzi concluded that "The rapid and considerable growth in public spending in more recent decades does not seem to have resulted in significant additional gains in socio-economic objectives"[8]. Several newly industrialising countries have achieved levels of educational attainment, freedom from crime, life expectancy and income equality which are comparable to those in the west, despite much lower spending.

It's not just awkward facts that are ignored. New Labour is also guilty of assuming that hard knowledge exists even where it doesn't.

The minimum wage provides a great example of this. If this is such a good idea, why not increase it massively?

The answer, of course, is that this would destroy jobs. There is, therefore, a point at which a trade-off does emerge between equality and efficiency. But how can we tell when this point is reached? How can we set the minimum wage at a level that does not destroy jobs, so we achieve equality without economic damage?

To see how, look again at diagram fig 6 illustrating monopsony in chapter 5. It shows that even where monopsony exists, and a minimum wage can actually create jobs, there comes a point – W_k in the diagram – above which it destroys them. To reconcile equality and efficiency, therefore, we must set the wage within the range W_m-W_k. A wage below W_m will not be egalitarian enough. And a wage above W_k will destroy jobs.

But how do we find out what this range is? New Labour thinks this is a simple task. The minimum wage will be introduced "at a level which will avoid adverse employment effects" Tony Wright assured voters before the 1997 election.[9]

But it's not as easy as this. Even if we assume that monopsony is really widespread, and that some minimum wage will be efficient and egalitarian, there's no reason to suppose that this wage will be the same across the country. The best minimum wage for barmen in Bournemouth may be very different from that for security guards in Swindon or farm workers in Falmouth. "Even if we accept that the labour market is riddled with monopsony, the requisite information that the technocrats would require to correct it is unavailable" says Deepak Lal.[10]

You might think the Low Pay Commission would have solved this problem – that's what it was set up for. Not a bit of it. As we saw in chapter 5, its first report couldn't even find out how many people were low paid at all.[11] David Metcalf, a member of the Low Pay Commission has said that the Commission "has been badly let down by the Office for National Statistics".[12]

In fairness, the Commission was aware of these uncertainties. Its first report stressed that "the impact of the National Minimum Wage cannot be predicted precisely" and that it was "a journey into uncharted waters".[13] The words of Neil Kinnock to the 1985 Labour party conference – that "you cannot play politics with people's lives" – spring to mind.

The key point here, though, is that New Labour thought governments and experts could obtain hard knowledge which was in fact unavailable.

And the minimum wage is not the only example of this. There are countless others. Will the demand for university graduates increase greatly in coming years? What is the best tax and benefit system for increasing the labour supply? How can universities be financed without deterring students from disadvantaged backgrounds? Can we really have an immigration policy that distinguishes between "desirable" and "undesirable" immigrants? Did Iraq have weapons of mass destruction?

In all these cases the definitive facts have been more elusive than the government has thought.

The limits to New Labour

We are now in a position to identify New Labour's failings, and to show how they justify declining voter turn-out. There are three related problems.

"We know it all"

New Labour has a massive and hubristic confidence in governments' cognitive skills. In this respect, it continues a long tradition. Thomas Sowell has called this ideology the "vision of the anointed." James Buchanan has called it "the presuppositions of Harvey Road" (the Cambridge street in which John Maynard Keynes lived). It's the idea that our social and economic problems can be solved, if only men of sound judgment and goodwill apply their minds to them.

New Labour forgets – or, more likely, never knew – the warnings of Hayek and Oakeshott, that centralised knowledge and rationality are weak and feeble guides to action, and that the consequences of any policy can be foreseen only dimly, and the full consequences not at all. What's more, it ignores the vast body of evidence which shows that even highly-trained experts make systematic errors when making judgments under uncertainty. And it ignores the fact that rationality is in fact much weaker and ambiguous than is generally recognised. I shall return to these points in chapters 13 and 14.

So, when the Prime Minister tells us he has "no reverse gear" we do not admire his steadfastness. We think him a blithering idiot for being so confident when the facts don't justify being so.

"The vision thing"

I have argued that the defining feature of New Labour is its belief that there are no significant trade-offs. It believes cleverly designed policies can overcome the trade-off between equality and efficiency. It seems to reject John Rawls' view that: "only ideologues and visionaries fail to experience deep conflicts of political values and conflicts between these and non-political values"[14]

This belief that we can have it all – justice and efficiency – stops the party from making coherent statements about fundamental values. After all, why bother to define and argue for particular conceptions of justice or efficiency if we can have them all?

This failure has already got New Labour into trouble. In consistently failing to make an explicit case for redistributive taxation it gives the impression (which is easy enough to get anyway) that taxes are merely state extortion. The upshot has been vigorous protests against fuel duties and council taxes. 'Stealth taxes' – imposts designed by cunning technocrats in the hope that people would not notice them – cannot fool people for long.

There is, though, a more grievous error. In failing to articulate clear fundamental values, New Labour simply gives us no ethical reason to engage with politics.

Mr Blair himself has recognised this. He has complained that "sometimes it can seem as if were a mere technocratic exercise, well or less well managed, but with no over-riding moral purpose to it".[15]

True. But things don't improve if we look for a statement of "over-riding moral purpose."

Consider this from a speech Mr Blair made in 2002: "Our goal is a Britain in which...we achieve true equality – equal status and equal opportunity[16]."

But these two ideals are inconsistent. From a position of equal opportunity, the successful will believe they deserve their success. They'll become smug, self-satisfied and contemptuous of the less successful, whose failure must, they believe, be due to their own lack of merit. This surely would undermine our sense of equal status.

A moment's thought, then, shows that you can't have both equal opportunity and equal status; I'll return to this in chapter 12.

That Blair believes otherwise merely shows that he hasn't really thought at all about the fundamental moral question underpinning political activity – what is the point of it?

And this in turn corroborates the suspicion that politicians are concerned with power, not principle.

Effectiveness versus excellence

This raises an important distinction made by Alasdair MacIntyre, between the goods of excellence and the goods of effectiveness.[17]

The latter are extrinsic goods – wealth, power, winning the game. The former are intrinsic qualities, of being a master of a particular practice. So, a pop singer who makes good-selling trashy music achieves the goods of effectiveness, but the singer who cultivates her talent but doesn't achieve such popularity achieves the goods of excellence.

The managerialist aims only at the good of effectiveness. As MacIntyre put it: "the manager treats ends as given, as outside his scope; his concern is with technique, with effectiveness."[18]

The intrusion of this attitude into politics means that the pursuit of excellence, of virtue gets lost. Two examples should show what I mean.

First, when Tessa Jowell was accused of benefiting from bribes paid to her then husband, she replied: "rules have not been breached. I obey the House of Commons rules. I always have and I always will."[19]

This presumes that good behaviour consists in a prissy, pedantic following of rules. Jowell never said that she behaved with dignity, nobility and virtue. And, scandalously, she was never asked.

Secondly, New Labour often claim that they have been better than the Conservatives. This is like me claiming that I'm a better guitarist than Abu Hamza. It's just stupid. The question is: am I as good a guitarist as I could possibly be? Likewise, the question for New Labour is: are you as good a government as you could possibly be?

This lack of interest in higher values leads naturally to a debased politics. New Labour often gives the impression that it wants to concrete over all of England, dragoon us all into mindless workaholism, harass the poor and immigrants, and kill thousands of innocent foreigners so that the British can get a spurious increase in their own security. Add to this Mr Blair's contemptible hard man posturing ("no reverse gear"), his kow-towing to powerful men like George Bush and Rupert Murdoch, and we get a clear but repulsive image. Politics is not a dignified activity, to be conducted by people of intelligence and decency. It is just an arena in which mentally disturbed bullies work out their neuroses.

The start of politics

It is, therefore, no surprise that people are renouncing party politics. And we should remember just how many millions of us are doing so. At the 2005 election, 17.1 million people did not vote.[20] Only 9.6 million voted Labour.

So, what's the alternative? The rest of this book tries to lay the foundations for such an answer. In chapters 13 and 14 I'll try and show why managerialism fails – because the tools of the managerialist – knowledge and rationality – are far weaker than politicians pretend.

Before then, though, I'll show why we need to put the politics back into politics. Politicians must talk about fundamental values because there are competing conceptions of values which cannot co-exist. As Raymond Plant says:

Values such as liberty, equality, fraternity/ fellowship/ solidarity/ community...contain internal tensions and contradictions and part of politics is about trying to establish the dominance of interpretation of the meaning of a value over others[21].

This is correct, except that Plant has omitted efficiency from his list.

As this seems to be one of New Labour's most cherished values, we should investigate just what it means. The next two chapters will try and do this.

Notes

1. *The Vision of the Anointed,* p102.

2. "How can economic policy strike a balance between economic efficiency and income equality?" p323.

3. Speech to Labour party conference October 4 1994, reprinted in *New Labour, New Britain,* p44-45.

4. *The Constitution of Liberty,* p323.

5. "The effects of taxes and benefits on household income 2004-05" table 3.

6. For example, Michael Portillo, *Sunday Times* 26 November 2006.

7. *Poverty and Inequality in Britain: 2006,* p42.

8. *Public Spending in the Twentieth Century,* p76.

9. *Why Vote Labour?* p170.

10. *The Minimum Wage: No Way to Help the Poor,* p31.

11. *The National Minimum Wage: First Report of the Low Pay Commission,* table A2.2, p174. In fact, these figures were later revised down by National Statistics. As if this is not unclear enough, there is a third source of data – the British Household Panel Survey – which the report overlooked. This estimated that 12.5 per cent of workers were low paid at the time. See Mark B. Stewart, "Low Pay in Britain" in Paul Gregg and Jonathan Wadsworth (eds), *The State of Working Britain.*

12. *Financial Times,* November 11 2002, p2.

13. *The National Minimum Wage: First Report of the Low Pay Commission,* p5, 19. See also pages 29, 80 and 89.

14. *Political Liberalism,* p44. Note that none of this is to suggest that there are always trade-offs everywhere. Such a position has been caricatured, rightly, by John Allen Paulos, who tells the story of a Congressman in Wisconsin who argued against daylight saving on the grounds that there were trade-offs associated with any policy, and that this one would cause curtains and fabrics to fade more quickly. *(Innumeracy,* p99.) I merely want to argue that we should be far more aware of the prevalence of possible trade-offs than we really are.

15. "The next steps for New Labour", speech at London School of Economics, March 12, 2002.

16. "On tackling poverty and social exclusion", September 18, 2002.

17. *Whose Justice? Which Rationality?* p32.

18. *After Virtue,* p30.

19. Quoted in the *Daily Express,* March 27 2006.

20.This is the difference between the electorate and the turnout. In fact, because the electoral register is always a little out of date, the number exaggerates the true number of abstentions. But the point holds – that many more abstained than supported New Labour.

21. "Blair and Ideology" p563 in Anthony Seldon (ed), *The Blair Effect.*

10.

No Matter of Congratulation

The government's central economic objective is to achieve high and stable levels of growth and employment. (H.M.Treasury, March 2001).[1]

I know not why it should be a matter of congratulation that persons who are already richer than anyone needs to be, should have doubled their means of consuming things which give little or no pleasure except as representative of wealth (John Stuart Mill).[2]

Money can't buy back your youth when your old
Or a friend when you're lonely
Or a love that's grown cold
The wealthiest person is a pauper at times
Compared to the man with a satisfied mind
(The Blue Sky Boys, "A Satisfied Mind")

The defining feature of New Labour, I have argued, is its belief that equality and efficiency are compatible. But what exactly is "efficiency"? It is tempting to think it is a hard, technocratic, uncontroversial ideal. But it's not. As we shall see in this chapter and the next, "efficiency" has several contested meanings.

The most obvious meaning, at least to a non-economist, is rapid economic growth. This has been New Labour's "central economic objective." And it's been the goal of all governments for decades to make us richer.

Just recently, though, this identification of efficiency with growth has been challenged. Conservative leader David Cameron has said: "It's time we admitted that there's more to life than money, and time we focused not just on GDP but on GWB – general well-being."[3]

The economic justification for this view has been publicised by Richard Layard. "Economic growth has not increased welfare as much as we expected" he says.[4] If we think true efficiency consists in making us happier, then, the pursuit of economic growth might not be efficient.

Money can't buy happiness

The evidence for this was first reported rigorously by Richard Easterlin. He found that in many countries huge gains in GDP per head have almost no impact upon happiness, as measured by surveys of people's well-being. For example, between 1958 and 1988, GDP per head in Japan sextupled. It was one of the greatest economic miracles in human history. And yet surveys suggest the Japanese people felt little happier at the end of the period than at the start.[5]

This is not a peculiarity of the Japanese psyche. It is also true of the US, UK and western Europe.[6]

Now, we should be careful here. It's certainly true that higher national incomes increase happiness in poor countries.[7] And some studies have found a small upward trend in happiness in rich countries.[8] But the general picture seems clear. Over the long run, big rises in incomes in developed countries have been associated with only small (if any) rises in aggregate well-being.

This is surprising. Just consider the things we have now that didn't exist 30 years ago: the internet, cheap foreign travel, better cars, more TV channels, more variety of food, Civ III and iPods. But we're not much happier for these. Why not?

One possibility is that we're stuck on a "hedonic treadmill." Higher incomes, and new consumer goods, do make us happier immediately after we get them. But the novelty soon wears off, so we start wanting even more: "The more we have the more we seem to feel to need" says Robert Frank.[9] And over time, what were originally considered luxuries – TVs, telephones, central heating – come to be thought of as necessities. Easterlin points out that the incomes which workers in New York believe they require to achieve a "minimum comfort" have risen consistently for most of the century; they have generally been around half of average GDP per head.[10]

What's more, some goods are inherently scarce. However wealthy our economy becomes, only the richest of us will be able to afford servants, or homes with unspoiled views, or works of fine art. Relative prices of such goods will rise as incomes rise. For some people, therefore, the goods they most want will get more unattainable as they get richer.[11]

Another possibility is that income is a positional good. We want it to feel, in the words of Harry Enfield's brummie, "considerably richer than yow." Hence the old joke about the worker asking his boss: "if you can't afford to give me a pay rise, could you at least give everyone else a cut?" There's little doubt that, at any point in time, richer people tend to be happier than poorer ones.[12]

Research by Sara Solnick and David Hemenway shows just how prevalent positional goods are. They asked staff and students at the Harvard School of Public Health the question: Would you rather earn $50,000 a year when others earn $25,000, or $100,000 a year when others earn $200,000, where prices are the same in both cases? 56 per cent said they preferred the $50,000.[13]

The key feature of positional goods is that demand for them can never be satisfied by rises in incomes across the board. If I want a high income in order to feel that I have more than you, a rise in aggregate income will never satisfy me, because your income rises at the same rate.

Oddly, it has taken economists 200 years to rediscover this. Eighteenth century thinkers were well aware of it. In 1755 Jean-Jacques Rousseau wrote:

> If one sees a handful of powerful and rich men at the height of greatness and fortune whilst the mob grovels in obscurity and misery, it is because the former prize the things they enjoy only to the extent that others are deprived of them; and because, without changing their position, they would cease to be happy, if the people ceased to be miserable[14].

All this makes people sound rather nasty; the pleasure we get from wealth lies in the knowledge that others lack it. But there are ways in which others' wealth hurts us even if we aren't spiteful. They lie in what economists call consumption spill-overs. When everyone else has a car, the roads are unpleasantly congested so the pleasures of driving a nice car wane. If people buy houses near to the best schools, overall education standards don't change, but some people are priced out of good areas. Or if some people buy huge people carriers, it raises the chances of others dying in road accidents. These therefore have incentives to buy huge cars.

Deepening the Easterlin paradox

If all this sounds like a convincing explanation of why aggregate income growth doesn't make us happier, it shouldn't. There's another possibility. Maybe economic growth does make us happier. It's just that other developments over the last 30 years have made us less happy – for example, rising crime and divorce rates.

A paper by Rafael di Tella and Robert MacCulloch has considered this question[15]. And they found something very queer.

First, they found, rising average incomes do make us happy. Indeed, GDP per head has as much effect upon our happiness as our own income. This contradicts the notion that income is a positional good. Sure, we'd be unhappier if we fell behind others. But a rise in everyone's income makes us happier.

Secondly, they found that happiness should have increased much more over the last 30 years than it actually has. Yes, they found, rising crime and divorce have made us less happy. But falling pollution, shorter working hours, lower inflation and increased life expectancy should all have made us even happier.

But they haven't. In this sense, the Easterlin paradox becomes even more puzzling.

What can explain this? Here are some possibilities:

- *Omitted variables.* Perhaps there's something Di Tella and MacCulloch left out that has made us unhappier over the last 30 years. One possibility could be the decline of religion.

- *Economic growth doesn't make everyone richer.* Robert Frank points out that the incomes of the worst-off 20 per cent of the US population have fallen in real terms in the last 20 years, so we'd expect these to have become unhappier.[16]

- *The loss of community.* Friends make us happier. If we've become more solitary, therefore, we'd become less happy. And there's evidence that Americans at least have become much more isolated in recent decades.[17]

- *The hedonic treadmill is speeding up.* Maybe the growth in TV advertising or increased interest in celebrity lifestyles mean that we make more comparisons today between what we have and what we want than we did 30 years ago. So a given relative income makes us less happy now than it did then.

- *We have unsatisfied minds.* Maybe the very attributes of our personality that are necessary for economic growth are also those which stop us enjoying the fruits of that growth. Economic growth requires men and women with a strong work ethic, with a capacity to postpone gratification, with self-control, with an ability to rationally calculate the best use of their time, with single-minded devotion to the task in hand, and above all with a desire for more, more, more. Can one imagine a personality less equipped to enjoy the here and now?

- *Increasing materialism and the decline of the hippy.* Robert E. Lane reports that people who are motivated by materialistic concerns tend to be unhappier than less materialistic folk.[18] If materialistic attitudes have increased, this means we would, other things equal, become less happy.

The bottom line here is that, over the long run, GDP growth has not made us much happier. The best we can say is that it's made us a little happier, and would have made us more so had other factors not intervened. The worst we can say is Robert Frank's words: "Across the board increases in our stocks of material goods produce virtually no measurable gains in our psychological or physical well-being. Bigger houses and faster cars, it seems, don't make us any happier."[19]

In search of a fallacy

All this suggests there is little justification for the almost obsessive interest some politicians – and journalists – have in economic growth. This, however, merely raises a question. If rising GDP doesn't make us happier, at least in nations as advanced as ours, why do so many people pay so much attention to it?

The question gains force from the fact that some of the finest minds to have applied themselves to this question thought the desire for growth to be rather deplorable. In 1848 John Stuart Mill wrote:

> I am not charmed with the ideal of life held out by those who think that the normal state of human beings is that of struggling to get on; that the trampling, crushing, elbowing and treading on each others' heels, which form the existing type of social life, are the most desirable lot of human kind, or anything but the disagreeable symptoms of one of the phases of industrial progress...The best state for human nature is that in which, while no-one is poor, no-one desires to be richer, nor has any reason to fear being thrust back by the efforts of others to push themselves forward...It is only in the backward countries of the world that increased production is still an important object.[20]

Almost 60 years later the sociologist Max Weber wrote:

> A man does not "by nature" wish to earn more and more money, but simply to live as he is accustomed to live and earn as much as is necessary for that purpose. Wherever modern capitalism has begun its work of increasing the productivity of human labour by increasing its intensity, it has encountered the immensely stubborn resistance of this leading trait of pre-capitalistic labour.[21]

In the 1930s, in his essay *Economic Possibilities for our Grandchildren*, Keynes took a similar view. He foresaw, correctly, a huge rise in labour productivity, but he could not envisage these productivity gains being used to produce more goods, simply because he could not foresee a demand for them. "The economic problem is in sight of a solution" he said.[22] As a result, he thought, the working week would fall to around 15 hours. To him, the problem we would face at the start of the 21st century would not be how to produce more goods, but rather how people would adjust from wanting more money to enjoying the wealth and leisure they had.

Although he thought the transition from the one state of mind to the other would be painful, he had little doubt it would be beneficial in the end, not least because he shared Mill's contempt for acquisitiveness:

> The 'purposive' man is always trying to secure a spurious and delusive immortality for his acts by pushing his interest in them forward in time. He does not love his cat, but his cat's kittens; nor, in truth, the kittens, but only the kittens' kittens, and so on forever to the end of catdom.[23]

To Keynes and Mill, the notion that people would be as purposive and desperate to "get on" in the 21st century as they were decades previously was unthinkable. And, I suspect, the idea that such striving would receive official encouragement from the government would have horrified them.

Why then, are we still so desperate for growth? There are, it must be admitted, some good reasons:

- Perhaps economic growth does make us better off, but the time lags between incomes and the quality of life are so long that the link cannot be measured by statistical methods. William Easterly points out that the huge improvements in public health in OECD countries in the 20th century are partly due to advances in nutrition and sanitation which began in the 19th century[24]. Unfortunately, because we tend to take for granted the advances made many years ago, we do not feel happier for them. Maybe growth increases our objective well-being, but not our subjective well-being.

- A rise in income per head, insofar as it betokens a rise in labour productivity can never be a bad thing, simply because increased productive power means we have more options, whether we exercise them or not.

- Growth may be necessary to reduce unemployment – although as we learned in the early 1980s, it is certainly not sufficient.

- Growth may be a sign that resources are being allocated properly over time. If returns on capital exceed interest rates – as they do in most countries – it makes sense for society to sacrifice some consumption today in order to invest. This is because the future consumption we can get by expanding the capital stock exceeds the rate at which that consumption is discounted. Such additions to the capital stock imply that output rises over time.

- Our greater wealth has been responsible for improved working conditions and a reduction in pollution – simply because higher incomes create a demand for more workers which strengthens their bargaining power, and for cleaner air.

- It may even be the case that economic growth creates a more civilised society, because when overall incomes are rising one person's gain is not necessarily another's loss. Even the most obnoxious Wall Street banker doesn't make a habit of chopping people's hands off.

• We need economic growth because the alternative – falling off the hedonic treadmill – would be very painful. When economic growth slowed in the 1970s, social conflict increased sharply, even prompting talk of a crisis of the legitimacy of government.

Whether these explanations account for all our desire for economic growth is, however, doubtful. Perhaps there are also some inferential errors at work.

One is a version of what psychologists call the availability heuristic – the habit of focussing our attention upon what is most obvious. GDP figures are easily available and widely publicised, and there are countless numbers of people willing to tell journalists about every minor move in them. It's easy, though fallacious, to believe that something that gets so much attention must be important.

Another cognitive error is to mistake correlation for causality. There's no doubt that economic growth has been accompanied by improvements in many aspects of our objective well-being, ranging from a greater respect for human rights through to better healthcare. Maybe people have inferred from this that growth causes improvements in the quality of life. But correlation is not causality. William Easterly has estimated that of 61 indicators of the quality of life which improve during economic growth, most do so because of the passage of time, rather than because of higher incomes[25]. Instead of improvements in the quality of life being due to economic growth, maybe they are due to the same things that cause growth – namely increases in our knowledge.

Modern minds are so used to seeing knowledge and incomes rise together that it is worth pointing out that this need not always be so. Mill, well aware of this, said:

It is scarcely necessary to remark that a stationary condition of capital and population implies no stationary state of human improvement. There would be as much scope as ever for all kinds of mental culture, and moral and social progress; as much room for improving the Art of Living, and much more likelihood of its being improved, when minds ceased to be engrossed by the art of getting on.[26]

A third inferential error is that we fail to anticipate the fact that we will get used to our higher incomes. "People's ability to predict their future tastes is sometimes quite poor" say Kahneman and Varey.[27]

A final error that biases us towards exaggerating the merits of economic growth is the fallacy of composition. Fred Hirsch complained that people think of aggregate growth as being merely "individual advance writ large".[28] So, for example, we imagine that if we were richer we could buy the country cottage with good views, or the high-performance car, but we forget that if everyone were richer, the price of that cottage would be bid up beyond our means, whilst the lustre of the expensive car would wear off if the roads were too congested to take advantage of it.

If all this were the full story of why we want economic growth so much, it would be a cause for sadness, but not anger. Regrettably, however, it may be that the concern with growth also has less pleasant motivations.

One is the desire of governments to take credit for what might happen anyway. It's a fair supposition that, left to itself, the economy would grow. In making growth an object of economic policy, governments can therefore claim to have achieved some spurious success. At a time when the very legitimacy of our managerialist rulers is in question, this is handy.

Also, economic growth is an easy way to raise more tax revenue. Without this, governments could not claim credit for increased spending on health or education.

Another unsavoury reason for governments to want economic growth is that it is often seen as an alternative to genuinely egalitarian policies. "Economic growth has acted to deflect questions of redistribution" says Jon Mulberg[29]. If income can grow at 2.5 per cent a year for 50 years, it will more than triple by 2050. That implies a minimum wage of over £15 an hour, in today's prices, or almost £600 a week. It seems therefore that growth can help the poor without the rich having to dig into their own pockets.

Some have argued that growth is not only an attractive alternative to redistribution, but a necessary one. This is because there is a potential tension between capitalism and the relief of poverty. Capitalism might require that the rich are taxed only lightly, in order to encourage them to invest. But the relief of poverty might require that they are taxed heavily. Economic growth can appear to solve this dilemma, by offering a way of curbing poverty without imposing onerous taxes. It's a way of avoiding the conflict of interest between the rich and the poor.

Conclusion: alternatives to growth

None of this is an argument for governments actively pursuing zero growth. The fact that growth does us little good does not imply that its absence would make us happier – maybe quite the opposite. The point is merely that governments should not pursue growth as an over-riding objective.

This view is much closer to intelligent defences of economic growth than you might think. "Maximising economic growth per se is simply a silly objective", wrote Wilfred Beckerman in his *In Defence of Growth*.[30] He added that affluent countries were reaching the point where governments should put more emphasis upon creating a civilised society, and less upon stimulating growth. As real GDP per person has risen 75 per cent since he wrote that, shouldn't we be past this point now?

But what should governments do instead of promoting growth? Here are some higher priorities.

Internalizing externalities

The only true cost of economic growth, said Wilfred Beckerman, is the consumption we sacrifice now in order to build capital goods. All else is due to the misallocation of resources and the failure to correct for externalities.[31]

This suggests governments should concentrate upon ensuring, so far as possible, that the misallocations of resources that often accompany growth do not happen. They should ensure that the external costs and benefits of economic activity are internalised, so they equal the social costs and benefits.

This has three possible implications. First, that pollution and congestion must be priced. This does not mean it should be a direct aim of policy to reduce these. It merely means that policy should aim at ensuring that the private benefits of the activities that give rise to these should not exceed the social benefits of them. This argues for carbon taxes or road pricing.

Second, consumption externalities must be recognised. As we have seen, spending on many goods has adverse effects upon others. To internalise these effects, there is, as Robert Frank has argued, a case for a progressive consumption tax[32]. It's better to tax Paris Hilton than hard-working but frugal folk.

Thirdly, there might be a case for intervention to improve the workings of capital markets. Welfare is increased by investment whenever returns on capital exceed the rate available on savings. This means that capital market imperfections reduce welfare, by raising the cost of capital relative to the return on savings. There is therefore a case for eliminating them. So, it is quite reasonable for the government to inquire whether small businesses are being starved of finance, and to do something about it if they are. It is equally reasonable to give tax breaks for research and development spending if the social return on this exceeds the private return. What is not reasonable, however, is to pretend that such policies are motivated by a need to increase growth. Growth is a by-product of welfare-increasing behaviour, not an end in itself.

All this might sound trivial. But it's not. As we saw with the public protests against high petrol duties in September 2000, people are reluctant to pay the full social costs of their actions. There's a potential trade-off between efficiency in the sense of equalizing private and social costs on the one hand, and popularity on the other.

Increasing autonomy

People are happier, says Mihaly Csikszentmihaly, when they are "in control of their own lives[33]." But this is exactly what is not the case in the workplace. It's no surprise, therefore, that the self-employed are much happier than the employed.[34]

This argues for breaking down the bureaucratic hierarchies which disfigure our working lives, and perhaps even transferring control from bosses to workers.

It also argues for greater democracy. Bruno Frey and Alois Stutzer have shown that people are happier in regions where there is more direct democracy[35]. Even if people don't actually vote in referenda, or don't like the outcome, they are happier for feeling consulted.

Freedom matters

One study has found that "life satisfaction decreases with higher government spending".[36] And Johan Norberg writes:

A system in which individuals had few opportunities to improve their lives, and where people were totally dependent on the state – communism – was disastrous to well-being. A lot has been made of the fact that post-communist countries reported lower happiness levels immediately after the fall of communism...Less attention has been drawn to the fact that communist countries were much more miserable than other countries.[37]

Maybe, then, people are happier when the state leaves them alone.

Help the unemployed

Being out of work destroys happiness. This is not merely because it reduces our income. Indeed, Liliana and Rainer Winkelmann have estimated that the non-pecuniary harm done by being unemployed – boredom, isolation and loss of self-esteem – accounts for over 90% of the unhappiness associated with joblessness, with the loss of income accounting for less than 10%.[38]

This would be a case for increasing economic growth, insofar as this creates jobs. But other policies – such as increasing training, improving job search, subsidising the employment of the long-term unemployed, or even perhaps raising welfare benefits – will also be necessary.

Help us make friends

A government seriously committed to increasing the well-being of its subjects would pay more attention to our need for companionship. As Robert E. Lane says, in affluent societies it is this – in the sense of having loving friends and spouses rather than just a vague feeling of community – that is the main source of well-being.[39]

This, though, raises the question of what, if anything, governments can actually do to promote such companionship. Maybe there is a case for limiting working hours. Or for discouraging long commuting times, so that people have more time to socialize.

Invest in goods that do increase happiness

One reason why economic growth does not make us happier is that we become accustomed to our nice cars, big homes and fancy TVs. But there are some things we do not become so quickly accustomed to. These include clean air, uncongested roads and good public transport. There is, says Robert Frank, a strong case for the government to encourage the development of these goods.[40]

I have been deliberately vague about these proposals. One reason for this is that some of them might be mutually inconsistent; one complaint about the field of happiness research is that it's often just a mirror: "we look into the data and see our ideology reflected."[41] Another reason is that, as we'll see in chapter 11, I'm not sure it is the job of governments to create happiness at all.

If, however, you don't share these doubts, there is one thing to be noted about policies such as these – that they could, paradoxically, end up boosting growth. This is because, as Charles Kenny suggested, it may be happiness that causes growth, rather than vice versa.[42]

One reason for this is that the same freedom that makes us happy also causes growth; communist countries prioritized growth over freedom, and ended up with neither. Also, happy people trust their fellow citizens. And trust can help reduce the transactions costs that can be a barrier to economic activity. Markets for used cars and builders are limited because few people trust used car sellers or builders. Moreover, happiness leads to less absenteeism and fewer arguments at work, which can raise productivity directly. And finally, happiness is associated with greater social contact with others and a responsiveness to requests for help. In an economy increasingly dependent upon knowledge and communication, such contacts may be a valuable way of stimulating growth, by encouraging the development and dissemination of new ideas.

Perhaps, then, economic growth is the by-product of institutions and policies that make us happy, not the cause of happiness. In this sense, growth should not be a goal of policy, and is not efficient in itself.

Notes

1. *Productivity in the UK: Progress Towards a Productive Economy,* p5.

2. *Principles of Political Economy,* p749.

3. Speech to Google Zetigeist Europe, May 22 2006.

4. *Happiness: Lessons From a New Science,* p229.

5. "Will raising the incomes of all increase the happiness of all?", Journal of *Economic Behaviour and Organisation,* 27, January 1995, p35-47, p41.

6. See for example Charles Kenny, "Does growth cause happiness or does happiness cause growth?", *Kyklos,* 52, January 1999, p3-6, p21, or Rafael di Tellla and Robert MacCulloch, "Gross National Happiness as an answer to the Easterlin paradox", April 2005, or David Blanchflower and Andrew Oswald, "Well-being over time in Britain and the USA".

7. *Happiness,* p32.

8. Michael Hagerty and Ruut Veenhoven, "Rising happiness in nations 1946-2004", *Social Indicators Research,* 2006, vol 77, p1-16.

9. *Luxury Fever,* p74.

10. "Will raising the incomes of all increase the happiness of all?" p41.

11. *Social Limits to Growth,* p29.

12. *Happiness,* p31.

13. "Is more always better?" *Journal of Economic Behaviour and Organisation,* 37, 1995, p373-83, p378. Note that this finding is not as strong as it seems, however. I find it very hard to conceive of a world in which absolute and relative prices are the same in both states. If others share my difficulty, they would plump for the $50,000 not out of a desire to feel better off than others, but to benefit from the more favourable prices in that state.

14. Discourse on the Origin of Inequality, in Donald A Cress (ed), *Jean-Jacques Rousseau: The Basic Political Writings,* p78.

15. "Gross National Happiness as an answer to the Easterlin paradox."

16. *Luxury Fever,* p4.

17. See, for example, Robert Putnam, *Bowling Alone* or Miller McPherson, Lynn Smith-Lovin and Matthew Brashears, "Social isolation in America: changes in discussion networks over two decades."

18. *The Loss of Happiness in Market Democracies*, p147.

19. *Luxury Fever*, p6.

20. *Principles of Political Economy*, p748-49.

21. *The Protestant Ethic and the Spirit of Capitalism*, p24. I'll return to this theme in chapter 14, where I'll argue that economic rationality – in the sense of wanting more and more – is a recent historical construction.

22. *Essays in Persuasion*, p326.

23. *Essays in Persuasion*, p330.

24. "Life During Growth", p5.

25. "Life During Growth", p8.

26. *Principles of Political Economy*, p751.

27. "Notes on the psychology of utility", p133.

28. *Social Limits to Growth*, p169.

29. *Social Limits to Economic Theory*, p147.

30. *In Defence of Growth*, p18.

31. *In Defence of Economic Growth*, p28.

32. *Luxury Fever*, ch 14.

33. *Flow: The Psychology of Happiness*, p10.

34. Matthias Benz and Bruno Frey, "The value of autonomy: evidence from the self-employed", University of Zurich Institute for *Empirical Research in Economics working paper 173*, November 2003.

35. Bruno Frey and Alois Stutzer, "What can economists learn from happiness research", University of Zurich Institute for *Empirical Research in Economics working paper 80*, October 2001.

36. Christian Bjornskov, Axel Dreher and Justina Fischer, "The bigger the better?", October 2005.

37. "Happiness paternalism: blunders from a new science", September 2006, p11-12.

38. "Why are the unemployed so unhappy?", *Economica*, 65, 1998, p1-15.

39. *The Loss of Happiness in Market Democracies*, p7.

40. *Luxury Fever*, p75.

41. Will Willkinson, "Growth matters", *Prospect*, October 2006.

42. "Does growth cause happiness or does happiness cause growth?"

11.

Some Defunct Philosopher

I think there is a danger sometimes that we look at everything just in terms of what its utilitarian value is. (Tony Blair).[1]

Economic growth doesn't make us much happier. This raises a question. If "efficiency" or the "national interest" does not obviously mean higher national income, what does it mean?

There are at least four possibilities: utilitarianism; Pareto efficiency; majority rule; and maximising primary goods or capabilities. All these have big flaws, and they all conflict with each other, and some with principles of justice or freedom.

This means the "national interest" or "economic efficiency"are not the self-evidently good objectives that managerialists believe. They are moral values with multiple meanings. We must therefore think about which we want. We cannot take ends as given.

To see this, let's consider these four conceptions in turn.

An English fantasy

"Practical men, who believe themselves to be quite exempt from any intellectual influences, are usually the slaves of some defunct economist."[2] So, famously, wrote Maynard Keynes. He omitted to add that they are also the slaves of some defunct philosopher. That philosopher is Jeremy Bentham, the founder of utilitarianism, who said that policies should aim at maximising the greatest happiness of the greatest number. This principle – recently endorsed by Richard Layard's popular book, *Happiness: Lessons from a New Science* – dominates policy making today, as Blair recognised himself.

There are countless examples of this. Consider just three:

- *Inflation targeting.* Bank of England economists calculate that cutting inflation by two percentage points a year would create welfare gains equivalent to 0.21% of GDP a year, the net present value which is 6.5% of GDP[3]. The costs of reducing inflation – a temporary loss of output and jobs caused by high interest rates – have a net present value of 6% of GDP, they estimate. Hence, the benefits of reducing inflation outweigh the costs. It promotes the greatest happiness of the greatest number.

- *Sacking civil servants.* The Comprehensive Spending Review of July 2004 proposed sacking 100,000 civil servants in order to increase spending on "front-line services." Presumably, the benefits of such spending outweigh the costs to the civil servants of losing their jobs.

- *The Iraq war.* The justification for this is that the benefits of war – the biggest of which was removing a brutal dictator – outweigh the costs, financial and human.

There is, however, a big problem with these policies, even if we assume that the aggregate benefits of them really do outweigh the costs.

The problem is that the gains and losses from these policies accrue to different people. Worse still, a few suffer immense losses so that the many can enjoy smaller gains. The Iraqi civilian who was killed by American bombers does not enjoy the benefit of freedom. And people who lose their jobs as a result of attempts to reduce inflation often don't get sufficient offsetting benefits. A 50 per cent cut in income for just 3 months, for example, implies a 12.5 per cent loss of income in one year. That swamps the gain from lower inflation, even ignoring non-pecuniary distress.

How can we justify imposing big losses onto some people so that others gain? Many economists have not even tried to do so, preferring to follow Nicholas Kaldor's advice in 1939:

> There is no need for the economist to prove – as indeed he never could prove – that as a result of the adoption of a certain measure nobody in the community is going to suffer. In order to establish his case it is quite sufficient for him to show that even if all those who suffer as a result are fully compensated for their loss, the rest of the community will still be better off than before. Whether the losers should in fact be given compensation or not, is a political question on which the economist, qua economist, could hardly pronounce an opinion.[4]

This idea – known as the Kaldor-Hicks compensation principle – is inadequate. The fact that every individual would gain from a particular policy if compensation were paid does not mean the policy is legitimate if compensation is not paid. A moment's thought will tell you this. I would readily consent to you taking the hideous grandfather clock which my great-aunt Dorothy left me in her will, if you pay me a small sum as compensation. If you break into my house and take the clock, the Kaldor-Hicks principle is therefore satisfied. But this is plain burglary, which is obviously wrong.

How then could so many intelligent people possibly take Kaldor's view seriously? It is because they assume that utilitarianism is merely the extension to the whole of society of the principles of individual rationality which economists take for granted. The defence of utilitarianism on which a generation of students was brought up asks:

> If it is rational for me to choose the pain of a visit to the dentist in order to prevent the pain of toothache, why is it not rational of me to choose a pain for Jones, similar to that of my visit to the dentist, if that is the only way in which I can prevent a pain, equal to that of my toothache, for Robinson?[5]

This is a silly question. It is obvious why I should consent to a trip to the dentist – because it is good for me in the end. But it is far less obvious why Jones should consent to his pain. After all, he may suffer something more painful than a toothache – even death itself in the case of the Iraqi war – and get no offsetting benefit. John Rawls put it well: "there is no reason to suppose that the principles which should regulate an association of men is simply an extension of the principle of choice for one man."[6] Society is not merely the individual writ large, as Robert Nozick forcefully pointed out:

> There is no social entity with a good that undergoes some sacrifice for its own good. There are only individual people, with their own individual lives. Using one of these people for the benefit of others uses him and benefits the others. Nothing more. What happens is that something is done to him for the sake of others. Talk of an overall social good covers this up (intentionally?) To use a person in this way does not sufficiently respect and take account of the fact that he is a separate person, that his is the only life he has. He does not get some over balancing good from his sacrifice, and no-one is entitled to force this upon him.[7]

Unless we can give Jones a reason for suffering so that others benefit, there is no justification for utilitarianism, and therefore for many economic policies we take for granted.

One reason we could give him lies in the principle of reciprocity. We should expect Jones to suffer so that Robinson benefits because there may come a time when we require Robinson to suffer for Jones' benefit. Indeed, if all policies fulfil the utilitarian requirement, then in the long run a representative individual will be better off, because what he loses in one policy area one day he may recoup in another the next day.

However, this only works if cost-benefit analysis applies to every single policy. But even many of its supporters do not believe cost-benefit analysis should apply to all policies.[8] After all, people have rights – there are some things we can't do to them, even if to do so would raise average happiness. And this means reciprocity breaks down. What if cost-benefit analysis is not applied to the policy questions where it would benefit Jones? Utilitarianism then is a pure cost to him. How can this be right?

The best attempt to answer this question came from John Harsanyi in the 1950s.[9] Utilitarianism, he said, is what people would choose if they were genuinely neutral and disinterested.

To see his point, imagine you had to choose a social system in complete ignorance of the position you would occupy in it. Let's assume the choice is two societies, each containing 10 members. They are identical in every way but one. Society A contains a central bank which controls inflation, at the expense of making one of its members more than usually vulnerable to unemployment. As a result, 9 of its members have a utility of 10, but one has a utility of just 5. Society B, by contrast, has a softer central bank, so everyone suffers a little from inflation and, we assume, has the same general probability of unemployment as a typical member of society A. Each has a utility of 8.

What would you choose? Harsanyi says you would reason as follows. In society A, I have a 90% chance of getting utility of 10 and a 10% chance of getting utility 5. This gives me an expected utility of 9.5 – that is, $(0.9 \times 10) + (0.1 \times 5)$. In society B, however, I have a 100% chance of utility of 8. 9.5 is clearly higher than 8. I should therefore choose society A.

There is, therefore, a justification for the inflation target. It's what we would choose, if we could slough off our vested interests, and choose on the basis of what Harsanyi calls our "ethical preferences", as distinct from our actual ones. It is therefore legitimate to impose costs on some so that others benefit.

Sadly, however, there are problems with this. One is that it assumes we have no desire to reduce risk. If we did want to do so, we might prefer a certain gain of 8 to an uncertain one of 9.5.

And justice requires that we would be risk-averse when making this choice between societies. Let's say the cost of inflation targeting would fall upon a particular individual – say, the one unskilled member of society. In the original position none of us knows, ex hypothesi, which of us would be this person. By definition, then, being an unskilled worker is something beyond our control. Most of us think it unjust, and certainly undesireable, that we suffer for things we can't control. As John Roemer has written, "the most powerful ethical criticism of utilitarianism is that it is insensitive to inequality of utility among individuals".[10]

In Harsanyi's original position, many of us would want to avoid suffering from this inequality. We might, therefore, choose the society which gave us a certain gain of 8 rather than a chance of just 5, even though aggregate well-being was higher in the latter society.[11]

It's far from obvious, therefore, that Harsanyi's "ethical preferences" lead to utilitarianism.

Not everyone accepts this criticism, however. Its supporters argue that utilitarianism has a bias towards equality, so perhaps risk-averse people would choose the utilitarian principle[12]. Richard Layard writes:

> If money is transferred from a richer person to a poorer person, the poor person gains more happiness than the rich person loses. So average happiness increases. Thus a country will have a higher level of average happiness the more equally its income is distributed – all else being equal.[13]

This is doubtful. It is often the case that if we have more of anything, we gain less from a given increment; the sixth pint never tastes as good as the first. But it doesn't follow that a transfer of income from rich to poor will raise average happiness. This is because rich and poor might well have different utility functions. Indeed, many of the rich are rich precisely because they attach great importance to money; this is why they keep working. This, along with the endowment effect and loss aversion (which we'll meet later) might well mean the rich would lose more than the poor would gain.[14]

Layard is therefore using a weak empirical claim to duck a philosophical question raised by Amartya Sen. He points out, if person A, who is disabled, gets only half the utility from a given income that B, a pleasure-wizard, gets, utilitarianism favours redistribution from the disabled towards the pleasure-wizard[15]. Can that be right?

The moral justification for utilitarianism – imposing costs on some so that others benefit – is therefore weak. For this reason, serious thinkers from many different perspectives have been hostile to the theory. John Roemer writes: "The continued interest in Harsanyi's aggregation theorem among economists, I believe, is sustained only by an incomplete understanding of these ideas."[16] Justice, says John Rawls "does not allow that the sacrifices imposed on a few are outweighed by the larger sum of advantages enjoyed by many." Utilitarianism, he continues "does not take seriously the distinction between persons."[17]

Alasdair MacIntyre says:

> The notion of the greatest happiness of the greatest number is a notion without any clear content at all. It is indeed a pseudo-concept available for a variety of ideological uses, but no more than that.[18]

And Serge-Christophe Kolm has dismissed it as "an English fantasy", which has only ever been taken seriously by economists and English-language philosophers.[19]

Impossibility and all that

If the utilitarian conception of economic efficiency is unacceptable, what can take its place?

To economists, the natural alternative is the notion of Pareto efficiency. This says that policies are efficient if and only if they make at least one person better off and no-one worse off. Unlike utilitarianism, it rules out imposing (uncompensated) losses onto some so that others may gain.

Unfortunately, however, it has problems of its own.

To see them, consider the question of whether the UK should join the European single currency. Imagine three individuals. Person A believes the UK should reject entry now. Failing that, he would prefer to wait and see if the conditions for entry improve. His worst option is to enter. Person B would prefer to wait and see. If he had to make a decision now, however, he would prefer to enter. Person C would prefer to enter now. However, because he believes the costs of waiting – because the uncertainty it creates for businesses leads to lower investment – are high, he would prefer to rule out entry forever than to wait.

These preferences are shown in table 20. What should society choose? The answer is: it's impossible to say. Two out of the three (A and B) prefer waiting to entering. And two out of the three (B and C) prefer entering to staying out. However, two of the three (A and C) also prefer staying out to waiting. There is no clear answer.

Table 20. An impossibility theorem

	Person A	Person B	Person C
1	No	Wait	Yes
2	Wait	Yes	No
3	Yes	No	Wait

This example is no accident. In an important monograph written in 1951, Kenneth Arrow proved that there was no method of voting which resolved paradoxes such as these, as long as four apparently innocuous conditions were fulfilled:[20]

- Weak Pareto optimality. That is, if all citizens prefer one thing to another, so does society.

- Independence of irrelevant alternatives. If a fourth option becomes available in the above case, no-one changes their ranking of the three existing options.
- Non-dictatorship. Everyone's vote counts once, and none more than once.
- Unrestricted domain. We have a free choice over all alternatives.

This result – known as Arrow's impossibility theorem – has some devastating implications. It means the only economic policies that can be clearly deemed to be in the national interest are those upon which everyone is agreed. Anything else would mean that some person's preference is overridden, which Paretianism forbids. And this, in turn, means that economists, if they are to stick to the Pareto principle, might have nothing to say at all. As Kotaro Suzumura has said: "since almost every economic policy cannot but favour some individuals at the cost of disfavouring others, there will be almost no situation of real importance where the Pareto principle can claim direct relevance."[21]

This is because Paretianism, in rejecting the possibility of interpersonal comparisons of welfare, has no means of adjudication when two people's preferences conflict.

Amartya Sen points out just how impoverished is the information Paretianism tries to get away with.[22] Imagine, he says, a Paretian wants to find out who are the best-off people in society. How does he do it? Does he look at who has the most money? No, because money is only one of many goods that give us welfare, and people with lots of money may have few other goods. And even if they have plenty of everything, they may have low welfare simply because they are poor at converting goods into utility. So this won't do. Does he look at who has the most utility? He cannot, because interpersonal comparisons of utility are ruled out. Or does he look at who has the lowest marginal utility with respect to any particular good? Again, no – because this requires both interpersonal comparisons and cardinal welfare. A thoroughgoing Paretian cannot therefore even identify the best-off and worst-off members of society.

And even if he could identify inequalities, he would do nothing about them. It is Pareto-efficient for a man to starve to death in a society of millionaires, if the only way of stopping him doing so is to make one of these millionaires worse off, even if by only a penny.

Majority rule and its variants

Problems such as these have led to efforts to get away from Paretianism. One way of doing this is to relax the conditions which produce Arrow's impossibility theorem. A common relaxation is to permit dictatorship, at least by the majority. "Giving the public what they want" is surely efficient, isn't it?

No. One problem is that the "will of the majority" can be rescued from incoherence only by the choice of an arbitrary voting rule. To see how, return to our imaginary Emu referendum, represented by table 1 (page 44).[23] Now imagine there are nine voters. Four have A's preferences, two have B's and three have C's. This gives us:

4 - No, wait, yes
3 - Yes, no, wait
2 - Wait, yes, no

What does this society choose? It all depends on the voting rule they have. Under a simple first-past-the-post or plurality system, the No option wins. This seems irrational – because the majority would prefer yes to no, given a straight choice between the two.

Alternatively, the choice might be made under the alternative vote system. Here, the wait option is eliminated on the first round of voting, because it gets the fewest first choices. The second preferences of those who chose this option are then transferred. The upshot is that yes wins by five votes (the two second preferences plus the three first preferences) to four.

A third possibility is the so-called Borda count. Given three alternatives, this allots two marks to every first preference and one to every second preference. On this rule, "no" wins, with 11 marks versus 8 each for yes and wait.

The message is clear. Majority rule will not always yield clear-cut results. There are conflicting ways of finding out what the majority wants.

What's more, there is a potential conflict between majority rule and efficiency in the utilitarian sense.[24] Imagine a democratic local council is considering three projects; building a new library, traffic-calming measures, and a swimming pool. Each of these would cost £33 per taxpayer. Assume for simplicity there are three taxpayers. The gross benefits of each scheme to each voter are shown in table 21.

Table 21. How majority rule conflicts with utilitarianism

Benefits, £	Swimming pool	Library	Traffic calming
A	35	35	0
B	35	0	35
C	0	35	35

If there were referenda on each individual project, all three would go ahead – as two voters out of three in each case believe the benefits to them outweigh the £33 cost of each. However, the upshot is that each individual gets only £70 of benefits, but has to pay £99 of taxes – so everyone loses.

There is, of course, a further problem. Majority rule, like utilitarianism, might require that some lose out in order that others benefit. And this is no mere theoretical possibility. For decades ethnic minorities and gays suffered under majority rule. So too do the very worst-off, because governments prefer to redistribute to median voters.

For these reasons, Amartya Sen might well be right: "The method of majority decision is a most peculiar way of dealing with conflicts of interest."[25]

"So good a judge as the man himself"

The problems don't stop here. There's another difficulty which afflicts majority rule, some forms of utilitarianism and Paretianism. All assume that individuals are the best judges of their own interests. As Bentham put it: "No man can be so good a judge as the man himself, what it is gives him pleasure or displeasure."[26]

Mainstream economists, brought up on the notion of consumer sovereignty, take this idea for granted. It is after all, the foundation for free markets. What then could possibly be wrong with extending this principle to policy-making in general?

Plenty. People's preferences can be a poor guide to their true interests. Maximizing efficiency (whatever that means) in terms of preference fulfilment, therefore, might not be the same as maximizing efficiency in terms of people's interests. "It is a mistake to equate the satisfaction of preference with what is good for an agent" say Hausman and Macpherson. "It takes no great philosophical talent to see that giving a powerful motorcycle to a reckless teenage boy does not necessarily make him better off."[27]

There are several reasons why preferences and interests might not coincide.

Ill-informed preferences

The most obvious is simply that preferences may be ill-informed. Imagine there are waste dumps in two towns. In Happyville, the dump is perfectly safe but residents believe it is dangerous, and that if left uncleared it will cause 100 deaths from cancer. In Blissville, however, the dump really is dangerous. If left untreated, it really will kill 100 people. But the residents are blissfully unaware of the risk.[28]

Assuming funds are so limited that only one dump can be cleared, which should the government remove? If we are to satisfy people's stated preferences, it must be Happyville's. If we are to maximise interests, it's Blissville's.

It is not just a lack of information that can cause ill-informed preferences. So too, as I'll show in chapter 13, can cognitive biases; we simply lack the rationality to judge risks correctly.

The endowment effect and loss aversion

Elementary economic theory says the amount we are willing to pay for a benefit should be the same as the amount we would accept as compensation for losing that benefit. The value we put on, say, clean air, should be the same in both cases.

But it isn't. Surveys have found that the minimum amount we are willing to accept (WTA) in compensation is many times higher than the amount we are willing to pay (WTP).[29]

This difference means the perceived efficiency of a project will depend upon the initial distribution of property rights. Whether it is in the public interest to build a by-pass will depend upon whether residents have a right to an unspoilt environment or whether road-builders have a right to build roads. In the former case, high willingness to accept the bypass may mean it does not get built, whereas in the latter case low willingness to pay the road-builders to stop building may mean the by-pass goes ahead.

Adaptive preferences

People often adapt their preferences to their circumstances, so they want only what they can get. Battered slaves, tamed housewives, the broken unemployed may be too easily pleased. As a result, says John Roemer, "counting only their self-conceived senses of welfare in the social calculus would give them too little".[30]

If women had been happy with being underpaid – say, because they felt inferior to men – the Equal Pay Act would never have been passed by a non-paternalistic utilitarian. Nor would such a utilitarian set free a happy slave.

Many believe this shows that preference satisfaction is a poor guide to policy. As Jon Elster asks: "Why should individual want satisfaction be the criterion of justice and social choice when individual wants themselves may be shaped by a process that pre-empts the choice?"[31] What matters, he says, is not merely the existence of preferences, but their origin. Only autonomous preferences should count.

Moral and immoral preferences

It's trivial that some preferences, such as racist ones, can be nasty and should be ignored. But benevolent ones can be a problem too. Some believe morally motivated preferences should also be excluded from the cost-benefit approach, because these introduce a form of double-counting.[32] If I oppose a by-pass not because it will do any harm to me, but because it would upset my friend, my friend's preference counts twice – once in her estimate of the costs and benefits, and once in mine.

All these problems mean that we will not always maximise people's interests by following their preferences. So what do we do?

One possibility of course is that, where we have good evidence that preferences are distorted, policy should be motivated by what experts know our true interests to be.

This won't do. We'll show in chapters 13 and 14 that experts can be as stupid as the rest of us.

Indeed, it's very hard to tell whether preferences are ill-informed or irrational. Will Kymlicka asks:

> How do we know what preferences people would have if they were informed and rational? What religious beliefs, for example, would informed people hold? How do we know when a desire to follow a traditional gender role is an authentic expression of the person's good, as opposed to a merely adaptive preference? What sort of time-discounting is rational – ie, is it irrational to care more about what happens to me today than about what will happen to me tomorrow? The issues involved are complex, yet we need an answer in order to begin the utilitarian calculations.[33]

To see a practical example of this, recall the debate in 1998 about whether young people who preferred to stay off government-supported training schemes should have their welfare benefits cut.

Those who supported this idea said that youngsters' desire to loaf around the house all day was not a true, or well-informed preference. If youngsters were sensible, they said, they would realise a training scheme was best for them. However, many pop stars and actors argued that welfare payments had financed their training and career development. Some youngsters were not lazing around, but developing skills that would later benefit society in the form of high taxes and artistic achievements. Their preference for staying on the dole was therefore reasonable, and in society's interest too, because the taxes paid by one or two millionaire pop stars can pay for thousands of dole payments. Who was right?

Needs, primary goods and capabilities

Luckily, there might be a solution to all these problems. Maybe we should not define efficiency in terms of maximizing welfare at all, in the sense of fulfilling people's preferences or true interests. Maybe we should instead define an efficient society as one which best satisfies people's most urgent needs, or which gives them bundles of primary goods.

This avoids many of the problems involved in measuring and comparing individual well-being by taking a narrower conception of what well-being is, or at least of the extent to which governments should increase well-being.

This view is closely associated with John Rawls. He proposed that policy-makers should focus not upon well-being but instead upon "expectations of primary social goods." These are those things "which it is supposed a rational man wants whatever else he wants".[34] Elsewhere he defined them as: basic liberties; freedom of movement and choice of occupation; positions of responsibility and powers of office; income and wealth; and the "social bases of self-respect":[35]

Now, Rawls did not propose merely maximizing primary goods. He was concerned with their distribution as well – which is why his most famous book was called *A Theory of Justice*, not *A Theory of Efficiency*. Nevertheless, we might think of efficiency in terms of maximising primary goods rather than a fuller conception of well-being.

Such a conception of efficiency conflicts with other conceptions. For example:

- *Economic growth.* Maximizing national income requires society's most talented people to be forced to work very long hours. The primary goods conception of efficiency rules this out, as freedom of choice of occupation is a primary good.

- *Preference fulfillment.* Primary goods efficiency will give people education and healthcare, whether they want them or not.

- *Pareto optimality.* Primary goods efficiency may require that some goods that enhance subjective well-being – for example the incomes of the rich – be destroyed in order to increase the numbers of primary goods. This makes some people worse off, in important senses, so that others might benefit.

Sadly, however, this theory has its own flaws. One says Amartya Sen, is that the focus on primary goods is fetishistic. What matters, he says, is not what goods we have, but what goods do for us. He says:

Two persons holding the same bundle of primary goods can have very different freedoms to pursue their respective conceptions of the good...To judge equality – or for that matter efficiency – in the space of primary goods amounts to giving priority to the means of freedom over any assessment of the ends of freedom.[36]

Some people – such as the disabled – need more goods to achieve the same level of functioning as the rest of us. Allocating goods without regard for what they do for people might not therefore be very efficient or equitable. He proposed replacing a concern with primary goods with one with capabilities; this would require giving more goods to those, such as the handicapped, who were bad at converting goods into functioning as full members of society.

There is another problem, pressed by John Roemer[37]. Different people, he says, will need different primary goods or capabilities to fulfil whatever life-plans they have. Some, for example, can live happily without positions of office or power, whilst needing a high income. Others have the opposite need. And many – especially in far eastern societies – seem to get by happily without the extensive liberties upon which Rawls laid such emphasis. Indeed, Michael Walzer has gone so far as to argue that "there is no single set of primary or basic goods conceivable across all moral and material worlds".[38]

What's more, some primary goods may conflict with each other. Giving people a high income regardless of their contribution to society, for example, might reduce their sense of self-esteem.

How, then, do we decide which bundle of primary goods is allocated? One possibility is for the government to give everyone a bundle, and let them trade. But this won't do, because many of the goods are untradeable. I cannot, for example, sell to you my right to vote or my right to free health care, even if I would like to. The alternative, therefore, is that the allocation of primary goods be related to individuals' conceptions of their own welfare. But this leaves us with exactly the problems of measuring individuals' welfare that we are trying to get away from.

To Thomas Scanlon, this misses the point.[39] What matters, he says, is not just what the individual wants, but what society has an obligation to provide. Society (meaning other people) is obliged to give us the basic means of achieving a good life. But it's not obliged to make us happy.

Efficiency as process

So far, we've considered efficiency in terms of outcomes. But is this right? Mightn't it be better to think of an efficient outcome not as one that satisfies some pre-ordained outcome, such as maximising happiness, well-being or wealth, but rather one that has arisen from free agreements based upon acceptable institutions? In other words, the role of government is not to maximise any end, but to provide the framework in which individuals can pursue their own ends. John Gray has stressed this:

> The aggregative method of...welfare economics has an inherent collectivist bias, in that it seeks to enhance imaginary maxima rather than to reform or extend markets so as better to enable individuals to achieve their diverse and incommensurable goals.[40]

To see what this entails, imagine there are just two of us. We would both freely agree to any schemes that make us both better off, in whatever sense we choose to conceive of this term. And we would both reject proposals that make us worse off. The only possible sticking points come with schemes that would make one of us better off and the other worse off. In such cases, we would negotiate. If the gains to you outweigh my losses, we will soon find some payment that would benefit us both. We just don't need any measure of aggregate well-being.

Why, then, does this process not work for large groups? One important reason is that property rights are not clearly assigned. It is unclear whether country dwellers have a right to an unspoiled neighbourhood or road-builders have a right to build roads. With this issue unresolved, questions of efficiency are often mixed up with questions of rights.

Secondly, there are transaction costs – there are often simply too many of us to reach agreement.

Thirdly, and relatedly, there are some cases where winners simply cannot compensate losers, often because the two groups simply cannot be identified.

There are possible solutions, or at least ameliorations, of these problems. One is to create markets in contingent securities which would ameliorate the losses. If there were unemployment-contingent assets, or bypass-contingent assets, people who stood to lose from an inflation target or road-building scheme would be able to buy compensation against the possibility of losing out.

Secondly, if property rights were assigned clearly, there would be a basis for negotiation between possible winners and losers.

Thirdly, governments must ensure that potential losers are as content as possible. Where compensation cannot be paid, these must at least feel as if their voice has been heard, their interests given full consideration, and the reasons for the policy fully and sympathetically explained to them. This means these must be treated as fellow members of society, rather than as the "enemy within" or the "underclass."

And above all, it means policy-making processes must be open and truly democratic – so that losers really can be heard. This should be no great loss – because if there is no coherent end-state conception of efficiency, there can be no justification for policies being handed down from on-high by know-all technocrats.

A dream of dentists

The message of all this is straightforward. There is no single notion of what's efficient, or what's in the national interest, which can justifiably command our assent. Blair's famous claim that "what matters is what works" is therefore incoherent. It invites the question: works by what standard? And it requires that this particular standard be justified. That requires political and philosophical argument, not mere assertion.

The arguments should be about three issues.

One is: what is it that's really good for us? Is it the fulfilment of our preferences, whether these are well-informed or not? Or objective well-being even if we don't like it much? Or a set of primary goods such as freedom, self-respect and income? Or just capabilities?

Secondly, how can we trade off one person's welfare (however this is defined) against another's? And what right do we have to impose losses onto some so that others benefit?

Thirdly, what should government do for us anyway? Should it really be concerned with making us happy? Or should it provide only our basic needs? Or should it merely lay down a framework of institutions and liberties that allow us to best pursue our own ends?

In practice, though, these arguments don't happen. Instead, our rulers have a pick'n'mix attitude to efficiency. Sometimes – such as in the choice of an inflation target – policies are justified on paternalistic utilitarian grounds. Other policies – such as the provision of free health and education – are motivated by a Rawlsian desire to provide the maximum possible level of primary goods. Yet others – such as greater support for the disabled or older pensioners – have in mind Sen's view that individuals' capabilities should be increased in cases where people are bad at converting goods into functionings. And others – such as the desire to cajole the young or long-term unemployed into work or training schemes – rest on a view that policy should be guided by idealized rational preferences, rather than actual ones. And very rarely, policies are guided by more than one criterion of efficiency. The decision to join or stay out of Europe's single currency will be taken first by a paternalistic utilitarian assessment of whether entry would be in "the national economic interest" – where this is defined simply as maximising output – and then by majority rule.

You might think this melange represents a decent, tolerable, response to the fact that different concepts of efficiency have different strengths in different areas.

But is it? Is it instead evidence that what Alasdair MacIntyre said of morality may also be true of efficiency?

> What many of us are educated into is not a coherent way of thinking and judging, but one constructed out of an amalgam of social and cultural fragments inherited both from different traditions from which our culture was originally derived...and from different stages in and aspects of the development of modernity.[41]

The bottom line here is clear. Keynes was wrong. He dreamed that one day, economists would be thought of as "humble, competent people, on a level with dentists".[42] But this is an impossible dream. Not only is there no agreed-upon ideal of a healthy mouth, but each tooth has its own life to live and interests to pursue. To pull some out so that others may thrive is, for a dentist, a straightforward task. For an economist, nothing could be harder, either technically or morally. They cannot be mere technicians. They misunderstand their discipline if they imagine otherwise.

And of course, the same is true for politicians. The managerialist idea that "efficiency" is a clearly defined obvious value is a fiction.

And it's a dangerous fiction. As Martha Nussbaum has written, cost-benefit analysis provides a ready answer to the question: "what should we do?" But, she says, there is a second question: are any of the courses of action open to us free from serious moral wrong-doing?[43] Often, the answer is no. When we raise interest rates to reduce inflation, we throw some people out of work so that others can benefit. When we build a new road we destroy the dreams of rural tranquillity that local residents cherished for lifetimes. And when we cut welfare benefits we make life tougher for some so that others may gain.

In all cases harm is done. People are hurt. Talk of "efficiency" or the national interest disguises this fact. And it distracts us from the need to talk directly to these losers, and to justify the pain we inflict upon them. At best, this is socially divisive. At worst, it's downright cruel. You can't keep moral questions out of politics.

Notes

1. Quoted in *Sunday Telegraph,* March 18 2001.

2. *The General Theory of Employment, Interest and Money,* p383.

3. Hasan Bakhshi, Andrew Haldane and Neal Hatch – *Some Costs and Benefits of Price Stability in the United Kingdom,* Bank of England working paper 78, March 1998. Strictly speaking, their analysis does not justify the current inflation target. This target is symmetric, so undershoots of the target are as much to be avoided as overshoots. According to the Bank analysis, though, efforts to raise inflation are anti-utilitarian, as the costs outweigh the benefits. I shall not pursue this point, except to note that it just shows how even apparently technocratic policies are less rooted in research than our rulers like to pretend.

4. "Welfare propositions of economics and interpersonal comparisons of utility", *Economic Journal,* 49, September 1939, p549-52, p550.

5. J.J.C.Smart – "An outline of a system of utilitarian ethics" p37 in Smart and Williams, *Utilitarianism: For and Against.*

6. *A Theory of Justice,* p28-9.

7. *Anarchy, State and Utopia,* p32-3.

8. See for example Adler and Posner, "Implementing CBA when preferences are distorted", p275 in Adler and Posner (eds), *Cost-Benefit Analysis.*

9. What follows draws on "Cardinal welfare, individualistic ethics and interpersonal comparisons of utility", *Journal of Political Economy,* 63, August 1955, p309-21, and "Morality and the theory of rational behaviour", in Sen and Williams (eds) – *Utilitarianism and Beyond.*

10. *Theories of Distributive Justice,* p160.

11. This, of course, was the insight which led John Rawls to argue that choices in the original position would lead not to utilitarianism, but to his "difference principle", in which inequalities were acceptable only if they benefited the least advantaged members of society. See *A Theory of Justice* p14-15. The two dominant philosophical positions of our age, it seems, rest upon assumptions about the utility function of hypothetical uninformed individuals.

12. R.M. Hare, "Ethical theory and utilitarianism", p27, in Sen and Williams (eds).

13. *Happiness,* p52.

14. I'm erring on the side of generosity to Layard here. There are many other problems with his claim. What about the "leaky bucket", whereby cash

transfers from rich to poor get lost as bureaucrats grab their share? Do the rich have a right to the money they've earned? And what's unique about money? Why not force beautiful women to have sex with lonely men, as this too would raise average happiness?

15. "Equality of what?" p 357, in his *Choice, Welfare and Measurement*.

16. *Theories of Distributive Justice*, p145.

17. *A Theory of Justice*, p4, 27.

18. *After Virtue*, p64.

19. *Modern Theories of Justice*, p187, 405.

20. *Social Choice and Individual Values*, p59.

21. "Paretian welfare judgments and Bergsonian social choice", *Economic Journal*, 109, April 1999, p204-220, p204.

22. "Personal utilities and public judgments: or what's wrong with welfare economics?" in *Choice, Welfare and Measurement*, p336.

23. The following draws on Robert Sugden – *The Political Economy of Public Choice*, p138-40.

24. What follows draws on James Buchanan, *The Limits of Liberty*, p155.

25. *Introduction to Choice, Welfare and Measurement*, p13.

26. *The Principles of Morals and Legislation*, p172.

27. *Economics and Moral Philosophy*, p63-4, p73.

28. "Risk equity" p31, in Matthew Adler and Eric Posner (eds), *Cost-Benefit Analysis*.

29. See Daniel Kahneman, Jack Knetsch and Richard Thaler, "Experimental tests of the endowment effect and the Coase theorem", p168, in Richard Thaler, *Quasi-Rational Economics*.

30. *Theories of Distributive Justice*, p190.

31. Jon Elster – "Sour grapes: utilitarianism and the genesis of wants" in Sen and Williams (eds) – *Utilitarianism and Beyond*, p219.

32. Adler and Posner, "Implementing CBA when preferences are distorted", p276 in Adler and Posner (eds), *Cost-Benefit Analysis*.

33. *Contemporary Political Philosophy*, p16-17.

34. Rawls argued that a just society was one which maximised the bundle of primary goods owned by the least advantaged. In what follows, we shall focus only upon whether primary goods, rather than welfare, are a superior measure of welfare for policy purposes. We shall return to Rawls' distributive theory in chapter 12.

35. "Social utility and primary goods" in Sen and Williams (eds) – *Utilitarianism and Beyond*, p162.

36. *Inequality Re-examined*, p8.

37. *Theories of Distributive Justice*, p167.

38. *Spheres of Justice*, p8.

39. "The moral basis of interpersonal comparisons" p39 in Elster and Roemer (eds), *Interpersonal Comparisons of Well-being*, p36.

40. *Post-Liberalism*, p55.

41. *Whose Justice? Which Rationality?* p2.

42. "Economic possibilities for our grandchildren" in *Essays in Persuasion*, p332.

43. "The costs of tragedy; some moral limits of CBA", in Adler and Posner (eds), *Cost-Benefit Analysis*.

12.

A Wild Goose Chase

Egalitarian devices are a wild goose chase after the unachievable (Joseph Raz[1].)

Men will never establish an equality which will content them. (Alexis de Tocqueville[2])

It's often said that Blair has abandoned Labour's commitment to equality. This is wrong. As we saw in chapter 3, Old Labour failed to achieve equality. And, if we are to judge him by words, Blair is quite egalitarian:

Our goal is a Britain...in which we achieve true equality – equal status and equal opportunity rather than equality of outcome. It must be a Britain in which we continue to redistribute power, wealth and opportunity to the many, not the few.[3]

New Labour pursues, in word or deed, four types of equality:

- *Equal status.* This is the notion that, whatever the differences between us, we are all in some sense equal members of the community, deserving of equal regard. This idea, Tony Blair has said, "is what has driven me all my political life".[4]
- *Equal opportunity.* This, says Gordon Brown, "lies at the core of our beliefs".[5]
- *Equal incomes.* Although New Labour rarely argues explicitly for this, and it has not reduced income equality yet, it is clearly the goal of many of its policies. Tax credits, the National Minimum Wage, the target of abolishing child poverty and the pensioners' minimum income guarantee are all aimed at reducing inequalities of income.
- *Endowment equality.* Traditionally, the welfare state has attempted to equalize incomes and power whilst leaving the sources of these inequalities untouched. However, New Labour is going deeper than this. One reason for its concern to increase basic educational standards is to reduce inequalities in skills – to increase endowment equalities.

This raises lots of questions. What – if anything – is so good about these equalities? Are they mutually compatible or do they conflict with each other? What other conceptions of equality is New Labour missing? And why, after

10 years in office, are we so far away from achieving these equalities?

I'll argue in this chapter that – again – managerialism is a big part of the problem. New Labour's managerialist ideology stops it thinking clearly about the fundamental moral question of which equality is desireable and why? Its commitment to hierarchy means equal status and a redistribution of power will never be achieved. And its faith in the state and continual busyness are obstacles to equality.

Let's start by considering the appeal of these different equalities.

Equality of resources

What is the moral case for redistributing income to poorer working parents?

You wouldn't guess from New Labour's rhetoric, but the best case was put by Ronald Dworkin[6]. He proposed that inequalities resulting from inequalities in natural talents should be reduced by redistribution.

The thinking here is that people with a lack of natural talent are victims of two market failures.

First, they are suffering from a missing insurance market. Being born with a poor genetic endowment, or into a bad family, or even into an era when our skills happen to be in low demand, are forms of individual bad luck. In theory, this is something we should be able to insure against. However, we cannot do so in practice, because we cannot buy insurance before we are born.

To see the second market failure, imagine a future world in which artificial intelligence has advanced so far as to make human intelligence redundant, and in which genetic engineering has rendered physical beauty commonplace. In such a world, intelligence and beauty would command no premium. But perhaps brute physical strength or stupidity would.

However, because mankind has not yet invented time travel, the strong and stupid cannot move into this era, where their attributes are most valued.

This is a sort of market failure, called factor immobility. Just as labour markets fail to work properly if people cannot move to areas where their skills are in demand, so they fail to work if people cannot move to times when their services are most valued.

Now, it is a perfectly legitimate task of government to correct market failures. Dworkin proposes that it does just this. It should, he says, organise a redistribution of resources between people that replicates the inter-personal transfers that would have occurred, had people been able to take out insurance before they were conceived.

Before being born, people would take out insurance against having low skills. In today's world, therefore, there should be transfers from skilled people to unskilled ones.

The virtue of this, says Dworkin, is that it recognises a place for individual responsibility. We would not insure against being lazy so we should not get any benefit from society by being so. The distribution of income would be "endowment insensitive" but "ambition sensitive." People would not suffer if they are born without talents or into a bad home, but they would suffer if they make bad choices or are lazy.

This is what New Labour has tried to do. The thinking here is that, in conditions of reasonably full employment, you can get a job if you really want one. The unemployed are therefore lacking ambition or have a taste for leisure. We shouldn't transfer resources to them because of this. However, a low wage is a sign of a lack of ability but no lack of effort. This is something we would want to insure against before we are born, so it is legitimate to transfer resources to such people. Hence the case for working tax credits.

Similarly, people obviously can't help being born into a poor home. It might therefore be something they would want to insure against, before being born. Hence the case for wanting to abolish child poverty.

Unfortunately, there are problems with Dworkin's idea. One is that redistribution might not go far enough.

Imagine two people, Ann and Barbara, who are identical before being conceived (we'll ignore the awkward metaphysical problems this raises)[7]. Both insure against being born with low skills. Ann, however, escapes the handicap of low skills, while Barbara doesn't. Under Dworkin's scheme Ann transfers cash to Barbara. However, unless the transfer is so big as to equalize their final levels of well-being, Barbara has suffered from no fault of her own.

Is this really equitable? If not, redistribution doesn't go far enough.

A second problem is that Dworkin's distinction between endowments and ambition might not be meaningful or robust.

Consider Jim Royle, who lounges around the house all day. We think he's lazy, got no ambition. In Dworkin's (and New Labour's) thinking, he doesn't particularly deserve redistribution.

But then, imagine a "hard work gene" were discovered, which Jim happens to lack. Suddenly, he's gone from lacking ambition to lacking a valuable endowment.

The distinction between endowments and resources rests, therefore, upon a conception of human nature that might change over time.

There's a solution to this, though. It's to recognise that Dworkin was onto something when he tried to distinguish between what we are responsible for and what we are not, but that he put the distinction in the wrong place. As Julian Le Grand says: "The relevant distinction for equity purposes is not between preferences and resources, but between factors that are beyond an individual's control and those that are not."[8]

Two versions of equality of opportunity

This distinction leads naturally to the principle of equality of opportunity. If we give people equality of opportunity, we equalize the factors beyond their control. Inequalities will then be due to factors within their control. This seems fair, doesn't it?

Sadly, there are lots of problems here. One is that equal opportunity is ambiguous. There are two different conceptions:[9]

1. Non-discrimination, or the idea that careers should be open to all talents. This requires that in the competition for positions, all candidates with relevant attributes be considered – that no-one be excluded from a university place or job for which they are qualified on the grounds of race, gender or class.

2. Levelling the playing field. This requires that those from disadvantaged backgrounds should get help to raise their chances of success to the same level as others.

To see the difference, consider a university admissions tutor who has to select a candidate for one vacancy. Charlotte comes from a wealthy, settled family and a good school. She has high exam grades. Kylie comes from a poor home and went to a bad school and has worse grades. However, the tutor judges that to achieve these grades required much harder work than Charlotte displayed.

Whom should the admissions tutor select? Non-discrimination says Charlotte. Even if her merit is largely the result of her favourable background, we should not discriminate against her on the grounds of class. But levelling the playing field requires him to select Kylie, because he should compensate for differences in the candidates' backgrounds which have affected their relative chances of success.

This highlights a crucial difference between the two conceptions of equal opportunity. According to the non-discrimination principle, what matters is the candidate's merit. Whether she worked hard to attain this merit, or it came naturally, is irrelevant. According to the levelling the playing field principle, however, effort is important. Kylie is more entitled to a place than Charlotte by virtue of her hard work. After all, says the levelling the playing field principle, it is unfair to penalise an individual for something – the quality of her education – for which she is not responsible. And if people are responsible for their effort, it makes sense to reward the harder working candidate.

New Labour seems to support both these versions of equal opportunity. When Laura Spence – a bright middle-class student from a northern state school – was rejected by Oxford University in 1999, Gordon Brown described it as a scandal. But he did not fuss about the rejection of hard-working candidates with worse grades from poorer schools. That suggests he favours the non-discrimination principle. On the other hand, however, New Labour is keen to improve the worst schools, which suggests they accept a levelling the playing field principle.

Despite this conflation, it is sensible to consider the two versions separately.

Equal opportunity as non-discrimination

So, what can be said in favour of equality of opportunity as non-discrimination? Mr Brown claims it is economically beneficial. He's said: "our economy can never reach its full potential unless everyone in our country has the opportunity to develop their talents to the full."[10]

This raises several questions. One is: why should maximizing income have priority over justice? After all, as we've seen in chapter 10, the ethical value of economic growth is dubious.

The second problem is that there's no reason to suppose that jobs will expand to maximise the use of people's full talents. As we saw in chapter 6, over-qualification is common, even at recent levels of education.

What's more, there's a long tradition which says that economic success depends upon us not using our talents to the full. Adam Smith – whom Brown claims to have read – wrote:

> In the progress of the division of labour, the employment of the far greater part of those who live by labour, that is, of the great body of people, comes to be confined to a few simple operations, frequently to one or two...The man whose whole life is spent in performing a few simple operations, of which the effects are perhaps always the same, or very nearly the same, has no occasion to exert his understanding or to exercise his invention...He naturally loses therefore the habit of such exertion and generally becomes as stupid and ignorant as it is possible for a human creature to become.[11]

And there's a long Marxist tradition – of which Harry Braverman's classic *Labour and Monopoly Power* is the zenith – which points out that capitalists are incessantly trying to routinize the labour process in an effort to de-skill – and therefore disempower – workers.

Brown's view that maximal development of talents is an "economic necessity"[12] is therefore dubious. It rests upon the sort of futurological claim of which managerialists are fond – but which might not be true.

There's a further problem. Why should we be rewarded for our talents? Sure, there's usually an economic case for paying talented people more, or for giving university places to the smartest applicants. But the case in justice is weak.

Many believe our talents and abilities are a matter of luck. We cannot be responsible for them. We are merely members of what Michael Young called "the lucky sperm club".[13] And why should we benefit from this? It would be abhorrent for me to prosper because I have a white skin. So why should I prosper because I have some natural talent? Both are things I have through no merit of my own.

To John Rawls, this is a clinching argument against regarding equal opportunity as a sufficient egalitarianism – because it "permits distributive shares to be improperly influenced by ... factors so arbitrary from a moral point of view".[14] It puts the line between responsibility and luck in the wrong place.

Levelling the playing field

Levelling the playing field (LPF) attempts to address this problem. It goes to great pains to distinguish between what an individual can control and what he cannot. The aim of LPF is "to fully compensate people precisely for that aspect of their situations for which they are not responsible." says John Roemer. "Society should indemnify people against poor outcomes that are the consequences of causes beyond their control, but not against outcomes that are the consequences of causes within their control."[15]

In equalizing those things for which individuals are not responsible, LPF ensures that the remaining inequalities reflect free choices. "Before the competition starts, opportunities must be equalized, by social intervention if need be, but after it begins, individuals are on their own" says Roemer.[16]

I guess this might be intuitively appealing to many social democrats. But we only need to see how Roemer proposes to implement LPF to see how far removed it is from what New Labour has done.

Imagine we are deciding how to allocate educational resources – although the same process can apply to a wide variety of problems. Roemer proposes that this is done in three steps.

First, we divide children into types, where types are defined according to circumstances beyond a child's control which influence her ability to process educational resources into achievement. These types may be race, class, or family structure.

Second, we ensure that within each type, each child gets the same resources. If this is the case, differences in achievement within each type will reflect differences in effort.

Third, we spend different amounts on different types, to ensure that average achievement is equalized across types.

If this process is followed, says Roemer, "the influence of children's backgrounds on the difference in abilities to combine effort and resources into future output should be entirely compensated for in the distribution of educational resources".[17]

Sounds reasonable? No. Such a process would mean, say, that black boys from single parent families do as well, on average, at school as white girls from two-parent families. This is what it means to eliminate the involuntary disadvantage of being born black in a white society.

To achieve this, though, would require massive increases in spending on educating black boys. One US study has estimated that up to 10 times as much would have to be spent, per capita, on blacks as on whites[18]. It might also require cutting spending on the education of people who currently do well at school – such as those of Indian and Chinese backgrounds. Sceptical readers might not think this practical.

Indeed, it might well be cheaper to tolerate the inequalities of educational opportunities between blacks and Indians, and redistribute income through the tax system.

This highlights a counter-intuitive fact about equality of opportunity. People often think of it as "equality-lite", an easier and more practical form of equality than equality of income. But this is not so.

There's a further problem. Why, asks Hillel Steiner, should it be society that should compensate the individual for her involuntary disadvantages[19]? If a student gets a bad education, or suffers disadvantage from being born into a single parent family, why should the rest of us pay compensation rather than the parents or poor teachers involved?

John Stuart Mill was clear on this – parents should pay. He proposed that people only be allowed to have children if they could show that they could afford to educate them, and advocated that fathers be fined if their children were unable to read and write.[20]

But it's not just practical problems that bedevil Roemer's scheme. There's also a moral problem – why should we reward effort rather than talent or being born into a rich home?

Our instinct is that it's because we are responsible for our effort, but not for our talents or family background.

But is this true? One problem is that a capacity for hard work might be a talent just like any other. Maybe some people have a talent for self-discipline and effort. Such a talent might be, in Rawls' words, "arbitrary from a moral point of view."

Also, natural talents and hard work are often complements. If we think we have a particular talent, we naturally work hard to cultivate it. If our natural talents are undeserved, our effort will then be undeserved. Allowing outcomes to depend on effort therefore does not necessarily put the line between responsibility and luck in the right place, because effort too may be a matter of luck.

It seems, therefore, that LPF might be unjust as well as expensive. It is hard to disagree with Fluerbaey's conclusion. Any principle of equal opportunity, he says, is "empty, inefficient, unfeasible and it relies on a shaky sociological and philosophical basis".[21]

Equality of status

New Labour's other ideal of equality is Blair's notion of equal status. Inequality is bad because it is a form of social exclusion. R.H.Tawney expressed this 70 years ago:

> What is repulsive is not that one man should earn more than others...It is that some classes should be excluded from the heritage of civilisation which others enjoy, and that the fact of human fellowship, which is ultimate and profound, should be obscured by economic contrasts.[22]

Again, it seems that equality is not a fundamental goal in itself, but rather a means to an end – in this case, a sense of community. New Labour, Blair has boasted, "is building a community where citizens are of equal worth".[23]

But what's so valuable about a community? Community, Blair's said "is where they know your name and where they miss you if you're not there." This might be a nice ideal for a local area. But it's either meaningless or deeply sinister when applied to a whole country.

And it might not even be such a nice idea for small areas. When they know your name, they often take a censorious and illiberal attitude to your personal life. For decades, gay men would move from small areas to big cities, where no-one knew their name – where they were free. And tight-knit communities can be hostile to new-comers, to immigrants.

This trade-off between community and liberty is clear in the policy proposals of some social egalitarians. Mickey Kaus has advocated replacing the voluntary army with conscription, introducing civilian national service, and coercing the unemployed or single parent families into low-paid work.[24] Such measures may be necessary to break down social barriers and integrate the "underclass" into society. But let's not fool ourselves into thinking they can be achieved at no cost to freedom, or without creating a potentially destabilising degree of resentment.

There's not just a conflict between social equality and liberty, though. There's also a conflict between managerialism and social equality.

The essence of managerialism is flatly opposed to social equality. Managerialism says there are some people – leaders, experts – who can transform society for the better. It therefore invites us to give such people more respect, worth and power than others – to do the exact opposite of Blair's rhetoric, and redistribute power to the few, not the many.

It's no surprise, therefore, that there's a gulf between rhetoric and action. The salient fact about New Labour is that it has done nothing whatever to equalize status within the organizations it runs. The civil service is as inegalitarian – lethally so – as it was in 1997. And there's been no effort to convert schools and hospitals into more egalitarianly managed structures. The state is far more hierarchical – far more opposed to the concept of equal status – than any investment bank.

Conflicts between equalities

It seems, therefore, that New Labour's different ideals of equality might not be as attractive as they seem.

And here's another problem – in some respects, they are mutually inconsistent. We can't have them all.

I say "in some respects" because this is not universally true. The ideal of more equal resources, for example, might well be a help, not hindrance, to the goal of equal opportunity. It seems that countries with a more equal distribution of incomes have more social mobility.[25]

In other respects, though, there are conflicts. As we've seen, the two conceptions of equality of opportunity conflict. Non-discrimination says we should merely hire the most talented candidate. Levelling the playing field says we should ensure that everyone has equal chance to be the most talented candidate.

There's also a conflict between equality of resources and equality of respect, especially in a society in which politicians are terrified of arguing coherently for redistribution. People who receive benefits are regarded as "claimants", whilst taxpayers are regarded as "contributors." There's inequality of respect there, mitigated only by the state's equal harassment of benefit recipients and taxpayers.

And there's a conflict between non-discrimination and equality of resources. It's trivial that equal opportunity will lead to inequalities in market rewards, as some get good jobs and others don't. What's more awkward for egalitarians is that the rhetoric of non-discrimination undermines the case for income redistribution.

Advocates of non-discrimination think it acceptable for someone to get a job on the basis of their talent, but not their family connections. Why the difference? The answer can only be, as Brian Barry has pointed out, that they believe in self-ownership[26]. They think a man's ability is legitimately his own, and that he is entitled to whatever flows to it, whereas a man's family connections are somehow not his, and so he is not entitled to what flows from them.

This invites the libertarian riposte: if my merits entitle me to a job with an income of £1 million a year, why should the state take a large chunk of that £1 million? How can I be entitled to a job, but not to the full benefits from it?

It is hard to defend both equal opportunity and redistributive taxation.

There's one final conflict – between either conception of equal opportunity and equal status.

If we had equal opportunity, the worst-off would be badly off because of their own fault, their inability to take their opportunities. Poverty would no longer be seen as an unfortunate accident or the result of injustice, but the result of their own failure. The poor would then suffer self-loathing and the lack of respect of others. Not for them the dignity and self-respect of the traditional working class.

Meanwhile, the successful would believe they deserve their success. That would lead to a ruthless contempt for the worst-off. As Michael Young put it "if the rich and powerful were encouraged by the general culture to believe that they fully deserved all they had, how arrogant they could become, and, if they were convinced it was all for the common good, how ruthless in pursuing their own advantage".[27]

All this would destroy any sense of community. "The only kind of solidarity likely to emerge ... is a certain arrogant esprit de corps of the successful and a shared depression amongst the unsuccessful" says John

Baker[28]. Equal opportunity combined with unequal rewards could, said Bernard Williams, "lead to a quite inhuman society".[29]

Can the state achieve equality?

So, New Labour's ideals of equality are of dubious merit, and mutually contradictory.

This might help explain why inequality has proved unattainable.

But there is, however, a deeper problem. Maybe the state is the wrong tool for achieving equality.

Social democrats have always believed that, if only they can control the state, greater equality would follow. However, there's abundant evidence that even social democratic states not only fail to achieve equality, but actually increase some inequalities. Consider the evidence:

- We take it for granted that the worst state schools are generally in the poorest areas of the country – this has been the case for decades. This means the state often transforms inequalities in children's backgrounds into inequalities of educational achievement – inequalities that affect entire lives.

- As we saw in chapter 9, the post-tax and benefit distribution of income has barely changed at all under New Labour.

- The police force is still racist. Blacks are eight times more likely than whites to be stopped and searched – although they are not eight times more likely to have committed crimes.[30] The state therefore violates even the most basic notion of equality – the idea of racial equality before the law.

- The "Whitehall studies" of the 1960s found that senior civil servants lived longer than junior ones. Within its own machinery the state creates inequalities of status that are literally deadly.[31]

- As we saw in chapter 3, the post-war welfare state increased inequality, as Tony Blair himself has recognised.

But why does the state fail to achieve equality? To the traditional left, it's because politicians have not been truly committed to the cause.

It's not as simple as this. There are deep reasons why the state is not a force for equality.

The trade-off between justice and democracy

Our supposedly abstract philosophical conceptions of equality can be coloured by the facts about which groups get politically organised and which do not. Before feminists and anti-racists became active in the 1960s and

1970s, social democrats tended to under-estimate the importance of racial and sexual inequalities and over-state the importance of earnings inequalities among organised white trades unionists. Racial and sexual inequalities were not less acute in the 1950s than in the 1970s – it is just that they were out of sight, out of mind.

This raises a disturbing possibility. Could it be that our egalitarianisms are perverted in favour of those disadvantaged people with voice and against those without it – that they therefore penalise the most disadvantaged people of all? Could it be that our neglect of the suffering of poor nations, or of indigenous peoples in the US and Australia, or of the mentally ill, or even of our so-called underclass, owes less to sociological and philosophical reasoning than to the fact that these just happen to be politically unorganised?

Perhaps, therefore, democracy itself rules out equality. Certainly, it does so in theory. Democracy permits – indeed requires – the wealthy 51% of voters to take resources away from the poorest 49%. Luckily, this rarely happens so crudely. But it can happen in scarcely less obvious ways – as, for example, when parents in an affluent areas campaign successfully for better schools whilst parents in poorer ones are less able to do so.

What's more, the most painful inequalities are often those suffered by minorities, which remain unredressed by democracies. Consider a stylized fact about how policies to help the poor may worsen the condition of the very worst-off.[32] As the numbers of poor fall, the first effect is to increase equality. However, as this happens, the poverty that remains is seen less and less as a social creation requiring a policy response, and increasingly as the result of individual failure. What's more, the culture of group self-help and the community ties that protected people can be destroyed as the numbers involved in them fall. In this way, a society in which many are well off and a few are badly off may contain more hurtful inequalities than a society in which many are poor.

This is no mere parable. Some believe the creation of the Beveridge Welfare State in the 1940s undermined friendly societies, charity and private insurance which had adequately protected many workers. And compare our attitudes to young people without qualifications now to those 50 years ago. Then, the perceived lack of education for all meant these carried no stigma. Today they do.

These are not the only problems. Democracy may compel governments to put the line between luck and responsibility in the wrong place. An acceptable egalitarianism might involve big redistributions towards people in third-world countries, as these are not responsible for their hardship. But it would not entail giving money to parents with big families, as their hardship is freely chosen.[33] Democracy, however, compels us to do the opposite of this. Democracy and justice may therefore conflict.

The state is the wrong size

Another problem is that the nation state is often the wrong size for the job of redistribution. A laboratory experiment by Norman Frohlich and Joe Oppenheimer shows one reason why.

They found that when people were put into small groups and asked to agree upon a system for distributing the rewards for work, there was widespread support for redistribution. Subjects were then put to work on a tiresome task – checking spelling errors in the writings of sociologist Talcott Parsons – being paid by the number of errors they spotted. After one work period, one subject realised that his colleague had not found a single error. In protest at having to subsidize him, the subject put down his pen and stared at him. On realising this person was in fact trying hard, and was simply a poor proof-reader, the subject frantically resumed work to make up for lost time.[34]

The message of this is that when we can see that other people are trying, we don't mind subsidizing them. In reality, however, the poor and unemployed are cut off from us. We can't tell whether they are trying to help themselves or not. Fearing that we may be taken for mugs by free-riders, we therefore resist redistribution towards them.

This raises a disturbing possibility for egalitarians – perhaps nation-states are often too big to achieve the fellow-feeling or sense of social equality which is necessary for there to be stable widespread support for redistributive policies. Is it really a coincidence that the most egalitarian nations tend to be small and traditionally mono-cultural, such as the Scandinavian countries?

The racist Welfare State

Being too big, though, is not the only problem with the state. It might be that the nation state is also too small to correct the greatest inequalities of all – those between rich and poor countries.

For this reason, some critics of the welfare state have alleged that it is simply racist – as it redistributes income towards it own members even though these are much richer than most of the world's people. As Hayek has taunted: "What socialists proclaim as a duty towards the fellow members of existing states, they are not prepared to grant to a foreigner."[35]

Why do we tolerate this state of affairs?

It's because some egalitarians believe there are good reasons for not extending equality to foreigners. These reasons don't often get an airing, so let's give them one.

One is that equality is a value because it builds community spirit. Inequality is bad because it implies social exclusion. As Nigerians are excluded from the UK anyway, there's no need to worry about inequality between us and them.

Secondly, needs are socially generated. In a society where most people have cars and TVs, social life is built around the assumption that everyone will have these. Those who lack them will therefore be worse off than they would be in a society where everyone lacks them. What's more, inequality within a country can lead to a loss of self-esteem, depression, drug and alcohol dependency in a way that inequality between countries does not. Research by Robert Frank has found that happiness depends upon relative incomes, not absolute ones[36]. Surveys suggest Nigerians are as happy as Germans or Americans, partly because they never compare themselves with wealthy Germans or Americans, and so do not feel any sense of deprivation. The same cannot, however, be said for poor Germans or Americans. Inequality within a nation-state is therefore a more pressing problem – because it breeds an unhappiness that inequality between nations does not.

A third argument comes from David Gauthier. Injustice, he said, "can arise only insofar as the actions of one person or group affect another"[37]. It follows that the only goods that are the legitimate subject of distribution are those created by social interaction; this is why we do not redistribute eyes, beauty or health. As long as inequalities between ourselves and Nigerians are not the result of any relations between the two countries, this means that we do not, in justice, owe anything to the Nigerians.

Are these arguments convincing? Some believe not. Some egalitarians, such as Kai Nielson and Hillel Steiner, have indeed argued for global redistribution.[38]

The key question here is: why do you want equality?

If you want it to increase social cohesion, or to promote happiness, there is a case for not redistributing assets overseas. If, however, you believe in equality in order to compensate people for suffering involuntary disadvantages, equality must apply globally. As John Roemer has asked: "From a moral point of view, does one deserve to benefit by virtue of being born in the US instead of Calcutta?"[39]

Conclusion: in praise of Marx

It looks then, as if Joseph Raz, who started our chapter, was right. The pursuit of equality is indeed a wild goose chase.

This is especially so when it's managerialists who are doing the chasing. Managerialism can be an obstacle to equality, in five ways.

One, as we've seen, is that its obsession with hierarchy makes meaningful equality of status impossible.

Secondly, managerialists rarely think clearly about ultimate values. The upshot is a failure to see that conceptions of equality can conflict not only with each other, but with other goals such as liberty or democracy.

Thirdly, the faith in the state as a means for good can blind managerialists to the fact that the state has in some ways magnified inequalities.

Fourthly, managerialists' over-confidence in their ability to resolve conflicts of interest lead them to exaggerate the feasibility of equality.

In this respect, managerialists are much more idealistic than Marx. He believed communism could only be achieved after capitalism had created material abundance, simply because if scarcity existed, equality would require superhuman sacrifices. As G.A.Cohen puts it:

> Marx thought that material abundance was not only a sufficient but also a necessary condition of equality. He thought that anything short of an abundance so complete that it removes all major conflicts of interest would guarantee continued social strife...It was because he was so uncompromisingly pessimistic about the social consequences of anything less than limitless abundance that Marx needed to be so optimistic about the possibility of that abundance.[40]

The problem is, though, that if we are stuck on the hedonic treadmill we met in chapter 10, we'll never achieve abundance. It will forever be one step ahead of us.

And herein lies the fifth problem with managerialist politics. It takes for granted our self-interest, and (as we'll see in chapter 14) assumes that instrumental rationality is the only rationality possible. In doing so, it does nothing to cultivate a virtuous citizenry – if indeed this is possible at all. And yet this is necessary if any justice is to be achieved.

This was recognised by Socrates 2500 years ago. A just state, he said, required just citizens: "The elements and traits that belong to a state must also exist in the individuals that compose it. There is nowhere else for them to come from."[41]

With people as they are, then, perhaps equality is just unattainable – at least through conventional means.

Notes

1. *The Morality of Freedom*, p234.

2. *Democracy in America*, p537.

3. Speech on tackling poverty and social exclusion, September 18 2002.

4. Sedgefield adoption speech, May 13 2001, available at www.labour.org.uk.

5. *The Times*, June 3 2000.

6. "What is Equality? Part 1: Equality of Welfare", *Philosophy and Public Affairs*, 10, summer 1981 p185-246 and "What is Equality? Part 2: Equality of Resources", *Philosophy and Public Affairs*, 10, fall 1981 p283-345.

7. John Roemer, *Theories of Distributive Justice*, p248.

8. *Equity and Choice*, p94.

9. I draw here on Roemer, *Equality of Opportunity*, p1. Others, such as John Baker *(Arguing for Equality*, p43-45) and Christopher Jencks ("What Must be Equal for Opportunity to be Equal?" p48 in Norman Bowie (ed), *Equal Opportunity*) have pointed out that there are more than two definitions.

10. Speech to Institute of Fiscal Studies, May 27 1999.

11. *The Wealth of Nations*, Books IV-V, p368.

12. *The Times*, June 3 2000.

13. *The Rise of Meritocracy*, pxvi.

14. *A Theory of Justice*, p72.

15. *Egalitarian Perspectives*, p4, 179.

16. *Equality of Opportunity*, p2.

17. *Equality of Opportunity*, p60.

18. John Roemer and Julian Betts, "Equalizing educational opportunity through educational reform", *University of California Davis working paper no.99-08.*

19. "Choice and Circumstance" p108 in Mason (ed), *Ideals of Equality.*

20. *On Liberty*, p177-79.

21. "Equal Opportunity or Equal Social Outcome", p27.

22. *Equality*, p154.

23. Speech to Global Ethics Foundation, Tubigen University, June 30 2000.

24. *The End of Equality*, p79-95, 125.

25. Markus Jantti et al, "American exceptionalism in a new light", *IZA discussion paper 1938,* January 2006.

26. "Equal Opportunity and Moral Arbitrariness" p30 in Bowie (ed), *Equal Opportunity*.

27. *The Rise of the Meritocracy*, pxvi.

28. *Arguing for Equality*, p46.

29. "The Idea of Equality" p130 in Laslett and Runciman (eds), *Philosophy, Politics and Society*.

30. *Independent*, November 8 2002.

31. In a series of papers Richard Wilkinson has argued that inequalities of income and status, not just poverty, are major causes of ill-health. See, for example, "Health, redistribution and growth" in Glyn and Miliband (eds), *Paying for Inequality*.

32. What follows comes from Serge-Christophe Kolm, *Modern Theories of Justice*, p290.

33. Egalitarianism may, of course, require that we help the children of such irresponsible parents.

34. *Choosing Justice*, p181.

35. *The Road to Serfdom*, p104.

36. *Choosing the Right Pond*, p28-31.

37. *Morals by Agreement*, p283.

38. *Equality and Liberty: A Defense of Radical Egalitarianism and Essay on Rights*.

39. *Free to Lose*, p4.

40. *Self-ownership, Freedom and Equality*, p11.

41. *The Republic*, 435e.

13.

The Rituals of Reason

On any matter not self-evident there are 99 persons totally incapable of judging it for one who is capable; and the capacity of the hundredth person is only comparative, for the majority of eminent men of every past generation held many opinions now known to be erroneous. (John Stuart Mill.[1])

We are afraid to put men to live and trade each on his own private stock of reason; because we suspect that this stock in each man is small, and that the individuals would do better to avail themselves of the general bank and capital of nations, and of ages. (Edmund Burke.[2])

Life is not too long, and too much of it must not be spent in idle deliberation how it shall be spent: deliberation, which those who begin it by prudence, and continue with subtlety, must after long expense of thought, conclude by chance. To prefer one future mode of life to another, upon just reasons, requires faculties which it has not pleased our creator to give us. (Samuel Johnson.[3])

Burke, Johnson and Mill all saw a vital truth – that human beings are not as wise, rational or clever as we like to think. This chapter will argue that the failure to recognise this fact has important implications for policy-making. Unless we recognise the limits of reason – which are much more tightly binding than generally supposed – we shall make poor use of what little understanding of human affairs we have. We shall, in Jon Elster's words, be condemned to practice the rituals of reason, not the substance of it.[4]

To see the problem more clearly, we need a little historical perspective. Return to the issue we discussed in chapter 3, the collapse of post-war social democracy. This created a crisis for western democracies. Fears emerged that nations had become ungovernable, and that democracy itself had become infeasible. Influential books appeared with titles such as *The Crisis of Democracy* and *Why is Britain Becoming Harder to Govern?*

Amongst the dwindling numbers who believed capitalism and democracy were still compatible, there were several responses to this crisis. These responses dominate politics even today.

One reaction has been to abandon the assumption that governments are an enlightened, selfless elite. Instead, government is seen as an economic activity like any other. This spawned a literature on "public choice" in which it is assumed politicians are concerned only to pursue their own self-interest.

A second reaction – the Thatcherite one – was to abandon the belief that governments should take responsibility for full employment. All governments can do, it is said, is to provide the climate in which enterprise can flourish – low inflation and low marginal tax rates. If people fail to take the opportunities this creates, it is no fault of the state's.

A third response to the crisis of demand management in the 1970s is New Labour's. Although it has abandoned faith in old-style Keynesianism, it retains the hope that a body of enlightened seers can intervene in the economy for good[5]. As we have seen, policies such as tax credits, the National Minimum Wage, and increased education all depend upon the belief that cleverly-designed policies can raise both efficiency (whatever this means) and equality.

An inventory of cognitive biases

There is, however, a fourth possible reaction to the 1970s crisis, which doesn't get the attention it deserves. This is that we should recognise that even the saintliest policy-makers are destined to make mistakes, simply because the capacities for judgment which they claim to possess are indeed faculties which it has not pleased our creator to give us.

There are, of course, endless examples of poor policy-making. But such failings, however numerous, are usually regarded as exceptions to the rule of enlightened policy. Perhaps, though, we should change our perceptions. Maybe – and here I exaggerate for effect – failure should be seen as the rule, and success the exception.

It is by now widely thought that stock market investors can be systematically irrational. A vast literature has emerged in recent years which studies how cognitive biases and deficiencies might affect share prices.

But if people can be systematically irrational when they face stiff competition and get immediate clear feedback – it's obvious if a share has been a good buy or not – aren't they more likely to be irrational when they don't have such stiff competition, and where they face more ambiguous and delayed feedback? If the people who work in EC1 can be irrational, it's even more likely that those who work in SW1 are.

But why is rationality so hard to achieve? There is a long tradition in western thinking which says all of us can think rationally, if only we can control our emotions.

There is much in this. Even apparently cold and calculating economic policies can be coloured by emotions.

One of these is wishful thinking. This might happen when policy-makers believe an economy's potential growth rate has increased (say, because of the supply-side policies it implemented earlier), so they hold down interest rates or increase government spending, with the result that an inflationary boom is unleashed. This is widely thought to have been a factor behind the Lawson boom of 1987-88.

Sometimes, wishful thinking might have fatal consequences. Perhaps the war in Iraq was motivated in part by an over-estimate of the US's ability to build a peaceful liberal democracy in the country after its liberation.

Another emotion that can cloud policy-making is weakness of the will. This happens when intentions that were sincerely formed at one date are not fulfilled when the time comes to implement them. Much of the literature on time inconsistency in monetary policy – whereby governments abandon a tough anti-inflationary policy when they see that private sector inflation expectations have not fallen – is a discussion of this problem[6].

All this, however, is only part of the story of irrationality in politics. Policy-makers, like the rest of us, often fall short of rationality even when they are not ruled by passion. There is, says Jon Elster "by now a massive body of evidence showing how belief formation can fail to be fully rational because people rely on misleading heuristic principles or, more simply, ignore basic facts about statistical inference".[7]

Let's look at some of these misleading principles, and how they might possibly infect political decision-making.

Representativeness and ignoring base rates

What are the chances that a particular event caused another event? What is the probability that an individual is a member of a particular profession? In answering questions such as these we often form a judgement of whether the individual is representative of that profession, or whether the effect is similar to the cause. When we do this, we use the representativeness heuristic.

This can lead us astray because, in focusing on similarities between causes and effect, or between a sample and a broader population, we may overlook other factors that affect probabilities. Not least of these factors is the base probability.

To see how easy it is to do this, consider the following question. A disease is present in one in a thousand of the population. A test for it has a false positive rate of 5 per cent, and everyone with the disease tests positive. If an individual, taken randomly from the population, tests positive, what is the chance that he actually does have the disease?

You may think the answer is 95 per cent. And this was the response given by around half the staff and students at Harvard Medical School when the question was put to them in 1978.[8]

If you gave this answer, you relied upon the representativeness heuristic. After all, testing positive for a disease must be highly representative of having the disease.

However, the true answer is only 2 per cent. This is because the probability of having the disease is a weighted average of the result of the test and the base probability of having the disease. And because the base probability is low, so the probability of having the disease is low even if you test positive.[9]

It's easy to see how the representative heuristic may colour policy judgments. Maybe the widespread belief that booms and slumps are the result of demand fluctuations rather than supply shocks rests in part on the view that weak demand seems more representative of what happens in a recession than is an adverse supply shock.

One particular use of the representativeness heuristic is the assumption that solutions to problems must resemble their causes. This is false – if a man's been run over by a bus, you don't restore him to health by reversing the bus. But it seems to affect thinking about poverty. Many in and out of New Labour think that because poverty (in the UK) is caused by low education, the solution must be better education. But this is not necessarily true. It might be cheaper to merely transfer cash to people than to spend money educating the ineducable.

Representativeness can be especially misleading when we try to predict the future, because we naturally believe the future must be representative of the present. For example, Star Trek's writers in the 1960s foresaw space travel but not the development of the hand-held computer. Their image of the future was representative of their present – a time in which there was space travel but not rapid development of computing power.

It's not just Star Trek writers who committed this error. Here are some famous examples:

"I think there is a world market for maybe five computers." (Thomas Watson, chairman of IBM, 1943)

"There is no reason anyone would want a computer in their home." (Ken Olson, president of Digital Equipment Corporation, 1977)

"Heavier than air flying machines are impossible." (Lord Kelvin, 1895)

"Guitar music is on the way out." (Decca Recording, rejecting the Beatles, 1962)[10]

Maybe New Labour is committing a similar error today. It believes globalization and technical change will increase demand for skilled workers and cut demand for unskilled ones in the future – hence its stress on improving education. But why should the future be representative of the recent past?

The four-box error

There is a simple solution to questions like the one I asked about the disease. We can present the data in the form of four boxes, as in table 22.

To do this, we convert probabilities into hard numbers. So let's think of 1000 people. Our information is that of these 1000, 50 – or 5 per cent – will test positive. So 950 will test negative. We also know that because everyone with the disease tests positive, no-one with it tests negative. Add to this the fact that one in a 1000 people have the disease, and we have the information necessary to fill the four boxes.

Table 22. An easy way of judging probabilities

	Test result	
	Positive	*Negative*
Disease	1	0
Healthy	49	950
Total	50	950

To know the probability that someone has the disease, given that he has tested positive, our task is now simple – just look in the column labelled positive. This gives us a figure of one in 50, or 2 per cent.

The message here is important. If we want to know that something is correlated with something else – either as a cause or a consequence – it is not good enough to look merely at cases where the two occur together. We must also look at cases where one occurs without the other.

Put like this, the logic is obvious. However, even rocket scientists commit the four-box error of failing to consider all four possibilities. Robyn Dawes says that after the 1986 Challenger space shuttle disaster, engineers were asked to study whether cold temperatures caused O-rings (a commonly used joint in the rocket) to malfunction. They looked at other cases of O-ring malfunction and found no correlation with cold temperatures. However, had they looked at cases where O-rings worked well, they would have discovered a correlation – because all these successes occurred at high temperatures.[11] Even very intelligent people therefore commit a gross error.

It is easy to see the policy applications of this. Many observers blamed rioting in Bradford and Oldham in May-June 2001 upon a combination of high Asian unemployment, poor policing and provocation by racists. Maybe they were right. But it is impossible to say this for sure unless we look at instances where these putative causes were present but there were no riots – and, indeed, where there were riots without these causes. And this requires that we look outside these towns to know what happened in them.

Some attempts to blame poverty upon the characteristics of the poor themselves also fall into the four-box error. Knowing that huge numbers of the poor are lazy or stupid or lacking in social skills is utterly irrelevant, unless we know that the rich do not possess these character failings.

The fallacy of local representativeness

One common application of the representativeness heuristic is the belief that a portion of a random sequence must itself be random – that is, representative of the bigger sample. This is wrong. Any sufficiently long random sequence is likely to have a regular-looking pattern in it somewhere; if we toss a fair coin enough times, it will show a long sequence of heads somewhere.

Representativeness, then, can lead us to misperceive randomness. Two examples will show the policy implications of this.

One is the Dangerous Dogs Act, passed after a spate of attacks on children by dogs. Another is the 1997 Protection from Harassment Act, passed after a few high-profile cases in which women were stalked.

Both are now widely regarded as mistakes. Many believe the infringements of freedoms of dog-owners and of obsessed suitors outweigh the benefits of greater safety of women and children.

Had governments been aware of the fallacy of local representativeness, they might have rejected both laws. They should instead have reasoned thus. Attacks by dogs and intrusive stalking are rare. All that is happening is that these rare attacks have clustered together – random events sometimes do. As a result, there's no need for action. If we wait, reversion to the mean will ensure that dog attacks and stalking become less common.

Availability and salience heuristics

"People's inferences and behaviour are so much more influenced by vivid, concrete information than by pallid and abstract propositions of substantially greater probative and evidential value" (Richard Nisbett and Lee Ross.[12])

This tendency – known as the availability bias, because we overweight the importance of easily available information – can also distort our judgment of probabilities.

The best known example is the fear of flying. Statistically, cars are a more dangerous mode of transport than planes. But because plane crashes get more publicity than car crashes, we fear the former more than the latter.

The availability bias can have pernicious effects. It can enhance public opposition to welfare benefits, as a few vivid reports of unemployed "scroungers" distort public perceptions of the character of the unemployed. Or it can inhibit social mobility, as youngsters from poor backgrounds, seeing that all those around them are also poor, under-estimate the possibilities of escape and feel little incentive to do well at school.[13]

The bias might also explain why there's so little objection to the minimum wage. The jobs destroyed by it are too few to show up in the macroeconomic data that get media attention – the job losses just aren't salient enough to matter.

It also colours the "debate" about "multiculturalism." The few Muslims who are deeply alienated from western values are hugely salient, whilst the millions who are well integrated don't get much attention. The upshot is that the degree of segregation can be over-stated, and plain (if horrible) criminality becomes a wider social issue.

Ignorance of revenge effects

If the availability effect causes us to exaggerate the importance of some information, it follows that other information gets under-weighted or ignored. This information often concerns what Thomas Homer-Dixon has called "revenge effects".[14] These occur when a clever solution to one problem merely begets another problem. For example:

- The installation of catalytic converters in cars in the 1980s reduced the amount of lead and smog in the air. But they increased emissions of nitrous oxide, a gas which contributes to global warming.
- The closure of many abattoirs in the early 1990s after the outbreak of BSE caused more long journeys for livestock. The upshot was that when foot and mouth disease broke out in 2001, it spread quickly around the country.
- The government's promise in 1997 to cut waiting lists caused doctors to treat patients with minor complaints, as these could be quickly removed from the lists. The result was that people with more serious conditions had to wait longer for treatment.[15]

- American support for Afghan resistance fighters in their fight against Soviet occupation in the 1980s provided guns, money and trained men which Osama bin Laden subsequently used to launch terrorist attacks against the US. And US support for Iraq during its war against Iran in the early 1980s helped strengthen Saddam Hussein's government.

Perhaps the most important effect of the combination of availability heuristics and the ignorance of revenge effects was described by Hayek. The value of freedom, he said, "rests on the opportunities it provides for unforeseen and unpredictable actions." This means it will be hard, or even impossible, to know what exactly we lose from any infringement of freedom. By contrast, the potential gain from the infringement will be clear. The result, he said, is that:

When we decide each issue on what appear to be its individual merits, we always over-estimate the advantages of central direction. Our choice will regularly appear to be one between a certain known and tangible gain and the mere probability of the prevention of some unknown beneficial action by unknown persons. If the choice between freedom and coercion is thus treated as a matter of expediency, freedom is bound to be sacrificed in almost every instance.[16]

Fundamental attribution error

The combination of the availability and representative biases can yield what psychologists call the fundamental attribution error. This is the tendency for us to attach too much importance to human agency and too little to environmental forces in assigning responsibility for actions.

It's easy to see how this error can influence policy debates. Perhaps managerialists' faith in the ability of leadership to change society is due to the fundamental attribution error. They attribute developments to deliberate individual agency more than to impersonal forces.

More particular examples of this error might include:

- The great US economic boom of the 1990s was widely attributed to the skilful economic management of Federal Reserve chairman Alan Greenspan. In fact it is more likely to have been the result of a mixture of faster technical progress in information and communication technology and massive borrowing by individuals and companies.

- Hostility to more redistributive taxation may arise in part because we over-estimate the extent to which wealth and poverty are the result of our own actions – in which case inequalities may be tolerable – and under-estimate the extent to which they are due to luck or circumstance.

- The failure of New Labour's plans to use "superheads" – headmasters with a track record of success – to improve under-performing schools may be because it failed to see that these headmasters succeeded because of luck and environmental forces rather than personal skills.

Indeed, Thomas Homer-Dixon has suggested that Western triumphalism – the rejoicing in the prosperity and technical achievement of Europe and the US – may be one big fundamental attribution error, because it "assumes agency where there may be mainly good luck".[17]

Adjustment and anchoring

This bias occurs when we arrive at an answer by adjusting our initial impression. To see how it works, give yourself five seconds to estimate the solution to this:

$$8 \times 7 \times 6 \times 5 \times 4 \times 3 \times 2 \times 1 = ?$$

The correct answer is 40,320. If you're like most people, your answer was an under-estimate. That's because you quickly saw that $8 \times 7 \times 6$ was something over 300, and then adjusted your estimate upwards from that. But you didn't adjust it enough.

This process might explain why managers and politicians over-estimate the chances of success of major projects.

Imagine there's a project whose success requires all of 20 smaller jobs to be completed. Each of these has a 95% chance of being completed on time and on budget. What's the probability of the whole project being successful?

It's just 35.8%, just over one in three. In other words, there's a two-thirds chance of the project failing. That's 0.95 to the power 20. Even if the probability of success of each job were as high as 98%, there'd still be a one-third chance of the project failing.[18]

Is it really surprising, therefore, that Wembley Stadium should be hugely delayed? Or that the 2012 Olympics are already running over-budget? Or that almost every big IT project fails?

Framing and redescription

Our choices are sensitive to the way they are framed.

An experiment by Richard Nisbett and Lee Ross shows this. They asked subjects to play a simple prisoners' dilemma game, in which they could choose to co-operate or defect, where co-operation offered a high reward if the other person co-operated, but a heavy penalty if the other person defected[19]. Before playing the game, subjects were read one of two stories, of a kidney donor or a nasty murder. People who heard the donor story were much more likely to co-operate than were people who heard the murder story – because the stories changed their opinion of whether others were basically decent, and thus likely to co-operate, or nasty, and so likely to defect.

Framing effects such as these are quite common in the economic arena. We know how easy it is to go on a spending spree soon after buying a house – because having spent tens of thousands of pounds, a few hundred pounds don't feel as valuable as they once did. Perhaps the same thing happens with public spending. A waste of a few million pounds seems tiny when framed within half a trillion pounds of public spending. But a few million here or there soon adds up to real money, as Matthew Elliott and Lee Rotherham show in *The Bumper Book of Government Waste*.

The fact that our choices are sensitive to contexts and descriptions explains why so much political effort is expended on controlling agenda and the media. It can also lead to misleading metaphors. When Margaret Thatcher argued for a tighter fiscal policy in the late 1970s she often spoke – to the horror of Keynesian economists – of the need for good housekeeping. And when industrialists speak of the need for a "manufacturing base" they are appealing to the common sense notion that a base should be strong and broad.

In both cases, we are invited to avoid the questions of whether fiscal policy really is analogous to housekeeping, or whether manufacturing really is analogous to a base.

Framing can also distort our attitudes towards equality and redistribution. Take the question: why am I rich? In a purely British frame, it's because I'm intelligent, educated and hard-working. In a worldwide frame, however, it's simply because I was born English rather than Ethiopian. The British frame can lead to opposition to redistribution, the worldwide frame to support for it.

Prior change of attribute weights

One important type of framing effect is the process whereby decisions look different with hindsight than they appeared at the time. In particular we may attribute more weight to the beneficial effects of a decision, relative to its costs, after the event than we did at the time. That car we were unsure about buying a few months ago may turn out to be a great bargain after we bought it, because over time we exaggerate its merits and downplay its defects. Jon Elster calls this process the prior change of attribute weights.[20]

This is not the only way in which we reframe our past decisions. There's also ego-involvement. We tend to believe a decision was a good one simply because it was made by us rather than someone else. David Craig and Richard Brooks say this is one reason why the government presses ahead with bad IT projects even when the evidence suggests they won't work:

The problem was that once millions, tens of millions or even hundreds of millions had been spent, there would be too much loss of face for the bureaucrats to pause and reflect whether maybe they had got things a little wrong.[21]

Ego-involvement can also lead to what Richard Downs called the law of increasing conservatism: "all organisations tend to become more conservative as they get older."[22] This happens because old organisations have built up a history of more decisions, which they feel compelled to stand by, regardless of their validity now.

Partial effects

Another way of persuading ourselves that decisions were better than they really were is to focus only upon some of their effects. This is especially easily done if these are more salient than other effects.

This can cost lives. After the Hatfield rail crash in 2000, which was caused by a broken rail, Railtrack closed many lines to check the track. That led people to switch from rail to road transport – although the death rates on the latter are many times higher than those on the railways. Also, in September 2002 the failure of the Criminal Records Bureau to check teachers' criminal records led to some schools being closed for a while. Children kept out of school were exposed to much greater dangers – from either child molesters or, more likely traffic, than they would have faced from unvetted teachers.

The hindsight bias

If all this has the effect of making close decisions seem more comfortable with hindsight than they did at the time, there is another cognitive bias which can have the opposite effect. This is the hindsight bias, whereby we regard events that actually happened as more probable than they in fact were before they happened.

One example of this is that the opinion today that sterling's exit from the European exchange rate mechanism in 1992 was inevitable. Before then, however, it was widely thought to be only a possibility.

Another example is the criticism that Chancellor Gordon Brown's decision to freeze public spending in 1997 was economically unnecessary and damaging to public services.[23] This ignores the fact that, at the time, there was a danger of the economy overheating and a large budget deficit, whilst New Labour's reputation for economic stability was insecure. There were, therefore, good reasons for Mr Brown's decision. It is only with hindsight that these reasons appear poor.

Perhaps the hindsight bias contributes to New Labour's belief that the future is linear and knowable. With hindsight, the past looks linear and predictable, with obvious effects following from identifiable causes. This leads us to over-estimate the predictability of the future.

Misperceptions of covariance

People are, say Nisbett and Ross, "extremely poor" at estimating covariance[24]. We tend to over-estimate covariances when there is a theoretical reason to expect covariance, and underestimate covariance when there is no theoretical basis for it.

Also, we tend to over-estimate correlations that are easy to remember, as an experiment by Loren and Jean Chapman showed[25]. They showed subjects a series of words flashed onto a screen. The left side of the screen showed one of the words: bacon, lion, blossom, boat. The right side showed one of the words: eggs, tiger, notebook. Although the experiment ensured that each possible pair of words appeared equally often, subjects over-estimated the frequency of the pairs "bacon-eggs" and "lion-tiger" – because these pairs are easy to remember.

Again, this bias can easily have policy implications. Inflation is serially correlated, with high inflation one month generally associated with high inflation the following month. As a result, it's easy to over-estimate the size of inflationary pressures – because the following month's numbers contain less new information than one might think. This is reinforced by the fact that press reports of inflation are also highly correlated with each other. Policy-makers can therefore find themselves raising interest rates too much in an inflationary boom. We now know – thanks to the hindsight bias? – that Nigella's dad did just this in 1988-89, with the result that the economy was plunged into recession.

Another policy implication lies in attitudes to public spending. Intuition tells us there must be a correlation between public spending on health or education and having more health or education. Naturally, therefore, there is a demand for more public spending. This demand is reinforced by the representative heuristic. Good education or healthcare must be representative of high spending, mustn't it? In truth, however, many believe the correlation between the two is weaker than you might think.[26] The upshot can be a tendency for government to get bigger and bigger without any great benefit.

Over-diversification

Here's a test[27]. I have a coin which is weighted so that it should come up tails 80 per cent of the time and heads the other 20 per cent. Predict the next ten tosses of the coin.

Most people write down eight tails and two heads in a random-looking sequence. This has only a 68 per cent chance of success; 0.8 x 0.8 plus 0.2 x 0.2. Calling ten heads would have an 80 per cent chance.

This shows that when people are faced with an uncertain outcome, they often spread their bets too thinly. This is no mere laboratory experiment. Richard Thaler and Shlomo Benartzi have shown that it bedevils the pension arrangements of airline pilots and university teachers – educated people making important decisions. They found that many of these spread their money evenly across a range of funds, with the result that those offered a range of bond funds but one equity fund over-invested in bonds, whilst those offered a range of equity funds but one bond fund over-invested in equities.[28]

Again, this may have policy implications. If governments don't really know what works, they may try a range of policies, which lead to excessive intervention and high administrative costs.

This may apply to policy towards poverty. Because this has no single cause, New Labour has a huge range of policies for tackling it; help for failing schools, the New Deal, tax credits, income support, the minimum wage and so on. Such a huge range could be sensible, but it could also impose more dead-weight costs than necessary.

The fallacy of affirming the consequent

Is the Chancellor of the Exchequer doing a good job? A common way to answer this question is as follows. All good chancellors will preside over a healthy economy. The economy is healthy. Therefore we have a good Chancellor. This is simple nonsense. It has the same structure as: all water buffalo are fat; John Prescott is fat; therefore John Prescott is a water buffalo. It is the fallacy of affirming the consequent – that is, of arguing from the second premise to the first.

In the second example, it's easy to see the error – because we know that although all water buffalo are fat, so too are many other things. The same is true of Chancellors. It's possible that a good Chancellor will have the misfortune to preside over a bad economy, and that a bad Chancellor will have the good luck to be in office at a time when the economy is thriving so well that it is little affected by his mismanagement.

Cynics will claim they avoid this fallacy because they know a Chancellor's most important quality is good luck. This is merely an example of the fundamental attribution error – of attributing to an individual what should properly be attributed to the environment. It's also an example of...

The illusion of control

People have more confidence in their predictions than should have. A neat experiment by Ellen J. Langer has shown this.[29] Subjects were sold tickets, at $1 each, in an office lottery. Some had tickets assigned to them, whilst others were allowed to choose them. The subjects were later asked how much they would be willing to sell the tickets for. For tickets which had been assigned to individuals, the average asking price was $1.96. But for tickets which subjects had chosen, the average asking price was $8.67. People seem to think they can predict even random events such as lotteries. They have the illusion that they can control things.

This has many possible political applications; maybe it underpins managerialist ideology itself, the notion that the world is controllable.

The most egregious examples of the fallacy are probably attempts to intervene in foreign exchange markets – where movements are often random. Perhaps the most disastrous such effort was not sterling's membership of the exchange rate mechanism of 1990-92, but the attempt to engineer a controlled devaluation of sterling in 1976 – an attempt which led to a collapse in the pound and the humiliating application to the International Monetary Fund for a loan.

Overconfidence

Closely related to the illusion of control is simple overconfidence – the belief that we can control or predict things better than others can.

Overconfidence seems to be rewarded. A paper by Magne Jorgensen and colleagues shows that software developers who offered their bosses overconfident predictions about projects were preferred to developers who offered more realistic, but less certain predictions.[30] Perhaps the same thing happens when the government hires contractors or promotes civil servants.

Indeed, perhaps politicians are selected for their overconfidence. People who exaggerate their chances of being able to improve the world are disproportionately likely to enter politics. And politicians who offer voters solutions, rather than the truth that affairs are complex and unmanageable, are disproportionately likely to get elected.

Confirmatory bias and belief persistence

You might think that all these biases and errors that lead to incorrect thinking would eventually be eliminated, as people learn from their mistakes. Not necessarily. For one thing, as we'll see soon, the feedback that might cause us to correct our beliefs is often absent. And for another, we often fail to seek out rigorous tests of our beliefs. For example, in the early 1970s, Democrats were far more likely to want to read about the Watergate scandal than Republicans. Labour supporters in 1996-97 were far more willing than Conservative ones to read about accusations of "sleaze" against Conservative MPs. American supporters of the war in Iraq don't seem to want to see pictures of the coffins of dead soldiers. And Culture Secretary Tessa Jowell has been accused of only wanting to hear good news about progress in Olympics construction projects, and ignoring bad news.[31]

This habit is often due to emotions clouding our judgment. We use facts not as tests of our beliefs, but as crutches to lean on in times of uncertainty.

However, a "cold" inferential error might also be at work. This is the confirmatory bias. To illustrate this, Peter Wason proposed a simple experiment.[32] You have four cards. They reveal: A, D, 3, 7. Which cards should you turn over to test the statement: "if a card has an A on one side, it has a 3 on the other"?

Clearly, you need to turn over the A. Even highly educated people, however, believe you should also turn over the 3. This is wrong. In fact, you should turn over the 7. (To see why, consider how you would test the statement, "if p, then q". You need to observe a "not q". This is the role fulfilled by the 7.) The reason for this error is simple. We tend to look for evidence that confirms a hypothesis, rather than evidence that may disconfirm it.

This can easily lead to belief persistence – the process whereby evidence that might affect a belief before it is formed has no effect in weakening the belief after it has been formed. An experiment by Lee Ross and Craig Anderson showed how prevalent this is. They took a group of people who supported capital punishment and a group who opposed it, and showed them academic research on the merits and demerits of the idea. Research that favoured each group's pre-existing ideas was deemed more convincing than research which opposed it. The upshot was that, after considering the opposite side of the case, both groups' views became more polarised. This was contrary to any principle of inference. They concluded:

> Beliefs can survive potent logical or empirical challenges. They can survive and even be bolstered by evidence that most uncommitted observers would agree logically demands some reworking of such beliefs. They can even survive the total destruction of their original evidential bases.[33]

Hyper-rationality

A common reaction to all the above is to believe that, having learnt it, you can now act rationally. Don't be so sure. It's also important to guard against hyper-rationality – using rationality in contexts where it doesn't fit.

One way in which this can happen is that it may simply take too long to reach a rational decision. There is an old civil service joke that, by the time a Royal Commission has reported on a problem, everyone has forgotten what the problem was in the first place.

Sadly, this is no mere joke. A protracted decision can do huge harm. Jon Elster points out that in some child custody cases, the trauma of a long legal battle and judicial interference may do more harm to the child than would giving custody to the worse parent.[34] Sometimes, delay can even be deadly. The National Institute for Health and Clinical Excellence took 15 months to approve NHS use of the breast cancer drug Herceptin. During this time, some women died because they were denied access to it.

The collective unwisdom

There's an obvious objection to all this. So far, I've considered biases and errors in individual decision-making. But most political decisions are made by groups – Cabinet, ministers and their advisors , or men on Blair's settee. And it's possible that individual biases can cancel each other out within groups. Imagine two gamblers at a roulette table. "Red is on a roll" says one. "Black must be due soon" replies another. They then agree that red and black are equally likely to come up.

Sadly, however, there's plenty of evidence that groups can often make terrible decisions. In *Groupthink*, Irving Janis describes how some of the greatest disasters in American history – the Bay of Pigs fiasco, Watergate, or the failure to consider the warnings before the attack on Pearl Harbor – all arose because "groupthink" magnified individual errors.

Indeed, there's some evidence that groups do worse than individuals. The rise of investment clubs – groups of people who get together to buy shares – allows us to compare the performance of groups with those of individuals. Brad Barber and Terrance Odean have done just this. They found that between 1991 and 1996 the average investment club had an annual return after transactions costs of 14.1 per cent, compared to 16.4 per cent for the average individual.[35] In the real world, with real money at stake, therefore, group decisions are worse than individual ones.

There are reasons for this:

- The fallacy of correlated observations. Groups often comprise people of similar backgrounds and training. This means their opinions are likely to be correlated, because they're the result of the same education. If we fail to see this, however, we might over-rate the importance of the opinion of the third or fourth member of our group, as we fail to see that this information is redundant. For example, in the 1960s, thousands of economists believed it was possible to avoid recessions through fiscal fine-tuning. However, the 1000th expert who espoused this view gave us little additional reason for believing in the efficacy of fine-tuning, because his belief was the product of the same training and (limited) evidence as the belief of the 999 other experts. His belief was, therefore, redundant. In failing to recognise this, we put more faith in fine-tuning than we should have.

- The heuristic of social proof – the belief that, if a large number of people believe something we don't, they must know something we don't.[36] This is especially pernicious because it arises from the most reasonable motive – the recognition of our own ignorance. And yet it can lead us horrifically astray. In the 1940s, Solomon Asch showed that judgments of even trivial factual matters, such as the length of lines, can be influenced for the worse by peer pressure. So too can be even vitally important judgments, such as threats to one's own life. Amitai Etzioni cites experiments in which people in smoke-filled rooms were less likely to ring fire alarms if stooges in the room were relaxed than if the stooges panicked.[37]

- Concurrence-seeking tendencies.[38] These happen when we like our fellow group members and feel loyal to them, with the result that we want to agree with them.

- Boosting overconfidence. If nice, clever people agree with us, we naturally think we must be right. So we become overconfident.

All this, however, might be too gloomy. There's other evidence that groups can make better decisions than individuals. For example, in laboratory experiments in setting interest rates, researchers have found that committees do better than individuals.[39]

This might be because the structure of monetary policy committees is favourable to good decision-making, and biased against the sort of groupthink errors identified by Janis. For example:

- The committee has a pre-set objective – to set interest rates to control inflation. This avoids the problems of manipulating or withholding private information which arise when members have conflicting preferences. It also means members don't feel that loyalty to the group is an over-riding value.

- The committee has only one tool to use – interest rates. One problem with groupthink – the tendency to ignore the full range of policy options – does not therefore arise.

- Decisions are limited to one per period. This reduces the tendency towards over-activism caused by overconfidence.

- The committee has only one objective. This means overconfidence cannot cause it to engage in a range of adventurous policies.

Sadly, however, these circumstances conducive to good collective decision-making are quite rare.

How governments fail

If you think this is depressing, it is only part of the story. So far, we've assumed group decisions are taken democratically, with everyone having their say. Political decisions, however, are often taken by hierarchies. And this makes errors more likely.

One reason for this is that information can get lost in hierarchies. As Charles Lindblom points out, subordinates can withhold information from their superiors for many reasons, ranging from laziness, through a wish to avoid "blame the messenger syndrome", to a desire not to burden the minister with trivia.[40] And they tell him only what he wants to hear. The upshot has been described by Kenneth Boulding:

> Almost all organisational structures tend to produce false images in the decision-maker, and ... the larger and more authoritarian the organisation, the better the chance that its top decision-makers will be operating in purely imaginary worlds.[41]

Worse still, even under the most benign authority, people are willing to abandon their own judgment to the extent of inflicting terrible suffering on others. Experiments by Stanley Milgram in the 1960s established this. He told volunteers he was studying how punishment helped people to learn. To this end, the volunteers were told, some students were connected to an electric shock machine. The volunteers were then told to ask the students questions, and administer electric shocks to them after each wrong answer. Milgram found that huge numbers of volunteers agreed to administer massive shocks if he asked them to. We are, therefore, all too quick to subordinate ourselves to authority[42]. It is thought this process contributed to the large number of child deaths at the Bristol Royal Infirmary in the late 1990s, as senior heart surgeons' faulty decisions were not properly challenged by subordinates.

Also, in hierarchies, unlike in individuals, there is a big difference between making a decision and actually carrying it out. Individuals rarely spend much time worrying how to implement decisions they have already taken, or about how to co-ordinate the various desires they have. Governments, however, spend thousands of man-hours on this problem. Governments, unlike individuals, suffer from: bureaucratic inertia; a lack of legislative time; a need for "joined up government"; confusion over the relative roles of civil servants, ministers or chief executives of government agencies; and lack of clarity over the precise boundaries between central and devolved powers.[43]

As if all this were not enough, there are ways in which politicians are an unrepresentative sample of the population at large – ways which make them even less likely than the rest of us to make good decisions:

• Politics is a risky career, in which success does not always go to the most meritorious. This means the people attracted to political careers are more likely than the rest of us to be over-optimistic about their chances of success in uncertain ventures. And this, in turn, means they are likely to be more vulnerable to the fundamental attribution error, overconfidence and the illusion of control.

• Politics is a disreputable career. The mere fact that politicians are regarded as "Millbank clones", mouthing the sound-bites of a "control freak" government, deters intelligent people from entering the profession. Politicians are thus drawn from the dregs of the professional classes.

• Politicians are drawn not from a random sample of educational backgrounds, but from ones which badly prepare them to consider issues of choice under uncertainty. Gerd Gigerenzer has said that "many students who spend much of their life avoiding statistics and psychology become lawyers".[44] And, he might have added, people who aren't smart enough to succeed in the law drop into politics.

Finally, governments may be less likely than individuals to receive the timely feedback that corrects poor decisions.

If a company sets the price of its goods too high a loss of sales may quickly cause it to reverse its decision[45]. However, if a government sets a tax too high, the feedback will rarely be so timely or effective. Any tax receipts lost will be only a small fraction of overall revenue, and so will not jeopardise the government's viability. Opposition to the high tax will normally come from vested interests, which must therefore be discounted. All this is the ideal environment in which the habit of belief persistence can thrive – a habit which, in policy-making circles, is reinforced by the desire not to admit that one was wrong.

If, to this, we add the combination of the confirmatory bias, the difficulties of correctly analysing covariance, and belief persistence, it's easy to see why many sub-optimal policies persist, until catastrophic error forces a change.

Conclusion: when experts and technology fail

Now, I have exaggerated the extent – and costs – of irrationality here. Irrational beliefs are often correct. Events that leap readily to mind, for example, may do so because they are common. If so the availability and salience biases will be correct. And the hindsight bias may often be correct, because the fact that an event has happened is good evidence that it was more likely than we had thought. Indeed, Gerd Gigerenzer has emphasised that apparently irrational rules of thumb can often work well[46]. They're a good second-best.

What's more, people reason much better in concrete, everyday situations than they do in abstract laboratory experiments; Herbert Simon called this "intuitive rationality".[47] Experienced practitioners can reach correct answers not by logical deduction or statistical inference, but simply because the problems they encounter are familiar to them. A grandmaster can spot the solution to a chess problem better than the rest of us not merely because he has greater powers of deduction, but because he will recognise the problem. Knowledge and experience can, therefore, often be a good substitute for powers of inference and deduction.

Even with these caveats, the message of all this is clear. Individuals regularly make errors of judgment under uncertainty, and groups and hierarchies may be even more prone than individuals to such errors. It's easy, as I've shown, to map cognitive errors onto errors in policy making and analysis.

Which raises the question. How can we overcome our cognitive deficiencies? Optimists might reply that we have two advantages in the 21st century which our forefathers lacked: more experts and more technology. Surely, these can help us?

No. Take experts first. One finding of laboratory experiments into individual reasoning is that: "There is no inferential error that can be demonstrated with untrained undergraduates that cannot also be demonstrated in somewhat more subtle form in the highly trained scientist"[48]. This should not be surprising. Although experts are well schooled within their (increasingly narrow) specialism, they are rarely taught how to think. It is easy to become a trained economist, for example, without learning anything about Bayesian inference or all the errors cited above; I, for one, managed it.

Paul Slovic and his colleagues have described a series of ways in which experts can misjudge pathways to disaster.[49] These include:

- Overlooking simple human error.

- Over-confidence in current scientific information. Much of the faith in demand management in the 1950s and 1960s illustrated this failing.

- Slowness in detecting cumulative effects. This can be particularly true of environmental policies, where the damage done by acid rain or carbon emissions took years to see.

- Failure to foresee the human response to safety mechanisms. For example, putting dams into a flood-prone area can encourage people to live there by giving them a false sense of security. Similarly, as we have seen, the promise of full employment in the post-war years gave wage bargainers the confidence to make inflationary pay claims, thus making full employment impossible.

- Failure to anticipate "common mode failures" – whereby systems that are supposed to be independent fail simultaneously. A good example of this was the 1998 global financial crisis, when assets that were supposedly uncorrelated, such as US corporate bonds and Russian government debt all fell together. As a result, financial institutions who thought they had spread risk effectively incurred huge losses.

Relying on experts, therefore, is no solution to collective irrationality. Indeed, it could even exacerbate such irrationality, because if opinions have the backing of expert authority, it is easy to have more faith in them than we should.

If we cannot rely on experts, still less can we rely upon advances in technology to get us out of this pickle.

One reason for this is that there is a huge difference between information and intelligence. Technology puts far more information at our fingertips, but it does not follow that we shall use this wisely. What stops us making good decisions is not a lack of information, but a lack of wisdom.

Indeed, the sheer quantity of information may even lead to worse decisions, by giving us the erroneous impression that our decisions are founded upon genuine knowledge, when in fact much of the information is useless or redundant. Brad Barber and Terrance Odean believe day-traders – people who buy and sell shares very regularly – fall into precisely this error.[50]

This is not the only way in which new technology can worsen our cognitive functionings. Thomas Homer-Dixon cites three others:[51]

- "Information overload" can increase stress, as decision-makers are bombarded with information, much of it dissonant, from all corners. And stress can lead to worse decisions.

- Information overload also adds to the pressure for sound-bites and over-simplification to cut through the complexities. Not only are TV quotes from politicians getting ever shorter, so too are newspaper articles.
- Technical progress in the production of artificial light has massively exceeded the pace of human evolution. Consequently, millions of us suffer sleep deprivation, which impairs our cognitive capacities.

If experts and technology are no solutions to the problem of group irrationality, what is?

I have two suggestions, one conservative and the other radical. The conservative solution is simply to be much more humble about our collective opinions. We must see that today's knowledge can be tomorrow's stupidity. This means there's no place for the dogmatic pseudo-certitudes of our politicians.

The radical solution is to be much more democratic in our decision-making, by considering carefully every possible minority view. This is not because democracy guarantees better decisions but rather because no hierarchy can ever possess the wisdom that would justify usurping democracy. What's more, a fully democratic decision is one that at least represents the best application of due diligence. If, after taking as democratic a decision as possible, we still get it wrong, we can at least be sure that we tried our best. And we can ask of the minority who criticised the decision at the time: "if we were wrong, why did you fail to convince us?" If this question cannot be answered easily, we shall at least have made some progress.

You might think all this is too simple. You'd be right. So far we have assumed there is one clear standard of rationality from which we all fall short. This, however, is not the case. Rationality is in fact as ambiguous and elusive a notion as efficiency. Let's turn to this question.

Notes

1. *On Liberty,* p79.

2. *Reflections on the Revolution in France,* p1.

3. Quoted in Jon Elster, *Alchemies of the Mind,* p288-9.

4. *Solomonic Judgments: Studies in the Limitations of Rationality,* p37.

5. Gordon Brown, "The New Monetary Policy Framework", p2. Given as Mais Lecture on October 19, 1999.

6. Whether central banks have actually been as guilty of time inconsistency

as the literature assumes is a moot point. We can never be sure whether a tough anti-inflation policy is really intended to be carried through – in which case its abandonment would be weakness of the will – or whether it is merely an attempt to reduce inflation expectations, in which case it would not necessarily be weak-willed to abandon the policy once it is clear that this attempt has failed. Thomas Mayer, in *Truth versus Precision in Economics*, p63, and Alan Blinder, in *Central Banking in Theory and Practice*, p40-52, both doubt the real-world relevance of the time-inconsistency problem.

7. *Solomonic Judgments*, p24.

8. Amos Tversky and Daniel Kahneman, "Evidential Impact of Base Rates", ch 10 in Kahneman, Slovic and Tversky (eds).

9. The actual probability is calculated by using Bayes' theorem. This says that:

$$P(d/e) = [P(e/d) \times P(d)]_{/P(e)}$$

where P(d/e) is the probability of having the disease, given a positive test, P(e/d) is the probability of testing positive for the disease if you really do have it (which we assume to be 100%), P(d) is the probability of having the disease (ie 0.1%) and P(e) is the probability of evidence for the disease – a positive test – appearing anyway, which is 5%. If you find this counter-intuitive, imagine a fictitious disease which absolutely no-one has. If there is a false positive rate of 5% in a test for this disease, you do not assume there is a 95% chance of having the disease if you test positive for it. Instead, you know from the base probability that you don't have the disease. But why should you pay heed to a base probability of 0 per cent, but ignore a base probability of 0.1%?

10. These, and more, come from:

www.gmu.edu/departments/economics/bcaplan/progs.htm.

11. *Everyday Irrationality*, p8-9.

12. *Human Inference: Strategies and Shortcomings of Social Judgment*, p44.

13. When I was at school, I paid little attention to French lessons, as I believed people from my background would never be able to travel to France.

14. *The Ingenuity Gap*, p178.

15. *Independent*, July 26, 2001.

16. *Law, Legislation and Liberty, volume I: Rules and Order*, p57.

17. *The Ingenuity Gap*, p2.

18. Daniel Kahneman and Amos Tversky, "Intuitive Prediction: Biases and Corrective Procedures", in Kahneman, Slovic and Tversky (eds).

19. *Human Inference,* p37.

20. *Sour Grapes,* p120.

21. *Plundering the Public Sector,* p170. It's not clear whether what's happening here is the cognitive bias of ego-involvement, or a failure of incentives. Maybe civil servants stick by their past decisions simply because admitting failure would be bad for their careers. Which raises the question: what sort of organization is it that penalises honesty?

22. Quoted in Oliver Williamson, *Markets and Hierarchies,* p200.

23. See, for example, Philip Stephens, "The Treasury Under Labour", p204 in Anthony Seldon (ed), *The Blair Effect.*

24. *Human Inference,* p10.

25. "Test Results are What You Think They Are" p241 in ch 17 in Kahneman, Slovic and Tversky (eds).

26. Vito Tanzi and Ludger Schuknecht, *Public Spending in the 20th Century,* p89-92 and chapter 6. This should not be as surprising as it seems. The keys to living longer lie in diet, exercise and a stress-free life, not in higher taxes. And an educated nation is one with a culture which values learning, not merely high spending.

27. This comes from Raymond Boudon, *The Art of Self-Persuasion,* p236.

28. "Naive diversification strategies in defined contribution savings plans", *American Economic Review,* 91, March 2001, p79-99.

29. "The Illusion of Control", p236-37, in ch 16 of Kahneman, Slovic and Tversky (eds).

30. Magne Jorgensen, Karl Halvor Teigen and Kjetil Molokken, "Better sure than safe? Overconfidence in judgment-based software development prediction intervals", *Journal of Systems and Software,* 70, February 2004, p79-93.

31. *Times,* December 4, 2006.

32. Jonathan Evans, Stephen Newstead and Ruth Byrne, *Human Reasoning: The Psychology of Deduction,* p99-108.

33. "Shortcomings in the Attribution Process", p145, in ch 9 of Kahneman, Slovic and Tversky (eds).

34. *Nuts and Bolts for the Social Science,* p25.

35. "Too many cooks spoil the profits: the performance of investment clubs", August 1999.

36. Timur Kuran, *Private Truths, Public Lies: The Social Consequences of Preference Falsification,* p163.

37. *The Moral Dimension,* p188.

38. *Groupthink,* p10.

39. "Are two heads better than one?", *National Bureau of Economic Research working paper* 7909, September 2000 and Clare Lombardelli, James Proudman and James Talbot, "Committees versus individuals: an experimental analysis of monetary policy decision-making", *Bank of England working paper* 165, September 2002.

40. *Politics and Markets,* p67.

41. "The knowledge of economics and the economics of knowledge", *American Economic Review,* 56, May 1966, p1-13, p8.

42. Cited in *Private Truths, Public Lies,* p28-30.

43. A good discussion of these issues can be found in Rod Rhodes, "The Civil Service", in Anthony Seldon (ed), *The Blair Effect.*

44.*Reckoning with Risk,* p159.

45. I am not arguing here that market processes always succeed in weeding out inefficiencies. Sometimes they do not. The companies that are closed down by recession need not necessarily be the most inefficient, and large company, simply by virtue of their size, often have advantages over their smaller competitors that make the latter more likely to fail. And even if the market's selection process did work perfectly, it could, like natural selection itself, only deliver a local, rather than global, optimum.

46. Gigerenzer and Selten (eds), *Bounded Rationality: The Adaptive Toolbox.*

47. *Reason in Human Affairs,* p22.

48. *Human Inference,* p14.

49. "Facts versus Fears: Understanding Perceived Risk", p477, in ch 33 of Kahneman, Slovic and Tversky (eds).

50. "The internet and the investor", *Journal of Economic Perspectives,* volume 15, winter 2001, p41-54.

51. *The Ingenuity Gap,* ps 321 and 88.

14.

The Idle Slave of the Passions

'Experts' frequently do not know what
they are talking about and 'scholarly
opinion', more often than not, is but
uninformed gossip. (Paul Feyerabend.[1])

In chapter 13, we assumed there was a single standard of rationality, from which people fell short due to human frailty. This assumption is wrong. Rationality, like its bedfellow efficiency, is a much less coherent concept that rationalist technocrats like to believe.

In this chapter, I shall first explore the ambiguities and inadequacies of the conventional modern-day idea of rationality. Then, I shall show that even where rationality is clear, knowledge – the material rationality has to work with – is often missing. The main tools of the manager and technocrat – knowledge and rationality – are therefore weaker than thought.

The ambiguity of rationality

Let's start with Newcomb's problem[2]. This shows that the basic rules which rationality recommends to us can conflict. "Rationality" is therefore ambiguous, and often cannot recommend a definite course of action.

The problem is as follows. There are two boxes. One contains $1,000. The second contains either nothing or $1 million. You have a choice; take what is in both boxes, or to take only what is in the second box.

However, the $1m will have been put in the second box by a superhuman being, the Predictor, if and only if he predicts you will take the second box only; if he predicts you will take both boxes, he puts nothing in the second box. You believe the Predictor is almost 100% reliable. And he knows you believe this. The pay-offs to your choice are shown in the table on the next page. What do you do?

There are two possible lines of reasoning.

The first is what Robert Nozick calls evidential expected utility theory. This says we should take only the second box. This is because the Predictor

Table 23. Pay-offs to Newcomb's problem

	A	*B*
Take second box	$1m	0
Take both boxes	$1m + $1000	$1000

will have anticipated this choice, and put the $1 million in the box. If on the other hand we choose both boxes, he will have predicted this, and we will be left with just $1,000. Our choice is therefore evidence of what the predictor has done.

The second line of reasoning is what Nozick calls causal expected utility. This says we should take both boxes. The idea here is that the Predictor has already made his choice, so the $1 million is either in the second box or not. If it is in the second box, and we take both boxes, we get $1m plus $1,000. And if it is not in the box, we will get $1,000 anyway. Either way, choosing both boxes dominates choosing just one box.

We therefore have a dilemma. You may think the way out of the puzzle lies in estimating the probability of the Predictor being right. After all, if the chances of him being right about our choice were just 60 per cent, most of us would choose both boxes. This, however, is a false solution. What's at stake here are two rules of choice. How can the validity of these allegedly logical rules possibly depend upon a mere contingent probability?

We have a genuine conflict between two genuine principles of choice. Rationality is therefore ambiguous.

This is no mere philosophical construct. It has practical applications. Take three.

Should we vote in general elections? Causal expected utility says no. The chances of our vote making a difference to the result are smaller than the chances of being run over on the way to the polling booth. So we should stay at home. However, evidential expected utility says we should vote. You might reason: "if I choose to vote, it's evidence that others like me will also choose to do so."

Should the UK restrict its carbon emissions? Causal expected utility says no, because our emissions are tiny and so won't on their own make any difference to global climate change. Evidential expected utility, however, says we should. Our choice to limit emissions is evidence that other countries, similarly situated, will also choose to do so. And together we can make a difference.

Should a central bank wishing to avert a recession cut interest rates? Causal expected utility theory says: "yes, obviously." But evidential expected utility theory suggests things are not as simple. Companies and consumers might interpret a rate cut as a sign that the economy is weaker than they had previously thought – because, they figure, "all those clever economists at the Bank must know something we don't." As result, a small rate cut may be counter-productive[3].

Actually, things aren't even as simple as this. So far, we've considered only two conceptions of rationality. But there's a third conception – symbolic rationality. There are some things it is rational to do not because they cause good outcomes, or are evidence of possible good outcomes, but rather because they signal to ourselves or others the kind of person we are.

Symbolic rationality, I suspect, is the key to understanding a vast amount of political activity (or inactivity). Take four examples.

- *State intervention.* Rigorous cold-headed belief rationality would conclude that policies as diverse as minimum wage laws, the "war on drugs" and ever-increasing spending on public services are hard to defend in terms of costs and benefits. And yet many politicians passionately favour them – more strongly than belief rationality would justify. This is probably because such policies have great symbolic value, as indicators of what sort of people we are.

- *Political protest.* The effort expended by protesters against fox-hunting or the war in Iraq cannot be justified by the effect such protests have on policy – which is tiny. Instead, its benefit lies in the symbolic value of demonstrating that they feel strongly about an issue. (This value does not just exist to the protestors themselves. Many of us are pleased to see that people are willing to stand up to the government, even if we're not wholly sure of their motives for doing so.)

- *Vietnam and Iraq.* Instrumental rationality tells us that in taking any decision we must ignore sunk costs. Bygones must be bygones. Only marginal expected benefits and marginal expected costs matter. However, sunk costs are a symbol of our past commitments. And it is quite reasonable to attach weight to these, because they define who we are. The classic example of this occurred in the late 1960s. By then, it was clear that the US could not win the Vietnam war. Instrumental rationality therefore dictated it should pull out. It didn't. This was in part due to a desire to honour sunk costs – to show that the dead had not given their lives in vain, and to show that the US would not be pushed around. Perhaps similar motives will keep US troops in Iraq.

- *The decline of voting.* I suspect a big reason for falling voter turnout is that the symbolic value of doing so has declined. Many people used to vote Labour because "Labour is the party of the working class and I'm working class." Or they voted Conservative because "the Conservatives represent good English traditions." Both these motives have declined in recent years. Politicians now expect us to vote for them out of causal expected utility motives. But these cannot justify voting.

"Rationality", then, is much more ambiguous than you might think. And this is just the start.

The Humean illusion

Let's now take a closer look at the conventional conception of rationality, instrumental rationality. There's a lot wrong with this. To see it, we first need to understand what exactly we mean by instrumental rationality. The conventional account has five elements.

First, desires are taken as given. They are matters of taste or preference, about which reason has little to say. As David Hume famously put it: "Reason is, and ought only to be the slave of the passions, and can never pretend to any office other than to serve and obey them"[4]. This has an analogue in public affairs. Technocrats often respond to ethical questions by claiming these are matters to be decided by the public or politicians, and that their purpose is merely to advise on how to achieve the goals of public policy. Their reason is the slave of public passions.

Secondly, our beliefs about how best to achieve our desires must be ruled by pure reason. If reason is impotent in determining desires whilst passion is omnipotent, exactly the opposite is true in determining beliefs. These must be decided by facts and reasoning, not by passion. There's no place for wishful thinking.

But how do we gather the facts to determine our beliefs? Herein lies the third precept of rationality. We must gather evidence up to the point where the marginal benefit of it just balances the marginal costs. Acting upon a belief for which you have not gathered evidence is irrational. But it can also be irrational to gather too much evidence, as when a man measures the length of each blade of grass before deciding whether his lawn needs cutting.

Fourthly, when our desires and beliefs are settled, we must choose the action which is expected to best fulfil our desires. To act otherwise is to display weakness of the will – which is irrational.

There is one final aspect of instrumental rationality which is often overlooked. As Amitai Etzioni points out, we must also cultivate the habits and personality which allow us to obey the precepts of instrumental rationality[5]. We must know how to separate reason and emotion, and to keep each in their proper place. And we must learn the rules of deduction and inference. As we saw in chapter 13, this takes more effort than is often realised.

This, or something like it, is the standard account of instrumental rationality. There is, however, much that is wrong with such a concept.

The first set of problems concerns its account of desires. The idea that our desires are things we just have that cannot be the subject of reason implies that it can sometimes be rational (or at least not irrational) to be addicted to drugs or alcohol. As Gary Becker and Kevin Murphy wrote: "Addictions, even strong ones, are usually rational in the sense of involving forward-looking maximisation with stable preferences[6]."

This sounds absurd. How can it be rational to behave in ways that can ruin our lives?

There's another absurdity. Douglas Allen points out that instrumental rationality means we are all "slaves of our preferences" – as these are beyond our reason[7]. This in turn has a disturbing implication – there's no such thing as free will. If our choices can be determined mechanically from prices and our preferences – as instrumental rationality implies – then "consumer choice" is a fiction. It makes more sense to talk of consumer slavery. As George Ainslie has said, if our "choices" are in fact determined entirely by expected utility, we never really decide anything – we merely discern incentives[8].

There's another problem. To see it, imagine you have three choices: to go for a run, to play a computer game or to go shopping. These actions can be judged according to three criteria: anticipated happiness, experienced happiness, and remembered happiness. What do you do?

You might reason as follows. The thought of going for a run is not appealing. It's cold out, and you know your muscles will ache. Anticipated utility is therefore low. But anticipated utility from shopping will be high; just think of the nice things you'll buy. Anticipated utility from playing the computer game falls between these two.

Now think of experienced utility – the happiness you'll get whilst doing the activity itself. Past experience suggests you won't enjoy shopping at all; the shops are too crowded, and they never have the things you really want. This is therefore the worst thing you can do. On the other hand, you know running won't feel so bad once you're out and warmed up. But playing the computer game will be best of all.

Finally, consider remembered utility. This will be low for the computer game, because you will feel guilty about wasting your time. It will be high for running, because you will feel as if you've gotten fitter. And it will be middling for the shopping – because you might come away with something nice, although you'll feel poorer.

These considerations generate a set of preferences as shown in table 24, where 1 represents first choice, and so on. Now, what do you choose?

Table 24. An intra-personal impossibility theorem

	Running	Computer game	Shopping
Anticipated utility	3	2	1
Experienced utility	2	1	3
Remembered utility	1	3	2

The answer is that if the problem is framed in this way, you cannot choose; table 24 has the same structure as Arrow's impossibility theorem, which we met in chapter 11. This theorem applies equally well to individuals as to society.[9]

In practice, our solution to this puzzle is simply to sometimes go shopping, sometimes go running, and sometimes play computer games. Instrumental rationality, however, tells us this is irrational. It decrees that when the pay-offs are the same, we should choose the same every time.

This is because it denies that the question should be framed as it is in table 24. It says that instead of merely ranking the pay-offs, we must attach precise numbers to them – that everything must be commensurable, not just comparable.

But is this the case? Do we – should we – really take the time to put precise numbers upon our choices? Surely not. Such an exercise would probably be arbitrary and superfluous – merely arranging the numbers to justify a decision we have already taken. And if it isn't, it would probably violate the third precept of rationality – that the costs of acquiring information must not exceed the benefits.

You might think this is trivial. Not so. It highlights a profound point. Any conception of rationality is, fundamentally, a conception of what it means to be a person. Instrumental rationality assumes that individuals are like hierarchical organizations. Orders flow down from the chief executive, who sets out desires. Operatives (our faculty for reason) merely find the best way to carry them out.

Perhaps some of the perceived legitimacy of hierarchy arises from this homology. We think of hierarchy as natural because we think of the self as a hierarchy, with reason being the slave of the passions. Or maybe it's the other way round. We think of the self as a hierarchy because hierarchical structures have been all around us.

Whether it's either or neither, the truth is that the self is not always a hierarchy. Sometimes, it's a group of equals haggling among each other; our "get fit" member bargains with our "play Civ III" member. The notion that the outcome of this bargaining maximises anything is a fiction.

Of course, it's not always the case that individuals are like groups. There are some choices we make that are much clearer and stronger than a temporary compromise among our different selves. Some choices define who we are.

However, instrumental rationality cannot explain these either.

Instrumental rationality predicts that, if we value two things, there must be some odds at which we would bet one for the other. If you value both £1 and a sports car, there must be some odds at which you would happily pay £1 for the chance of winning the car.

Sounds reasonable? It's not, points out John Searle. This theory predicts that he should accept some chance, albeit of the order of billions to one, of his son being killed in exchange for a penny. But, he says, there are no odds at all at which he would accept such a gamble.

Instrumental rationalists tell him he is being irrational. He replies that this merely shows that their rules "are not satisfactory at all"[10].

Their inadequacy lies in the fact that valuable things are not all commensurable. It is impossible to find terms on which they can be exchanged for each other. To even try to compare your son's life with any sum of money betrays a crass ignorance of what it means to be a father, even of what life itself means. Commensurability therefore violates some of our most precious values.

We reject such violations not only because we don't like their costs and pay-offs, but because of what they reveal about ourselves. Our actions don't just have material consequences, they have symbolic importance. Searle does not accept an infinitesimal chance of his son's death because to do so would raise the question: "what kind of person are you?" The pure instrumental rationalist who would accept such a chance is a monster, ignorant of the meaning of life and oblivious to the fact that we are human beings, not human choosings.

This discussion shows that the Humean notion of instrumental rationality contrives to be inconsistent with both our mundane everyday choices and our important life-defining ones. Instrumental rationality ignores that aspect of us which consists of an internal bazaar, in which ad hoc bargains are struck between different interests. And it ignores the fact that some things are not to be traded at all – they are beyond choice.

This is not the only problem with the treatment of desires in the conventional account of instrumental rationality.

Another is that it is often not the case that desires are logically prior to actions. Many only emerge after we have followed a practice for some time – because only then do we realise they are achievable. No normal child wants to be a professor of economics. It is only a few years after becoming an economist that the desire typically emerges. Similarly, today's policy objective of targeting a precise level of inflation has only arisen after years of striving to reduce inflation to some vague acceptable level. Practices, therefore, can produce desires, and not just vice versa.

Also, instrumental rationality assumes that desires can be achieved by direct means. But this is often not the case. If you want to fall asleep, for example, trying to do so will often be counter-productive. A similar thing may be true of the goal of full employment. As we saw in chapter 3, if workers believe the government is committed to securing full employment, they may get inflationary pay rises, which undermine full employment. Jobs for all, therefore, may be one of those things best achieved by not striving for it.

It is not only its treatment of desires that makes instrumental rationality silly, however. There's another difficulty. There are two different conceptions of rationality within instrumental rationality. On the one hand, rationality is what best fulfils our desires. On the other hand, rationality requires that beliefs are compatible with the evidence.

These can conflict. Imagine a man is found guilty, after a fair trial and with overwhelming evidence, of a series of brutal murders. Should his doting mother believe he is guilty, even if to do so would break her heart? Or consider recovering alcoholics. These often say "another drink will kill me." As a factual statement, this is plain wrong. But it is what the alcoholic must believe if he is to stick to his determined desire to stay dry.

These examples illustrate a contradiction. Instrumental rationality requires both that we pursue our own (self-defined) interests, and that our beliefs fit the facts. Sometimes, though, our most basic interests can best be served by having beliefs that don't fit the facts.

This helps explain a curious finding from social psychology – that, as Jon Elster puts it "the individuals who have the best judgment – who are, that is, most able to be guided by the reality principle rather than the pleasure principle – are clinically depressed people. They are sadder but wiser"[11]. Perhaps, then, it is not rational to be rational, because having rational beliefs might make us very unhappy.

This tension within the notion of rationality has economic implications. It means irrationality – in the sense of an over-confidence in our abilities – can be good for us, as it's the spur to creativity, innovation and economic growth. Richard Nisbett and Lee Ross have written:

> We probably would have few novelists, actors or scientists if all potential aspirants to these careers took action based on a normatively justifiable probability of success. We might also have few new products, new medical procedures, new political movements or new scientific theories.[12]

Equally, there's a tension between rationality in the sense of fulfilling our desire for more goods and rationality in the sense of our acquiring rational beliefs. This much was evident in Adam Smith's attitude towards the division of labour. This, he said, causes "the greatest improvement in the productive powers of labour"[13] but also makes workers "stupid and ignorant".[14] So, although the division of labour delivers the goods, it reduces the possibility of our ever acquiring rational beliefs.

There is one final set of problems with conventional instrumental rationality. These concern the fact that it is a rule-based rationality. There are rules of logical deduction, rules of statistical inference, and rules of decision theory.

This raises all sorts of problems. One, as we've seen, is that the rules conflict with each other. Another is that, as Ludwig Lachman points out, the notion of rationality as obeying rules of logic and inference ignores vast amounts of important human behaviour – anything that is spontaneous or creative, such as entrepreneurial activity.[15] Consider the Nobel prize in economics. Common sense says the winners of this are exemplars of human rationality. But this is not true, if by rationality we mean merely instrumental rationality. James Heckman won his prize not by following rules of inference, but by inventing new ones.

These considerations have led some thinkers to believe it is insufficient to define rationality in terms of abstract rules. Instead, they say, it is a virtue that can only be embedded in particular practices. "A cook is not a man who first has a vision of a pie and then tries to make it" says Michael Oakeshott. Instead:

> The characteristic of the judge, the carpenter, the scientist, the painter, the cook, and of any man in the ordinary conduct of life ...is a knowledge, not of certain propositions about themselves, their tools and the material in which they work, but a knowledge of how to decide certain questions...consequently, if 'rationality' is to represent a desirable quality of an activity, it cannot be the quality of having independently premeditated propositions about the activity before it begins.[16]

If this is right, then it kicks away the very foundation of managerialism. Management, as a separate practice, supposes that there are general rules along which any organization can be rationally run. But if rationality is inherently embedded in concrete practices, or if rules conflict, this supposition is plain wrong. "Management" can't be separated from the particular organization from which it arises. Early managers were much more aware of this than modern ones, As Protherough and Pick point out:

> Rightly, we honour the memory of managers such as Jesse Boot, Dr Barnardo, Florence Nightingale, Thomas Cook, the Joseph Rowntrees or W.H. Smith – people who have in past times created and run great and purposeful enterprises. But we do not admire them because of their excellence as personnel officers, resource controllers, production co-ordinators, relocation directors, downsizers or marketers – indeed they would not have understood the meaning of most of those terms – but because of the distinctive skill, dedication and prowess showed by each of them within their very different realms... The notion that they had in common a single talent which can be identified as "managerial skill", capable of ready transference between their different callings, is pure fantasy. That Dr Barnardo could equally well have run a chain of newsagents, or that Thomas Cook could just as readily have run a chocolate factory, is manifestly absurd.

Yet the modern world believes as fervently in the *transferability* of management as it believes that management skills are separate and identifiable realities[17].

Rationality as historical contingency

At this stage, you may be forgiven for being puzzled. How can it be that rationality – an idea we have taken for granted for so long – is so incoherent?

It may help overcome our dissonance if we recognise an often forgotten fact – that instrumental rationality is not a timeless attribute of human nature, but rather a relatively recent, and geographically limited, artificial construction.

This emerges clearly from Alasdair Macintyre's *Whose Justice? Which Rationality?* There, he shows that the modern Humean notion of rationality as the slave of the passions would have made little sense to the ancient Greeks. They saw rationality as the ability to discover what the true aims of a man should be – a question which Hume thought to be one for the passions to decide, not reason.

It is also clear, in a different way, in Michel Foucault's account of governmental rationality, or what he called governmentality.[18] This, he said, only emerged in the 17th and 18th century. Of course, thinkers had always discussed what sort of laws we should have, and Machiavelli had taught princes how to hang onto power. None, however, asked how to govern people, rather than territories. And none thought the state was in any meaningful sense analogous to a big household. It is only, said Foucault, after the centralised state emerged after the 16th century that such a paradigm emerged.

Economic rationality – in the sense of maximising output for given inputs – is also a relatively recent construction. This is clear from Marshall Sahlins' *Stone Age Economics*. He points out that primitive hunter-gatherer men are the exact opposite of modern economic men, because their wants are scarce whilst their means are plentiful. They do not therefore work long hours in an effort to acquire as much as possible, but rather do the bare minimum to ensure adequate nutrition. And what work they do is often easy-paced and relaxed. Sahlins writes:

> A good case can be made that the hunters and gatherers work less than we do; and rather than a continuous travail, the food quest is intermittent, leisure abundant, and there is a greater amount of sleep in the daytime per capita per year than in any other condition of society...The work process is sensitive to interference of various kinds, vulnerable to suspension in favour of other activities as serious as ritual, as frivolous as repose. The customary working day is often short; and if it is protracted, frequently it is interrupted; if it is both long and unremitting, usually this is only seasonal.[19]

It is not only the work patterns of primitive man that offend today's economic rationalist. So do the trading activities. Sahlins describes how trade is used not to get the maximum gain for the minimum sacrifice, but to make friends and cement alliances. Tribes are often more generous than they need be when they trade with each other.[20]

The triumph of Gradgrindian economic rationalism over this casual traditional approach to economic affairs was a difficult process. "A man 'by nature' does not wish to earn more and more money" wrote Max Weber.[21] Many factories went bust in the 18th century, simply because bosses could not get workers to do any more than the bare minimum necessary to get a subsistence wage. As economic historians such as Andre Gorz has shown, the "rationalization" necessary to stimulate economic growth consisted not merely in making production more methodical and "efficient", but was also a way of changing workers' preferences.[22]

In this sense, the triumph of economic rationalism required an inversion of Humean instrumental rationality – the "reason" of bosses had to become the master of workers' passions.

The traveller in the dark

The message of all this is simple. There's no ubiquitous, single coherent rationality. The appeal to "rationality" to justify a particular policy or action will therefore often be useless – because rationality can be so ambiguous as to recommend almost any action.

But let's assume this is false, and there is one coherent notion of rationality by which to judge and select policies. Let's assume also that all the biases and instincts that cause us to think irrationally are purged away. Could policy-making then be maximally effective?

Not at all – because even if rationality doesn't let us down, knowledge might. And as G.L.S. Shackle has pointed out, in the absence of good information, even the most rigorous rationality can be useless. Rationality, he said, "is an empty and idle term until the data available to the individual are specified. If they are incorrect, what is the good of his taking action which would be rational if they were correct? ... For the traveller in the dark, a bridge with a missing span is worse than merely useless".[23]

But what sort of knowledge is missing? There are two sorts. On the one hand, there are traditional ways of doing things. These are often very hard to codify but can contain hidden strengths. Here are three examples of how rationalism can conflict with these traditional ways:

- Attempts to introduce free market economies (or worse still centrally planned ones) into traditional societies can sometimes lead to the breakdown of these communities and their complex structures of adaptation and self-help. Russian history illustrates this most starkly. The famines of the 1930s after Stalin's attempts to collectivize agriculture, and the recession and social dislocation caused by the "shock therapy" of the early 1990s both testify to the damage done by different sorts of rationalism.

- The growth of the British welfare state in the 20th century sometimes supplanted charities, trades unions and friendly societies who had been providing decent support for thousands of people. Although this notion is now associated with New Right romanticism, it was once a quite "left wing" idea. Writing in 1958, Brian Abel-Smith said: "The single working man in sickness and unemployment had a better deal pre-war than he does today."[24]

- As Harry Braverman showed in *Labour and Monopoly Capital*, "scientific management" helped destroy traditional craft skills. Although his account is often seen as a story of how capitalists conquered workers, this did not always work in capitalists' best interests. If scientific management is such a good idea, why are "works to rule" considered a form of industrial action rather than the ultimate way of co-operating with management?

It is of course important not to over-romanticize traditional, unarticulated knowledge. Nevertheless, these examples show that an ignorance of such knowledge – and the attempt to supplant it with codifiable managerialist knowledge – can be very costly. This, according to David Craig and Richard Brooks in *Plundering the Public Sector*, is one of the mistakes New Labour made in trying to "modernize" the civil service. It over-estimated the expertise of management consultants, with their explicit codified rules of "rational" management, and under-estimated the traditional know-how of civil servants.

The second sort of information which often eludes rationalists is the knowledge of countless individual profit-making opportunities – the sort that lies in the answers to questions such as: how can I produce this thing cheaper? How can I get the best price for this good? How can I improve on this product, or this location? It is the fragmentary knowledge about how best to use scarce resources.

This knowledge – as Friedrich Hayek above all others pointed out – is often unavailable to any central agency. This is partly because there is so much of it, as it exists in millions of people going about their everyday business. It's also because knowledge is often, as in the case of a temporary profitable opportunity, merely transitory.

You might think Hayek's concern is now out-dated. After all, don't we live in an "information age" in which billions of pieces of information can be transmitted around the world in a micro-second?

This misses the point. Information technology gives us the impression that all knowledge can be broken into byte-sized chunks, codified, organised and transmitted. But this is not so. Knowledge may not be articulable at all. We know more than we can say: just try to write down a set of instructions for tying your shoelaces. "Knowledge management" is a contradiction in terms.

Herein lies the strongest case for free markets rather than government intervention. It rests not upon the notion that markets somehow reach an optimum allocation of resources, but upon the fact that they are far better able to use dispersed, tacit knowledge than central planners – because prices are a way of communicating such information. Markets might not always allocate resources efficiently, but they use knowledge efficiently.

This much is widely known – or at least should be. What is less well appreciated is that the role of fragmentary, tacit, information is central to any understanding of the economy.

It's such knowledge that causes entrepreneurship. Businesses are started (or closed) because individual entrepreneurs have local knowledge of what processes or products will work in particular places. It is the effort to profit from dispersed, peculiar and idiosyncratic information that generates innovation and entrepreneurial activity. Table 25 shows the importance of this. It shows that even during years of macroeconomic stability, a typical year sees almost one-tenth of all companies close, and another one-tenth open, as thousands of individuals exploit the knowledge that a profitable opportunity has opened or another closed. Underneath apparently stable macroeconomic aggregates lies huge disruption. As Joseph Schumpeter said:

> The capitalist economy is not and cannot be stationary...It is incessantly being revolutionized from within by new enterprise...Any existing structures and all the conditions of doing business are always in a process of change. Every situation is being upset before it has had time to work itself out. Economic progress, in capitalist society, means turmoil.[25]

Table 25. VAT registrations and de-registrations (thousands)

	Registrations	De-registrations	Stock at start-year
1998	182.2	145.8	1667.3
1999	176.9	150.3	1703.8
2000	178.9	155.8	1730.4
2001	170.0	155.9	1753.5
2002	176.9	162.4	1767.6
2003	191.2	165.5	1782.2
2004	183.8	163.4	1807.9
2005	177.9	152.9	1828.2

Source: Department of Trade and Industry press release, 24 October 2006.

This raises the question: what right do we have to speak of "the economy" as if it were much the same animal from one year to the next, when huge chunks of it are perpetually disappearing and being replaced?

No right at all, say some. Perhaps fragmentary, tacit, knowledge, it renders many concepts of macroeconomics – perhaps even the whole discipline – meaningless. Macroeconomic theory says David Simpson "is fundamentally inadequate and, when applied, gives conclusions which are misleading in practice".[26]

This is because the aggregate concepts on which macroeconomics rests, such as consumer spending or the price level, are in reality the results of millions of individual actions. And these actions are not necessarily repeated from day to day, or even from year to year. As a result, there's no reason to suppose they will be stable from one day or year to the next.

What's more, an aggregate or average need not be true of any of the particulars of which it is composed. This means it is dangerous to assume that macroeconomic variables somehow reflect an underlying reality. It makes far more sense to regard macroeconomic variables as the result of individual decisions than as the cause of them. As O'Driscoll and Rizzo say, we should forget talk of the "price level" or "output as a whole", because "neither aggregate has any real existence, or has any direct impact on economic decision-making".[27]

However, the fact that macroeconomic aggregates are, at best, merely a crude shorthand description of millions of individual actions means it is almost impossible to peer behind this description to grasp a deeper reality. For this reason says Shackle, economics is "fundamentally, essentially, imprecise and blurred".[28]

Roughly right versus precisely wrong

These are not the only problems standing in our way of understanding how economies work. Another is that it's often hard in economics to establish counterfactuals; one reason why we can't say how good a Chancellor Gordon Brown has been is that we can't agree upon what the relevant alternative is. There's also the problem of the Duhem-Quine thesis – that it's often impossible to test single hypotheses rather than conjunctions of them.[29]

There's also the fact that people, unlike the objects of study of most natural sciences have minds of their own. This opens up a host of problems for the economist which the physicist doesn't have. One is that beliefs determine behaviour. For example, if people believe an expansion in the money supply will lead to inflation, then it will lead to higher inflation expectations and therefore rising inflation. But if they believe it will lead to higher output, expectations of this will also be self-fulfilling.

Also, people learn. So if they discover that a central bank really is committed to delivering low inflation, whatever the cost, their inflation expectations will fall. Behaviour will therefore change, in a way electrons' behaviour cannot.

Thirdly, people have intentions. Only by understanding these can we make sense of behaviour. For example, if an employer is paying his workers more than a rival firm, is this a temporary disequilibrium that will soon be eliminated by competition? Or is it a disciplining device intended to reduce shirking? Or is it because working conditions are more unpleasant or prospects for career development less promising so workers need a higher wage as compensation? Or is it because these workers are white men and the employer is indulging a racial prejudice? Or is it because productivity is higher because of a more modern capital stock or more skilled workers? Only by answering these questions can we understand wage inequalities. And that requires a consideration of the employers' intentions. Physicists, by contrast, need only bother with observable behaviour.

The cliché-mongers say this means economics – and indeed the study of society generally – is an art, not a science.

But this is gibberish. As Deirdre McCloskey has said, anyone who thinks there's a clear distinction between art and science just hasn't read anything in the philosophy of science since 1955.[30] By some standards – does knowledge progress? – economics is obviously a "science". And by others – do we rigorously follow Popperian falsifiability? – the natural sciences are not "scientific."

Rather than get hung up on this silly issue, there's a more important message here. It's that the aims of social sciences should be modest. Rather than search for universal law-like generalisations that will help us control society, they should instead, as Jon Elster has said, content themselves with identifying mechanisms.[31]

This means it will often be easier to explain events than to foresee them. As we have seen in our discussion of macroeconomic stability, there are several mechanisms linking this to good or bad outcomes. We cannot foresee in advance which of these mechanisms will be triggered. The best we can hope – and even this may be too optimistic – is that we will be able to identify the dominant mechanisms after the event.

What is clear is that the aspirations of economics to be a "hard science" are misplaced. They might even be positively dangerous. This is because the search for precision can get in the way of the truth. If precision were the mark of a good scientific theory, we would prefer Archbishop Ussher's claim that the world began in 4004BC to modern cosmologists' belief that the universe is roughly 13 billion years old.

There are many examples of how it is, in Keynes' words, better to be "roughly right than precisely wrong." David Simpson has argued that the search for quantifiable, testable relationships has led economists to ignore important but unmeasurable facts such as entrepreneurship, innovation and many psychological factors.[32]

Writing in the mid-1970s, Hayek argued that this bias could be very costly. Unemployment, he said, may be due either to a lack of demand or to a mismatch between the distribution of demand and the distribution of labour and capital. The former claim may be more precise, because its proponents often argue that a certain quantity of extra demand will lead to a definite fall in joblessness, whereas proponents of the latter view cannot claim to know which structure of relative prices will reduce unemployment. However, the view that unemployment was a problem of deficient demand proved disastrous in practice, as it led to ever-increasing inflation and a willingness to overlook the growing sclerosis of the price system. Hayek concluded: "I prefer true but imperfect knowledge, even if it leaves much undetermined and unpredictable, to a pretence of exact knowledge which is likely to be false."[33]

Like lonely men

The message of all this is stark. Policy-makers and their advisors cannot be relied upon to act "rationally" even if they can avoid the countless cognitive biases to which we are all vulnerable. This is because rationality itself is a contradictory notion, and because even when it is coherent, we often lack the information necessary to use it adequately.

This means many everyday political judgments rest on flimsier foundations than generally thought. They are often, says Jon Elster "made under conditions of radical cognitive indeterminacy". He continues:

> No theories exist that allow us to predict the long-term equilibrium effects of large scale social reforms and ...trial and error cannot substitute for theoretical prediction. Theory is impotent and we cannot learn from experience and experiments.[34]

Is it any wonder, therefore, that, as we have seen, the long-run effects of macroeconomic stability, or increased education, or a national minimum wage should be so hard to assess?

In this context, a distinction made by Deirdre McCloskey becomes very useful. There is, she said, a big distinction between rationalism and rationality[35]. Rationalism believes we can solve all society's problems by using knowledge and reason. Rationality – in the vague sense of thinking carefully – tells us this is not so.

This raises a nasty question. If rationality is not the powerful tool we think it is for reaching good or correct policy conclusions, what exactly is its function?

Partly, we use it as a drunk uses a lamp-post – for support, not illumination. Like lonely men who exaggerate the virtues of their few friends, we exaggerate our capacity for rational behaviour to give ourselves false assurance. "What we boldly call rational evaluation is a way of steeling ourselves to endow our actions with the shimmering look of conviction" says Amelie Oksenberg Rorty. "It is our magic for acquiring a brave face and a sureness of manner".[36]

It's not just in policy-making that this is the case. Gerd Gigerenzer points out that it's also true of the medical profession. Meetings between doctors and patients, he points out, are rituals, in which patients seek reassurance as much as a rational cure for their illness. He quotes an anonymous doctor:

A physician who takes anxiety away from the patient is a good doctor. One has to do something; one cannot do nothing; the patient would be disappointed or even angry. Most prescriptions have no proven effect, but when the patient applies the ointment, the doctor, the patient and the pharmaceutical company are happy.[37]

Perhaps, then, the so-called experts differ from the rest of us not because of their superior knowledge or rationality, but because of their superior capacity for self-deception.

There is, however, another use of "rationality" – to give an appearance of legitimacy to what are merely claims to power. When reason is the slave of the passions, that passion is often a lust for power.

Both New Labour and the Conservatives also use "rationality" as a tool for gaining power. Both try to win votes by claiming that they have the rationality and expertise to manage the public services better.

Whether such claims are plausible or correct is not the point. What is the point is that the desire for power comes first, and claims to possess expertise will be merely the means to achieve power.

This is clear in the history of New Labour. Its leaders did not enter politics because they wanted to introduce tax credits or even the minimum wage, and still less because they wanted to make the Bank of England independent.

None of these policies were contained in the 1983 manifesto upon which Messrs Brown and Blair were first elected to parliament. Instead, they were adopted because they reconcile a desire for power with Labour principles. The claim that these policies are efficient or rational comes after the lust for power.

Political parties, though, are not the only ones to use fictive claims to "expertise" to legitimate power. As writers such as Stephen Marglin, Andre Gorz and Harry Braverman have shown, managers' claims to possess expertise within the workplace often rests not upon narrow technical considerations, but upon a desire to take control of production out of the hands of workers. Alasdair Macintyre has asked:

> What if effectiveness is part of a masquerade of social control rather than a reality? What if effectiveness were a quality widely imputed to managers and bureaucrats...but in fact is a quality which rarely exists apart from this imputation?... Do we possess that set of lawlike generalisations governing social behaviour of the possession of which Diderot and Condorcet dreamed? Are our bureaucratic rules thereby justified or not? It has not been sufficiently remarked that how we ought to answer the question of the moral and political legitimacy of the characteristically dominant institutions of modernity turns on how we decide an issue in the philosophy of the social sciences.[38]

Macintyre believes terms such as effectiveness, efficiency and rationality may function as some atheists believe "God" to function – as a fictitious belief, appeal to which disguises more important realities.

Now, you might object at this point that I am being unreasonably idealistic. Some forms of power are necessary in any society. They must be legitimated somehow. And it is a foolish counsel of perfection to call for this legitimisation to be wholly intellectually justifiable. Just as individuals need a little self-deception in order to carry on living, so too do societies.

This ignores the fact that the attempt to legitimate power by appealing to expertise and rationality carries some big costs.

Not least of these is that it threatens our very freedom. The easiest way for us to lose our liberties is to accept the claims of experts that some greater good will be achieved if we sacrifice them. And it is a small step – but a vitally important one – from claiming to know better than one's fellow citizens to imposing this often spurious knowledge upon them. As Hayek said: "The erroneous belief that the exercise of some power would have beneficial consequences is likely to lead to a new power to coerce other men being conferred on some authority."[39]

This is a very slippery slope indeed. Paul Feyerabend has argued that rationalism is very close to Nazism. He wrote:

I say that Auschwitz is an extreme manifestation of an attitude that still thrives in our midst. It shows itself in the treatment of minorities in industrial democracies; in education, education to a humanitarian point of view included, which most of the time consists in turning wonderful young people into colourless and self-righteous copies of their teachers...It shows itself in the killing of nature and of 'primitive' cultures with never a thought spent on those thus deprived of meaning for their lives; in the colossal conceit of our intellectuals, their belief that they know precisely what humanity needs and their relentless efforts to recreate people in their own sorry image; in the infantile megalomania of some of our physicians who blackmail their patients with fear, mutilate them and then persecute them with large bills; in the lack of feeling of many so-called searchers for truth who systematically torture animals, study their discomfort and receive prizes for their cruelty...As far as I am concerned, there exists no difference whatsoever between the henchmen of Auschwitz and these 'benefactors of mankind' – life is misused for special purposes in both cases.[40]

You might think this is an offensive exaggeration. I thought so too – until I recalled an essay by the "liberal" Maynard Keynes, where he wrote: "The time may arrive a little later when the community as a whole must pay attention to the innate quality as well as to the mere numbers of its future members."[41] Rationalism can easily lead to eugenics. And where does that lead?

It is not only freedom that is endangered by the arrogation of a fictitious rationality. Such claims can easily lead to an unwarranted shrillness in political debate. The notion of a single truth and a single rationality can only mean that if my truth differs from your truth, or my rationality from your rationality, one of us is being stupid. The upshot is that many political "debates" either become mere slanging matches – in which neither side realizes that their "rationality" is only one partial conception of the nature of rationality- or sides end up only talking among themselves.

Another problem with rationalism is that it can cause society to become too inflexible to cope with unpleasant surprises, because it encourages us to adopt, in McCloskey's useful distinction, "tricky policies rather than wise institutions".[42]

A paper by Joao Ferreira do Amaral shows how this can happen[43]. Imagine a company has no notion at all about the outlook for demand in its industry. It will therefore, for want of any better judgment, regard boom and slump as equally likely and plan accordingly. Its managing director then has an idea. Let's employ some consultants to forecast demand, so we can plan our output better. These consultants then tell him there is an 80 per cent chance of a boom. The MD therefore decides to build a new factory. But the boom never happens. This is not because the consultants were wrong but because 20 per cent chances do sometimes come up. Our MD is therefore burdened with an unprofitable factory. In rationally deciding to acquire more knowledge, and then rationally acting upon this knowledge, he has lost money.

The lesson of this, says Amaral, is that "it does not always pay to be rational." This is because as our knowledge increases, so too does the scope for surprises. And these surprises can be very unsettling, especially if we have invested on the basis of knowledge. It may be better, says Amaral, not to gather more information, but instead to ensure that our institutions are flexible enough to cope with surprises.

This, perhaps, is another argument for free markets over hierarchical central planning. The latter can be very brittle. We saw this when the Soviet Union collapsed suddenly. We saw it also when the breakdown of the post-war settlement in the 1970s led to a crisis of governance, and doubts about the very sustainability of western democracy. Compare those crises to the way New York recovered reasonably well after the terrible blow of 9/11. It did so partly because a city's economy and society are flexible, resilient networks rather than knowledge-dependent hierarchies.

The crisis of rationalism and an alternative

In light of all this, a paradox at the heart of governmental rationality becomes more understandable. This is that it promises to solve problems, and yet these problems remain. As Peter Miller and Nicholas Rose wrote, "whilst governmentality is eternally optimistic, government is a congenitally failing operation".[44]

Strangely, rationalists often exacerbate this problem, rather than seek a solution to it. As Michael Oakeshott pointed out, the intrusion of rationalism into politics means that political life "is resolved into a succession of crises, each to be surmounted by the application of reason"[45]. Such diverse but common occurrences as recessions, inflation, poor education, high crime rates, food scares, fears about asylum-seekers or inadequate health care are all regarded as crises to be cured by rational central administration.

And yet central administration, as we all know, fails so often.

So what's the alternative?

First, we should – as far as possible – abandon the belief that government manages society. Society is not a common enterprise moving in a single direction, requiring leadership and management. It's a bunch of diverse people with diverse aims. The function of government should be to minimize conflicts between legitimate goals. Government should be an umpire, not a player, in Oakeshott's phrase.[46]

Secondly, policy-makers should learn from the natural sciences. The great thing about these is not their stock of knowledge but their method of enquiry.

The essence of science, in its ideal form, was captured by Richard Feynman when he said that the difference between true sciences and pseudo-sciences lies in the fact that the former bend over backwards to be honest whereas the latter do not[47]. As Mark Blaug put it: "Science, for all its shortcomings, is the only self-questioning and self-correcting ideological system that man has yet devised. ..the scientific community as a whole is the paradigm case of the open society"[48]. Richard Dawkins – perhaps a dangerous man to quote in this context – describes the scientific ideal in his story of one of his professors of zoology:

> For years he had passionately believed, and taught, that the Golgi apparatus (a microscopic feature of the interior of cells) was not real: an artefact, an illusion. Every Monday afternoon it was the custom for the whole department to listen to a research talk by a visiting lecturer. One Monday, the visitor was an American cell biologist who presented completely convincing evidence that the Golgi apparatus was real. At the end of the lecture, the old man strode to the front of the hall, shook the American by the hand and said – with passion – "My dear fellow, I wish to thank you. I have been wrong these fifteen years."[49]

Of course, scientists themselves often fall short of this ideal. But that does not invalidate its appeal as a model for policy-making.

And the thing is, this ideal is totally opposed to managerialism, in four ways:

- It is open, whereas managerialism is secretive. The essence of proper research is that it's published, and therefore subject to scrutiny. As James Mirrlees once said: "economists, like real people, cannot be trusted to give advice unless it is subject to the checks of publishable analysis."[50]

- It is egalitarian, whereas managerialism is hierarchic. The thing about Dawkins' story is that the visiting lecturer was relatively junior, and yet he was encouraged to criticise his elders' ideas.

- There's no ego-involvement, as Dawkins' story shows. In the ideal of science, the test of an idea is: "is it true?" not "whose is it?"

- It recognises the limits of our own wisdom. Managerialism does not. We must remember that, as Deirdre McCloskey says, "the only certitude is that yesterday's timeless orthodoxy will become tomorrow's laughing stock".[51] As a result, policy-makers must, as Etzioni said "proceed carefully, ready to reverse course, willing to experiment; in short, humbly".[52] Contrast this with the arrogant stridency of the managerialist, for example Blair's contemptible claim that he "has no reverse gear."

The message here is that the ideal of the open society is fundamentally opposed to managerialism. And managerialism's claim to power – that it has the knowledge and rationality to control society for the better – is just plain fantasy.

Notes

1. *Farewell to Reason,* p16.

2. The problem is named after a physicist, William Newcomb, although it was introduced to the literature by Robert Nozick in "Newcomb's problem and two principles of choice," reprinted in his *Socratic Puzzles.* It is discussed in detail in the essays in Richmond Campbell and Lanning Sowdon (eds), *Paradoxes of Rationality and Co-operation.*

3. Andrew Caplin and John Leahy, "Monetary Policy as a Process of Search", *American Economic Review,* 86, September 1996, p689-702.

4. *A Treatise on Human Nature,* p462.

5. *The Moral Dimension,* p153.

6. "A theory of rational addiction", *Journal of Political Economy,* 96, winter 1988.

7. "The paradox of choice: with an application to freewill versus predestination," *Journal of Interesting Economics,* 2002.

8. *Breakdown of Will,* p130.

9. This point is made in Ian Steedman and Ulrich Krause, "Goethe's Faust, Arrow's Possibility Theorem and the Individual Decision Taker" p207 in Jon Elster (ed), *The Multiple Self.*

10. *The Construction of Social Reality,* p138.

11. *Nuts and Bolts for the Social Sciences,* p38.

12. *Human Inference: Strategies and Shortcomings of Social Judgment,* p271.

13. *The Wealth of Nations,* p109.

14. *The Wealth of Nations Books IV-V,* p368-9.

15. *Macroeconomic Thinking and the Market Economy,* p22.

16. "Rational Conduct", p110-11 in *Rationalism in Politics and Other Essays.*

17. *Managing Britannia,* p13, emphasis in original.

18. "Governmentality", in Graham Burchell, Colin Gordon and Peter Miller (eds), *The Foucault Effect: Studies in Governmentality.*

19. *Stone Age Economics*, p14, 56.

20. *Stone Age Economics*, p186, 303. Note that I may be exaggerating the difference between them and us. George Akerlof has shown that over-reciprocation may be economically rational in ongoing relationships, such as employee-employer relations, as a way of building trust and so reducing risk. See his "Labour contracts as partial gift exchange", reprinted in Akerlof and Yellen (eds), *Efficiency Wage Models of the Labour Market*.

21. *The Protestant Ethic and the Spirit of Capitalism*, p24.

22. *Critique of Economic Reason*, p21.

23. *Epistemics and Economics*, p37.

24. "Whose Welfare State?", p56, in Norman MacKenzie (ed), *Conviction*.

25. *Capitalism, Socialism and Democracy*, p31-32.

26. *The End of Macroeconomics*, p71.

27. *The Economics of Time and Ignorance*, p226.

28. *Epistemics and Economics*, p72.

29. W.V.O. Quine, *From a Logical Point of View*, p41.

30. *Knowledge and Persuasion in Economics*, p56. She adds that English is one of the few languages in which the question even makes sense. In many others, the word science means merely "disciplined study", which can apply equally to literature and physics.

31. *Alchemies of the Mind*, p1.

32. *The End of Macroeconomics*, p34.

33. "The Pretence of Knowledge, Nobel Memorial Lecture December 11 1974, reprinted in Chiaki Nishiyama and Kurt Leube (eds), *The Essence of Hayek*, p266-76, p268.

34. *Solomonic Judgments*, p181.

35. *Knowledge and Persuasion in Economics*, p323.

36. "Self-deception, Akrasia and Irrationality" in Jon Elster (ed), *The Multiple Self*, p118.

37. *Reckoning with Risk*, p19.

38. *After Virtue*, p75, 87.

39. "The Pretence of Knowledge, p276

40. *Farewell to Reason*, p313.

41. "The End of Laisser-Faire", p292, in *Essays in Persuasion*. You might reply, reasonably, that Keynes was only a creature of his time, as an interest in eugenics was a popular fashion amongst liberal and left-leaning

intellectuals in the 1920s and 1930s. This may defend Keynes, but it strengthens Feyerabend's point.

42. *If You're So Smart*, p4.

43. "Surprise and uncertainty: is it rational to be rational?", February 2001.

44. "Governing economic life", p84, in Mike Gane and Terry Johnson (eds), *Foucault's New Domains*.

45. "Rationalism in Politics" p9, in *Rationalism in Politics and Other Essays*.

46. "On Being Conservative, p427, in *Rationality in Politics and other Essays*.

47. Cited in Thomas Mayer, *Truth versus Precision in Economics*, p141.

48. *The Methodology of Economics*, 2nd ed, p42.

49. *The God Delusion*, p283-84.

50. "The economic uses of utilitarianism" p84 in Sen and Williams (eds), *Utilitarianism and Beyond*.

51. *Knowledge and Persuasion in Economics*, p67.

52. *The Moral Dimension*, p244.

15.

Conclusion

The message of all this is simple. The state shouldn't be run as if it were a hierarchical business. There are conflicts between values, and ambiguities within them, so the state cannot have a simple clear objective like businesses can. Governments don't have the knowledge to design tricksy policies that can intervene in the economy for the better. And they don't have the rationality to do so.

Hierarchy, management, and leadership, then, can't solve social problems. Politicians over-rate their importance.

Indeed, it's increasingly doubtful that management has a place even in business. So politicians' belief that they should act like company bosses is even more questionable.

The End of Hierarchy?

To see why management is inefficient, let's begin with a curious paradox. In the 1970s and 1980s, Conservatives told us, rightly, that no-one had enough knowledge and rationality to manage an economy. But they also told us that bosses had enough know-how to manage a firm; "management's right to manage" was a popular slogan among early Thatcherites. However, as Ronald Coase pointed out in 1937 in his seminal paper, "The nature of the firm", there is a close parallel between economic planning within a nation and economic planning within a firm. This raises the question: if centrally planned economies were a stupid idea, why are centrally planned companies a good one?

Coase's answer was that in some circumstances the cost of using the price mechanism exceeded the costs of planning production by a hierarchy. Hierarchies can reduce the costs of gathering information by making this a specialised function rather than one performed occasionally by everyone. They can reduce the problems of asymmetric information between buyers and suppliers by bringing both under the control of the same person. And the problems caused by bilateral bargaining can be replaced by management fiat.[1]

However, the benefits of hierarchical control of firms are falling.

Firstly, production processes have become more complex. When the first factories were established by Richard Arkwright and James Watt, it made sense for them to control production with an iron hand, because they knew the production processes inside out – they had invented them. In these conditions, it made sense for information to flow up the hierarchy, and for solutions and instructions to flow down.

Today, management doesn't have this know-how. Products, process and markets are too complex for anyone to know as thoroughly as Arkwright or Watt did. If knowledge is power, ignorance should mean impotence.

Instead, knowledge of the production process is scattered across the organisation. If you have a problem, it is often better solved by asking your fellow workers than asking the boss.

However, hierarchies can obstruct co-operation between workers. One reason for this is simply that pyramidical reporting lines often prevent workers from knowing and therefore using the skills of their colleagues. Another reason is that communication requires trust – the trust that a confession of your ignorance will not be used against you. And, says Diane Coyle, "Skewed corporate hierarchies will almost certainly not be high-trust organisations".[2] Worse still, the benefits of co-operation are often impossible to quantify, and so a management obsessed with budgets and targets does not encourage it. And the knowledge that such gains will flow to managers, rather than themselves, will inhibit workers from co-operating fully.

A second reason for the declining usefulness of hierarchies is that the technological costs of storing and communicating information have collapsed. When it was expensive to communicate or store data, it was sensible to keep them in one place, and to limit communication. This was best done by pyramidical management, in which information flowed only up or down the pyramid, and data was stored at the apex. Now that information and data storage are almost free, though, it is easy for it to flow across the pyramid, from co-worker to co-worker. Middle management is no longer necessary as a conduit between bosses and workers.

Indeed, it's a positive obstacle. Simple sums tell us this. Imagine there are six layers of hierarchy through which information must be transmitted. Then imagine that 10 per cent of information gets lost through simple misunderstanding or wilful misrepresentation at each layer. It follows that only 53 per cent of information will make it from top to bottom of the hierarchy, or from bottom to top. It's small wonder, therefore, that top decision-makers can operate in imaginary worlds. The fate of "Comical Ali", Mohammed Saeed al-Sahaf, the former Iraqi minister of information, teaches all bosses a lesson.

Once upon a time, the cost of these Chinese whispers was tolerable, as the cost of full communication was even higher. But is this still the case today?

A third reason for the declining usefulness of hierarchy lies in the growth of the knowledge economy. It was entirely reasonable for Arkwright to control production like a dictator because his employees were incapable of making decisions – they were illiterate seven-year olds. Many workers today, though, are skilled professionals, whose knowledge is essential to the company. Treating these as hired hands to be ordered around is just stupid. It merely demotivates them.

This leads us to another crucial cost of hierarchy. Hierarchies are rubbish at fostering innovation, because you cannot order creativity. It might make sense to give the order "be here by nine o'clock." But it's just gibberish to say, "be creative." Hierarchies inhibit research by alienating creative spirits or by swamping them in market research.[3] The culture of presenteeism can prevent the emergence of those new ideas that come to us in our leisure time, or from casual conversations. And managers' desire to employ like-minded people who won't challenge their spurious authority – what they call "team players" – prevents the emergence of ideas from the creative clash of competing cultures.

These aren't problems that can be removed by good management – though they can be ameliorated. They are an inherent feature of hierarchy, as Kenneth Cloke and Joan Goldsmith have pointed out:

> Through years of experience, employees learn that it is safer to suppress their innate capacity to solve problems and wait instead for commands from above. They lose their initiative and ability to see how things can be improved. They learn not to care.[4]

The responses of management to these rising costs of hierarchy are revealing.

One has been to create yet more managers. At the start of the 19th century, the Arkwrights employed just three managers to supervise over 1,000 workers, most of whom were paid complex piece-rates.[5] Today, a firm of this size would employ ten times as many managers. Elementary economics tells us that if more and more of an input is needed to achieve the same output, there must be severely diminishing returns.

And there are. The same things that caused Friedrich Hayek to deplore the centrally planned economy should therefore cause us to decry the hierarchical company. As Manuel Castells says: "The large, multi-unit corporation, hierarchically organized around vertical lines of command seems to be ill-adapted to the informational, global economy."[6]

Another reaction has been to redefine the function of management.

In the sense pioneered by Frederick W. Taylor, management meant the efficient organization of resources. This skill – gained through a detailed study of work practices – was a valuable but humble function, subordinate to professional judgment. Farm managers sowed crops decided by the land-owner, and hospital ward managers did as senior doctors suggested.

Today, these hard skills have been replaced by abstract ones. Managers don't organise efficient production. Instead, they manipulate symbols and abstractions. Managers, say Protherough and Pick, are hired for "a fabled ability to deal with such abstract matters as 'long-term strategy', 'market positioning' or 'rebranding.'" Modern management, they say, "like modern government, is increasingly concerned with fashioning attitudes, and less and less concerned with tangible goods and services".[7]

This response is the classic action a pseudo-science takes when presented with a challenge to prove its validity – it replaces a testable, falsifiable hypothesis with an untestable one that we are invited to take on faith. The claim that managers had a useful function because they knew the details of the production process was testable – we could test their knowledge, and measure how the changes they made to the process increased output. However, there's no such test of today's management's skills. How do you tell whether someone's skill at rebranding or long-term strategy has played a useful role?

All this raises two questions. One is: if hierarchy is so bad, why has the west's economic performance in recent years been so good? There are (at least) three answers.

First, the costs of hierarchy have been mitigated by intensified competition among them. General Motors has for years been a dysfunctional organization. But competition from other car producers has forced it to mitigate its dysfunctionality.

Second, some firms have begun to de-layer hierarchies. In the 1960s, IBM had 23 layers of hierarchy. Today it has just six. The same's true of Tesco, Britain's largest retailer. Its boss Sir Terry Leahy has said: "There are only six layers between the person who works on the checkout counter and me[8]."

Thirdly, much economic growth comes not from old hierarchical ones, but from new firms which spring up to exploit the opportunities created by the inefficiency and slowness of those old firms. Dell became a multi-billion pound business because IBM was slow to sell personal computers direct to households. Bloomberg's success was facilitated by Reuters' slowness and lack of innovation. Countless biotech firms are doing research which Glaxosmithkline and Astrazeneca are too inflexible to do. And in recent years hedge funds – most of which are partnerships – have grown at the expense of traditional hierarchically-organised fund managers who use out-dated and discredited investment techniques.

Even Oliver Williamson, an economist who generally stressed the benefits of hierarchy, conceded this point. He said: "Major new developments have historically come preponderantly from sources outside the large corporation."[9]

Striking empirical evidence for this comes from Bart Hobijn and Boyan Jovanovic. They estimate that the stock market value of US firms that existed in 1972 fell relative to GDP in the three subsequent decades.[10] And yet the value of the overall market more than doubled relative to GDP. This means that more than all the rise in the value of shares relative to GDP came from new firms. Old, existing firms, then, don't generally grow quickly, at least at times of rapid technical change.

All of this raises the second question: if corporate hierarchies are so bad, why do they persist?

To a large extent, they don't. The remarkable thing about stock market-quoted companies is just how few of them there are. As of this writing there are 3,255 listed on the London Stock Exchange, even including investment trusts. That's only one in 500 of the total number of firms in the UK. There are countless more co-operatively organised ventures.

Also, it's because of the power of vested interests. Managers have an obvious interest in hanging onto the huge salaries that hierarchies give them. And many workers like the lack of responsibility and indolence that hierarchy gives them.

We met a couple of other reasons in chapter 13. One is belief persistence. People carry on believing things long after the facts that justified such beliefs have changed. Another is the information cascade; people believe things because others do. As many companies are hierarchies, so we believe these must be rational. The upshot is what Anthony Downs called the law of increasing conservatism; organizations get more conservative as they get older.

Market forces don't grind so finely as to remove completely all these inefficiencies.

Alternatives to managerialism

Now, if managerialism doesn't work in companies, it works even worse in government. After all, the three things that mitigate the inefficiency of corporate hierarchies – competition, delayering and innovation from without – are largely absent in government.

So, what are the alternatives to managerialism? An answer would fill several books. I'll just sketch some of my favourite alternatives.

I stress that these are not blueprints for immediate implementation. That would be, well, managerialist. Think of them instead as contrasts to our existing institutions.

A citizens' basic income

The idea here is that all welfare benefits, tax allowances and subsidies be replaced with a single monthly payment to all adults. This is anti-managerialist in (at least) three senses. One is that it's simple to administer. The other is that it abandons the pretence that the state can or should know enough about individuals' needs and circumstances to target help properly. As Robert Goodin has said:

> Let's give up trying to second-guess how people are going to lead their lives and crafting categorical responses to the problems they might encounter. Instead, simply give them the money and let them get on with it.[11]

A third way in which a basic income would be anti-managerialist would be that – especially if it's accompanied by tax simplification – it would bring the question of equality back into prominence. If there were just two parameters for policy – the level of basic income and the tax rate – politicians would be forced to debate how much income equality there should be, and why, rather than try to hide behind managerialist stealth taxes and bribes to median voters under the guise of helping the worst-off.

Turn schools and hospitals into co-operatives

Look at those private sector businesses whose success depends upon professional talents and human capital – law firms, vets practices, accountancy firms and so on. Overwhelmingly, they are partnerships.

There's a simple reason for this, on top of the reasons why hierarchy fails. Power within a firm is often best exercised by the person who has control over the most valuable asset. If that asset is a valuable machine, it's the machine owner. But in human capital-intensive firms, the valuable asset is people. So these should run the firm.

In schools and hospitals, teachers and doctors are the most important asset. So give them control.

Introduce macro-markets

I argued in chapter 7 that Gordon's Brown's promise to deliver macroeconomic stability does not, and cannot, mean economic security for all individuals.

Instead, you can improve this by developing insurance markets. As Robert Shiller showed in *The New Financial Order* it is possible to have securities whose prices are related to national income, or to the incomes of particular occupations or professions. People who are worried by a downturn in their country or industry can, therefore, sell such securities, thus, in effect, buying insurance.

The simple-minded question here is: if these markets are such good ideas, why don't they already exist? The answer's simple. The costs of setting up such markets are borne by a few individuals, but the benefits accrue to many. This has long been a deterrent to financial innovation; index tracker funds, for example, only really took off in the 1980s, even though it was known for years before then that they were good ideas.

This naturally provides a role for government to stimulate the development of such markets.

Use demand-revealing referenda

Should Britain join the euro? Should we have gone to war in Iraq? There's a simple, non-managerialist way to answer questions like these – to use the Clarke-Groves method.[12] Instead of asking people to vote for their preferred option, this asks people to record the amount they would be willing to pay to see their preferred alternative win. These sums are then added up, and the decision goes to the option with the larger sum. Those who voted for this option must then pay a tax equal to the net benefits the other voters would have received, had he not voted.

Table 26 illustrates this. Imagine we are holding a referendum on whether the UK should join the euro. Person A would pay £10 to join, and person B would pay £20. Person C, however, would pay £40 to stay out.

Under simple majority rule, we would join, as A and B outvote C.

Table 26. A Clarke-Groves referendum			
Voter	Yes	No	Tax
A	10		0
B	20		0
C		40	30
Total	30	40	30

Under the Clarke-Groves method, however, we would stay out – because the £40 exceeds £30.

What happens next is important. Each voter must pay a tax according to whether their vote made a difference. A and B pay no tax – because we would have stayed out of Emu had they not voted. Person C, however, must pay £30 – because had he not voted, we would have joined Emu, and £30 of benefits would have accrued to A and B.

This method generalizes to lots of policy questions.[13] It has (at least) four advantages:

- It recognises – as majority rule does not – that the strong preferences of a minority can outweigh the weak preferences of a majority. If voter C gets his way, he can, in theory, compensate A and B in such a way that everyone gains. That's Pareto-efficient. Simple majority rule, by contrast, need not be – and in this case, isn't.

- It's good in itself. Bruno Frey and colleagues show that "procedural utility" – the question of how decisions are reached – matters for our well-being.[14] Direct democracy makes us happy.

- It gives the public the incentives to get decisions right. Making people pay is a way of making them think. If it works for shopping, why shouldn't it work for politics?

- It takes the heat out of political questions. In making people pay, we ask not just: what side do you support? but also: how strongly do you support them?

The trivial objection to all this is that such a method gives greater power to the rich. Which only goes to show that there might be another trade-off, between allocative efficiency and distributive justice.

The start of politics

You can, of course, think of countless objections to these ideas. And I can think of counter-objections. And you can think of counter-counter objections.

And that is the point. There is a place for debate about policies, institutions, and ideals. Our policies don't have to be mandated by economic necessity. There are alternatives to the unthinking, unreflecting managerialist ideology that rules us. Politics needn't be a mere soap-opera about characters insufficiently interesting for Coronation Street. It can be about the choices and values of real people.

Alasdair MacIntyre concluded *After Virtue* by saying: "the barbarians are not waiting beyond the frontiers; they have already been governing us for quite some time."[15] I shall conclude this much lesser work by saying: it doesn't have to be so.

Notes

1. Reprinted with further analysis in *The Nature of the Firm,* edited by Oliver Williamson and Sidney Winter.

2. *Paradoxes of Prosperity,* p159.

3. *Paradoxes of Prosperity,* p238. The fact that such market research is often of appallingly poor quality, conducted in ignorance of basic statistical methods, merely compounds this problem.

4. *The End of Management,* p10.

5. Harry Braverman, *Labour and Monopoly Capital,* p260.

6. *The Rise of the Network Society,* p209.

7. *Managing Britannia,* p33, p12.

8. Interview in *The Observer,* January 8 2006.

9. *Markets and Hierarchies,* p186.

10. "The information technology revolution and the stock market: evidence", *American Economic Review,* 91, December 2001, p1203-20.

11. "Something for nothing?", p93 in Philippe van Parijs (ed), *What's wrong with a free lunch?*

12. I draw here upon Dennis Mueller, *Public Choice II,* p124-26.

13. *Public Choice II,* p124-34.

14. Bruno Frey, Matthias Benz and Alois Stutzer, "Introducing procedural utility: not only what, but also how, matters", *Institute for Empirical Research in Economics working paper* 129, October 2002.

15. *After Virtue,* p263.

Index